MISSOURI NOTETAKING GUIDE

McDougal Littell
Algebra 1

Larson Boswell Kanold Stiff

McDougal Littell
A DIVISION OF HOUGHTON MIFFLIN COMPANY

Missouri State Reviewers

Vicki Bullard
Sikeston Junior High School
Sikeston, Missouri

Rhonda Foote
N. Kansas City Schools
Kansas City, Missouri

Linda Heckman
Jefferson City High School
Jefferson City, Missouri

Laura Harris
Ozark High School
Ozark, Missouri

Diane Schwarting
Joplin High School
Joplin, Missouri

Copyright ©2007 by McDougal Littell, a division of Houghton Mifflin Company.
All rights reserved.

Permission is hereby granted to teachers to reprint or photocopy in classroom quantities the pages or sheets in this work that carry a McDougal Littell copyright notice. These pages are designed to be reproduced by teachers for use in their classes with accompanying McDougal Littell material, provided each copy made shows the copyright notice. Such copies may not be sold and further distribution is expressly prohibited. Except as authorized above, prior written permission must be obtained from McDougal Littell, a division of Houghton Mifflin Company, to reproduce or transmit this work or portions thereof in any other form or by any other electronic or mechanical means, including any information storage or retrieval system, unless expressly permitted by federal copyright laws. Address inquiries to Manager, Rights and Permissions, McDougal Littell, P.O. Box 1667, Evanston, IL 60201.

ISBN 13: 978-0-618-77511-8
ISBN 10: 0-618-77511-0

1 2 3 4 5 6 7 8 9—QDI—10 09 08 07 06

A Note to the MISSOURI STUDENT

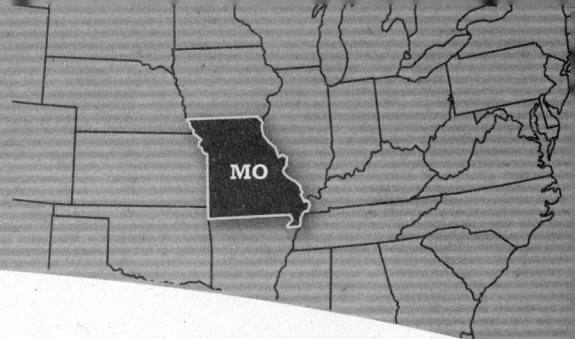

Dear Student,

This **Missouri Notetaking Guide** contains a lesson-by-lesson framework that allows you to take notes and review the main concepts of each lesson in your math textbook. It has been written so that you will have an organized set of **study notes** providing a place to go for review and to prepare for quizzes and tests.

The Notetaking Guide:

- reinforces the goal of each lesson, reviews vocabulary and provides a place for you to record key concepts.

- provides extra examples to use as a built-in set of practice problems.

- includes checkpoint questions to help reinforce the material that was taught.

The goal of this Notetaking Guide is to present the math in a way that you can understand!

Information on the **Missouri Mathematics Grade Level Expectations** and the **Missouri State Test (MAP)** is covered in the Student Guide and includes:

- a chart that explains what the standards mean and examples of the questions you will encounter on the **(MAP)** test

The **Additional Notetaking Lessons** present supplementary mathematical content. These lessons support state standards and align to the guidelines of the National Council of Teachers of Mathematics.

We wish you success in your math studies as you prepare yourself for a bright future. Think of this as a study guide to help you perform well on the **MAP** Test!

Missouri Algebra 1
NOTETAKING GUIDE

Table of Contents Preview

This Missouri Algebra 1 Notetaking Guide includes:

> A Student Guide to
  - Missouri Mathematics Grade Level Expectations
  - Missouri State Test (MAP)

> Lesson-by-Lesson Notetaking Support

> Additional Notetaking Lessons

Student Guide to the *Missouri Mathematics Grade Level Expectations* and *Missouri State Test (MAP)* ix

1 Expressions, Equations, and Functions
- **1.1** Evaluate Expressions 1–3
- **1.2** Apply Order of Operations 4–6
- **1.3** Write Expressions 7–9
- **1.4** Write Equations and Inequalities 10–12
- **1.5** Use a Problem Solving Plan 13–15
- **1.6** Represent Functions as Rules and Tables 16–18
- **1.7** Represent Functions as Graphs 19–21
- Words to Review 22

2 Properties of Real Numbers
- **2.1** Use Integers and Rational Numbers 23–26
- **2.2** Add Real Numbers 27–29
- **2.3** Subtract Real Numbers 30–31
- **2.4** Multiply Real Numbers 32–35
- **2.5** Apply the Distributive Property 36–38
- **2.6** Divide Real Numbers 39–41
- **2.7** Find Square Roots and Compare Real Numbers 42–44
- Words to Review 45–46

3 Solving Linear Equations
- **3.1** Solve One-Step Equations 47–51
- **3.2** Solve Two-Step Equations 52–54
- **3.3** Solve Multi-Step Equations 55–56
- **3.4** Solve Equations with Variables on Both Sides 57–59
- **3.5** Write Ratios and Proportions 60–62
- **3.6** Solve Proportions Using Cross Products 63–65
- **3.7** Solve Percent Problems 66–69
- **3.8** Rewrite Equations and Formulas 70–71
- Words to Review 72

4 Graphing Linear Equations and Functions

- **4.1** Plot Points in a Coordinate Plane 73–75
- **4.2** Graph Linear Equations 76–79
- **4.3** Graph Using Intercepts 80–82
- **4.4** Find Slope and Rate of Change 83–86
- **4.5** Graph Using Slope-Intercept Form 87–90
- **4.6** Model Direct Variation 91–93
- **4.7** Graph Linear Functions 94–97
- Words to Review 98–99

5 Writing Linear Equations

- **5.1** Write Linear Equations in Slope-Intercept Form 100–102
- **5.2** Use Linear Equations in Slope-Intercept Form 103–105
- **5.3** Write Linear Equations in Point-Slope Form 106–108
- **5.4** Write Linear Equations in Standard Form 109–112
- **5.5** Write Equations of Parallel and Perpendicular Lines 113–116
- **5.6** Fit a Line to Data 117–120
- **5.7** Predict with Linear Models 121–124
- Words to Review 125–126

6 Solving and Graphing Linear Inequalities

- **6.1** Solve Inequalities Using Addition and Subtraction 127–129
- **6.2** Solve Inequalities Using Multiplication and Division 130–133
- **6.3** Solve Multi-Step Inequalities 134–136
- **6.4** Solve Compound Inequalities 137–139
- **6.5** Solve Absolute Value Equations 140–142
- **6.6** Solve Absolute Value Inequalities 143–145
- **6.7** Linear Inequalities in Two Variables 146–148
- Words to Review 149

7 Systems of Equations and Inequalities

- **7.1** Solve Linear Systems by Graphing 150–152
- **7.2** Solve Linear Systems by Substitution 153–154
- **7.3** Solve Linear Systems by Adding or Subtracting 155–157
- **7.4** Solve Linear Systems by Multiplying First 158–159
- **7.5** Solve Special Types of Linear Systems 160–162
- **7.6** Solve Systems of Linear Inequalities 163–165
- Words to Review 166

8 Exponents and Exponential Functions
- **8.1** Apply Exponent Properties Involving Products 167–169
- **8.2** Apply Exponent Properties Involving Quotients 170–172
- **8.3** Define and Use Zero and Negative Exponents 173–175
- **8.4** Use Scientific Notation 176–178
- **8.5** Write and Graph Exponential Growth Functions 179–182
- **8.6** Write and Graph Exponential Decay Functions 183–186
- Words to Review 187

9 Polynomials and Factoring
- **9.1** Add and Subtract Polynomials 188–190
- **9.2** Multiply Polynomials 191–194
- **9.3** Find Special Products of Polynomials 195–198
- **9.4** Solve Polynomial Equations in Factored Form 199–202
- **9.5** Factor $x^2 + bx + c$ 203–206
- **9.6** Factor $ax^2 + bx + c$ 207–209
- **9.7** Factor Special Products 210–213
- **9.8** Factor Polynomials Completely 214–218
- Words to Review 219

10 Quadratic Equations and Functions
- **10.1** Graph $y = ax^2 + c$ 220–223
- **10.2** Graph $y = ax^2 + bx + c$ 224–226
- **10.3** Solve Quadratic Equations by Graphing 227–229
- **10.4** Use Square Roots to Solve Quadratic Equations 230–232
- **10.5** Solve Quadratic Equations by Completing the Square 233–235
- **10.6** Solve Quadratic Equations by the Quadratic Formula 236–238
- **10.7** Interpret the Discriminant 239–241
- **10.8** Compare Linear, Exponential, and Quadratic Models 242–244
- Words to Review 245–246

11 Radicals and Geometry Connections
- **11.1** Graph Square Root Functions 247–250
- **11.2** Simplify Radical Expressions 251–255
- **11.3** Solve Radical Equations 256–258
- **11.4** Apply the Pythagorean Theorem and Its Converse 259–261
- **11.5** Apply the Distance and Midpoint Formulas 262–264
- Words to Review 265–266

12 Rational Equations and Functions

12.1	Model Inverse Variation	267–270
12.2	Graph Rational Functions	271–275
12.3	Divide Polynomials	276–279
12.4	Simplify Rational Expressions	280–282
12.5	Multiply and Divide Rational Expressions	283–286
12.6	Add and Subtract Rational Expressions	287–290
12.7	Solve Rational Equations	291–293
	Words to Review	294–295

13 Probability and Data Analysis

13.1	Find Probabilities and Odds	296–298
13.2	Find Probabilities Using Permutations	299–301
13.3	Find Probabilities Using Combinations	302–304
13.4	Find Probabilities of Compound Events	305–307
13.5	Analyze Surveys and Samples	308–310
13.6	Use Measures of Central Tendency and Dispersion	311–313
13.7	Interpret Stem-and-Leaf Plots and Histograms	314–316
13.8	Interpret Box-and-Whisker Plots	317–319
	Words to Review	320–323

Additional Notetaking Lessons

These Additional Lessons have been written to provide enrichment and challenge opportunities and to support state standards.

A	Estimation and Accuracy of Measurement	A1–A3
B	Metric/Customary Conversions	A4–A6
C	Special Right Triangles	A7–A9
D	Triangle Inequalities	A10–A12
E	The Tangent Ratio	A13–A15
F	The Sine and Cosine Ratios	A16–A18
G	Vertex-Edge Graphs, Circuits, Networks and Routing	A19–A22
H	Introduction to Vectors	A23–A25
I	Introduction to Recursive Functions for Sequences	A26–A28
J	Introduction to Limits	A29–A30
K	Two-Way Tables of Probability	A31–A33
L	Quantitative vs. Qualitative Data	A34–A36
M	Causation vs. Correlation	A37–A39
N	Misleading Data Displays	A40–A42

MISSOURI STUDENT GUIDE

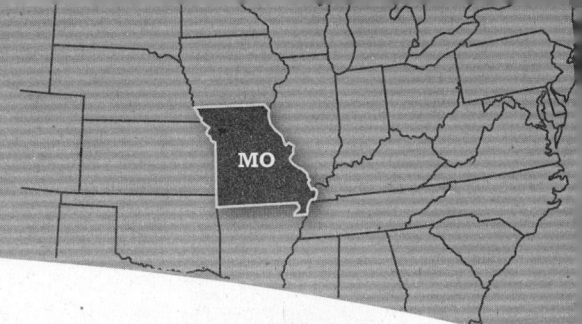

What are Math Standards?

The standards in your state are called the **Missouri Mathematics Grade Level Expectations.**

Think of **Math Standards** as a list of categories or topics, like *Number & Operations*, *Algebra*, *Geometry*, *Measurement* and *Data Analysis & Probability* that need to be learned by all students. Math Standards help you focus on a common foundation of mathematical concepts that will help in everyday life and later in the workplace.

Compare the word *standards* to a set of rules that must be followed in any sport event. When a sport is played, the participants need to know the actions that must be followed to either win or lose the game. For example, in a baseball game, the batter must move from first base to second base and then third base before proceeding to the home plate to score a run. Because the batter has learned this concept, he will be able to support his team to win the game. All the rules must be learned by the team players. Without the knowledge of how a baseball game is played, the team will not have the fundamental concepts to compete.

This is true when you learn mathematics. Learning and acquiring the common foundation of mathematics will provide you with opportunities to be highly successful in many areas of life. The need to understand and be able to use mathematics has never been greater. Your state standards have been written as a commitment to you, the student, to help you focus on the proper content to achieve both depth and understanding of mathematical knowledge.

Each state has a unique list of standards. When writing your standards, the state of Missouri utilized the National Council of Teachers of Mathematics *Principles and Standards 2000* as a reference in their development. These national standards provide the guidelines to help states meet both their individual curriculum standards and the state assessment objectives.

How Will You Learn the Missouri Mathematics Grade Level Expectations?

The math standards for **Missouri** are organized into the following five strands:
1. Number and Operations
2. Algebraic Relationships
3. Geometric and Spatial Relationships
4. Measurement
5. Data and Probability

Each strand is divided into the big ideas and then further broken down into concepts by grade level. This organization guides your teacher through the mathematical content that needs to be covered to help you be successful on the **MAP** test.

MAP stands for the Missouri Assessment Program. It is given in the spring to students in the 10th grade to evaluate your knowledge of the **Missouri Mathematics Grade Level Expectations.** Your teacher will be working with you throughout the year to help you prepare and be successful on this test.

Missouri uses a special numbering system to identify the strands, the big ideas, concept objectives, and grade level. Here is an example of a particular strand, big idea, concept objective, and grade level identifier.

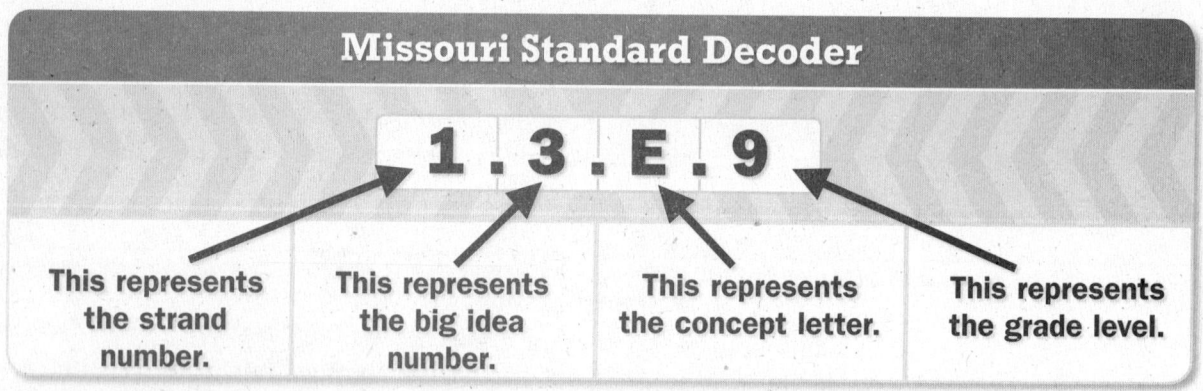

So, when you see 1.3.E.9, you know it belongs to:

Strand 1: Number and Operations

Big Idea 3 : Compute fluently and make reasonable estimates

Concept E: Solve problems involving proportions

Grade Level 9: Grade 9 expectation

The information that follows highlights the main strands, big ideas, concepts, and grade level, what they mean to you, and examples of what the selected response questions might look like on the MAP Test.

Strand 1: Number and Operations

Big Ideas:

1. Understand numbers, ways of representing numbers, relationships among numbers, and number systems

2. Understand meanings of operations and how they relate to one another

3. Compute fluently and make reasonable estimates

What It Means To You

A major learning goal for all students studying math is to develop an understanding of properties of, and relationships among, numbers. Numbers are the cornerstone of any mathematics curriculum and they penetrate all areas of life. This strand falls under the *Number and Operations Standard*.

Here is what questions might look like on the MAP Test:

1.3.E.9 Solve problems involving proportions

1. Tara ran 175 feet in 35 seconds. Leslie ran at the same rate for 25 seconds. How much farther did Tara run than Leslie?

   A 25 ft
   B 50 ft
   C 75 ft
   D 125 ft

Solution for Question 1

Write and solve a proportion to find the distance d that Leslie ran.

$$\frac{175}{35} = \frac{d}{25} \quad \begin{matrix}\leftarrow \text{distance} \\ \leftarrow \text{time}\end{matrix}$$

$$175 \cdot 25 = 35 \cdot d$$

$$125 = d$$

Leslie ran 125 feet. Tara ran 175 feet. Tara ran 50 feet farther than Leslie, so the correct answer is B.

2. A bag contains 25% red marbles, 15% green marbles, 30% blue marbles, and 30% yellow marbles. There are 180 marbles total in the bag. What is the total number of green marbles in the bag?

   F 15
   G 27
   H 45
   J 54

Solution for Question 2

Use the percent proportion $\frac{a}{b} = \frac{p}{100}$ where a is part of the base b and p is the percent.

$$\frac{a}{180} = \frac{15}{100}$$

$$100 \cdot a = 15 \cdot 180$$

$$a = 27$$

So, the correct answer is G.

Strand 2: Algebraic Relationships

Big Ideas:
1. Understand patterns, relations, and functions
2. Represent and analyze mathematical situations and structures using algebraic symbols
3. Use mathematical models to represent and understand quantitative relationships
4. Analyze change in various contexts

What It Means To You

All students need to learn algebra. Algebra is the branch of mathematics in which symbols, usually letters, are used to represent numbers. To learn how to think algebraically includes recognizing and analyzing patterns, studying and representing relationships, making generalizations, and analyzing how things change. This strand falls under the *Algebra Standard*.

Here is what a question might look like on the MAP Test:

2.2.C.9 Use and solve equivalent forms of equations and inequalities

1. The area of the triangle below represents the portion of Mrs. Simpson's driveway in which cement is to be poured. The area of the region is 73.5 square feet. Mrs. Simpson wants to surround the region with caution tape. How much tape does she need?

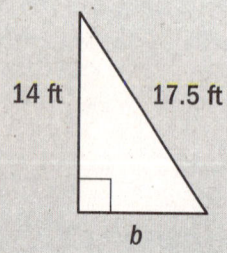

- F   10.5 ft
- G   31.75 ft
- H   39.9 ft
- J   42 ft

Solution

The height of the triangle is 14 feet. Use the area formula to find the base of the triangle.

$$A = \frac{1}{2}bh$$

$$73.5 = \frac{1}{2}b(14)$$

$$73.5 = 7b$$

$$10.5 = b$$

The base is 10.5 feet. Find the perimeter.

$$P = 14 + 10.5 + 17.5 = 42$$

The perimeter is 42 feet, so the correct answer is J.

Ⓕ   Ⓖ   Ⓗ   Ⓙ

Strand 3: Geometric and Spatial Relationships

Big Ideas:
1. Analyze characteristics and properties of two- and three-dimensional geometric shapes and develop mathematical arguments about geometric relationships
2. Specify locations and describe spatial relationships using coordinate geometry and other representational systems
3. Apply transformations and use symmetry to analyze mathematical situations
4. Use visualization, spatial reasoning and geoemtric modeling to solve problems

What It Means To You

The mathematics of geometry is the study of the properties, measurement, and relationships of points, lines, angles, surfaces and solids. The *Geometry Standard* teaches you all about geometric shapes and structures and how to analyze their characteristics. It also deals with spatial relationships, which provides an interesting insight into mathematics and into art and aesthetics. Transformations, which is an operation that maps or moves a figure onto an image, include translations, reflections, dilations, and rotations. The study of this mathematical concept leads to a better understanding of symmetry and congruence.

Here is what a question might look like on the MAP Test:

3.3.A.9 Represent translations, reflections, rotations, and dilations of objects in the coordinate plane

1. Hexagon *LMNOPQ* is similar to hexagon *UVWXYZ*. By what scale factor was hexagon *UVWXYZ* dilated to form hexagon *LMNOPQ*?

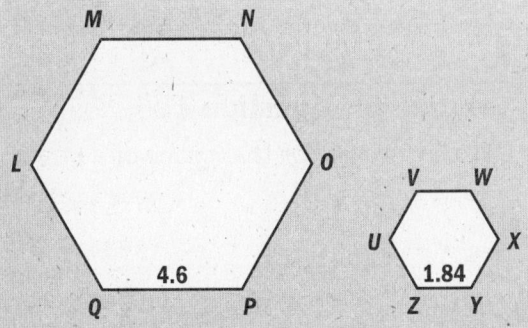

F 0.4
G 1.6
H 2.5
J 2.8

Solution

The scale factor of a dilation is the ratio of side lengths after the dilation to corresponding side lengths before the dilation.

Here, the known side length after the dilation is the length of segment *QP*. The known side length before the dilation is the length of segment *ZY*.

To determine the scale factor, x, write and simplify the ratio.

$$x = \frac{QP}{ZY}$$

$$x = \frac{4.6}{1.84}$$

$$x = 2.5$$

The scale factor is 2.5. So, the correct answer is H.

Strand 4: Measurement

Big Ideas:
1. Understand measurable attributes of objects and the units, systems, and processes of measurement
2. Apply appropriate techniques, tools, and formulas to determine measurements

What It Means To You

Measurement is the assignment of a numerical value to a characteristic of an object, such as the length of a football field. The major emphasis of this standard is to understand what a measurable characteristic is and becoming familiar with the units and the processes that are used to measure the characteristic.

Here is what questions might look like on the MAP Test:

4.2.C.9 Determine the surface area and volume of geometric figures including cones, spheres, and cylinders

1. A farmer is planning to paint the roof of his silo, which is cone-shaped as shown. What is the best estimate for the number of square feet the farmer must paint?

   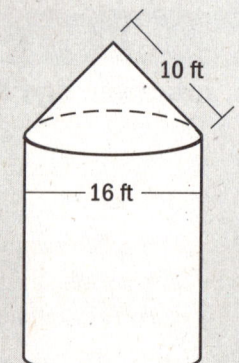

   A 250 ft²

   B 500 ft²

   C 750 ft²

   D 1000 ft²

Solution for Question 1

Because only the lateral surface of the cone is to be painted, use the formula for the lateral surface area of a cone.

$$S = \pi r l$$
$$= \pi(8)(10)$$
$$\approx 251$$

So, the area he must paint is about 251 square feet. The correct answer is A.

2. The net of a rectangular prism is shown below. What is the volume of the rectangular prism?

   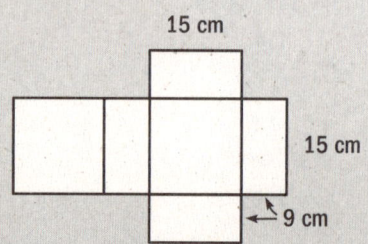

   F 135 cm³

   G 225 cm³

   H 990 cm³

   J 2025 cm³

Solution for Question 2

Use the formula for the volume of a prism.

$$V = Bh$$
$$V = (lw)h$$
$$V = (15 \cdot 15)(9)$$
$$V = 2025$$

The volume of the rectangular prism is 2025 cubic centimeters. So, the correct answer is J.

Strand 5: Data and Probability

Big Ideas:

1. Formulate questions that can be addressed with data and collect, organize, and display relevant data to answer them

2. Select and use appropriate statistical methods to analyze data

3. Develop and evaluate inferences and predictions that are based on data

4. Understand and apply basic concepts of probability

What It Means To You

Data Analysis involves learning how to process information gathered in order to draw conclusions, make decisions, and solve problems. Probability, the study of the likelihood that a given event will occur, is connected to many other areas of mathematics, especially, number and geometry. Both topics are important to know about in order to be able to reason statistically.

Here is what a question might look like on the MAP Test:

5.1.C.9 Select, create, and use appropriate graphical representations of data

1. Steven glanced at the graph below.

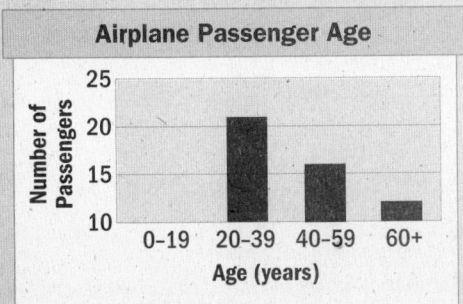

He concluded that there were no passengers under the age of 20 on the plane. Why might he be incorrect?

A The bars of the graph fall between the numbers shown in the vertical scale.

B The graph divides the passengers into too few age groups.

C The vertical scale starts at 10.

D The vertical scale ends too low.

Solution

The vertical scale of the graph starts at 10. So, if there are ten or fewer passengers in an age group this information will not appear on the graph.

It is possible that there are as many as 10 passengers in the 0- to 19-year-old range.

The most likely explanation of Steven's incorrect conclusion is that he failed to notice the vertical scale of the graph starts at 10. The correct answer is C.

 Evaluate Expressions

Goal • Evaluate algebraic expressions and use exponents.

Your Notes

VOCABULARY

Variable

Algebraic expression

> An algebraic expression is also called a variable expression.

Evaluating an expression

Power

Base

Exponent

ALGEBRAIC EXPRESSIONS

Algebraic Expression	Meaning	Operation
$7t$	7 times t	_____
$\dfrac{x}{20}$	_____	Division
$y - 8$	_____	_____
$12 + a$	_____	_____

Your Notes

> To evaluate an expression, substitute a number for the variable, perform the operation(s), and simplify.

Example 1 Evaluate algebraic expressions

Evaluate the expression when $n = 4$.

a. $11 \times n = 11 \times \underline{}$ Substitute ___ for n.

   $= \underline{}$ _____.

b. $\dfrac{12}{n} = \dfrac{12}{\square}$ Substitute ___ for n.

   $= \underline{}$ _____.

c. $n - 3 = \underline{} - 3$ Substitute ___ for n.

   $= \underline{}$ _____.

✓ **Checkpoint** Evaluate the expression when $y = 8$.

1. $7y$	2. $y \div 2$	3. $10 - y$	4. $y + 6$

Example 2 Read and write powers

Write the power in words and as a product.

Power	Words	Product
a. 12^1	twelve to the _____ power	_____
b. 2^3	two to the _____ power, or two _____	_____
c. $\left(\dfrac{1}{4}\right)^2$	one fourth to the _____ power, or one fourth _____	_____
d. a^4	a to the _____ power	_____

Your Notes

✓ **Checkpoint** Write the power in words and as a product.

5. 7^5	6. $\left(\dfrac{1}{3}\right)^2$	7. $(1.4)^3$

Example 3 **Evaluate powers**

Evaluate the expression.

a. y^3 when $y = 3$ b. a^5 when $a = 1.2$

Solution

a. $y^3 = \underline{}^3$ Substitute ___ for y.

  $= \underline{}$ $\underline{}$.

  $= \underline{}$ $\underline{}$.

b. $a^5 = \underline{}^5$ Substitute ___ for a.

  $= \underline{}$ $\underline{}$.

  $= \underline{}$ $\underline{}$.

✓ **Checkpoint** Evaluate the expression.

8. t^2 when $t = 3$	9. m^5 when $m = \dfrac{1}{2}$	10. x^3 when $x = 4$

Homework

1.2 Apply Order of Operations

Goal • Use the order of operations to evaluate expressions.

Your Notes

VOCABULARY

Order of Operations

ORDER OF OPERATIONS

To evaluate an expression involving more than one operation, use the following steps.

Step 1 Evaluate expressions inside _____ _____.

Step 2 Evaluate _____.

Step 3 _____ and divide from left to right.

Step 4 Add and _____ from left to right.

Example 1 *Evaluate Expressions*

Evaluate the expression $30 \times 2 \div 2^2 - 5$.

Solution

Step 1
There are no grouping symbols, so go to Step 2.

Step 2
$30 \times 2 \div 2^2 - 5 = 30 \times 2 \div \underline{} - 5$ _____ power.

Step 3
$30 \times 2 \div \underline{} - 5 = \underline{} \div \underline{} - 5$ _____.
$\phantom{30 \times 2 \div \underline{} - 5} = \underline{} - 5$ _____.

Step 4
$\underline{} - 5 = \underline{}$ _____.

---

4   Lesson 1.2 • Algebra 1 Notetaking Guide   Copyright © McDougal Littell/Houghton Mifflin Company

Your Notes

✓ **Checkpoint** Evaluate the expression.

1. $10 + 3^2$	2. $16 - 2^3 + 4$
3. $28 \div 2^2 + 1$	4. $4 \cdot 5^2 + 4$

Example 2 *Evaluate expressions with grouping symbols*

Evaluate the expression.

> Grouping symbols such as parentheses ( ) and brackets [ ] indicate that operations inside the grouping symbols should be performed first.

a. $6(9 + 3) = 6(\_\_\_)$ _____ within parentheses.

$= \_\_\_$ _____.

b. $50 - (3^2 + 1) = 50 - (\_\_ + 1)$ _____ power.

$= 50 - (\_\_\_)$ _____ within parentheses.

$= \_\_\_$ _____.

c. $3[5 + (5^2 + 5)] = 3[5 + (\_\_\_ + 5)]$ _____ power.

$= 3[5 + (\_\_\_)]$ _____ within parentheses.

$= 3[\_\_\_]$ _____ within brackets.

$= \_\_\_$ _____.

Your Notes

✓ **Checkpoint** Evaluate the expression.

5. $6(3 + 3^2)$	6. $2[(10 - 4) \div 3]$

Example 3 *Evaluate an algebraic expression*

Evaluate the expression $\dfrac{12k}{3(k^2 + 4)}$ when $k = 2$.

A fraction bar can act as a grouping symbol. Evaluate the numerator and denominator before dividing.

Solution

$\dfrac{12k}{3(k^2 + 4)} = \dfrac{12(\boxed{})}{3(\boxed{}^2 + 4)}$ Substitute ___ for *k*.

$= \dfrac{12(\boxed{})}{3(\boxed{} + 4)}$ _____ power.

$= \dfrac{12(\boxed{})}{3(\boxed{})}$ _____ within parentheses.

$= \dfrac{\boxed{}}{\boxed{}}$ _____.

$= \underline{}$ _____.

✓ **Checkpoint** Evaluate the expression when $x = 3$.

7. $x^3 - 5$	8. $\dfrac{6x + 2}{x + 7}$

Homework

1.3 Write Expressions

Goal • Translate verbal phrases into expressions.

Your Notes

VOCABULARY

Verbal model

Rate

Unit rate

TRANSLATING VERBAL PHRASES

Operation	Verbal Phrase	Expression
Addition	The _____ of 3 and a number *n*	_____
	A number *x* _____ 10	_____
Subtraction	The _____ of 7 and a number *a*	_____
	Twelve _____ than a number *x*	_____
Multiplication	Five _____ a number *y*	_____
	The _____ of 2 and a number *n*	_____
Division	The _____ of a number *a* and 6	_____
	Eight _____ into a number *y*	_____

> Order is important when writing subtraction and division expressions.

Your Notes

> The words "the quantity" tell you what to group when translating verbal phrases.

Example 1 — Translate verbal phrases into expressions

Translate the verbal phrase into an expression.

Verbal Phrase	Expression
a. 6 less than the quantity 8 times a number x	_____
b. 2 times the sum of 5 and a number a	_____
c. The difference of 17 and the cube of a number n	_____

✓ **Checkpoint** Translate the verbal phrase into an expression.

1. The product of 5 and the quantity 12 plus a number n

   _____

2. The quotient of 10 and the quantity a number x minus 3

   _____

Example 2 — Use a verbal model to write an expression

Food Drive You and three friends are collecting canned food for a food drive. You each collect the same number of cans. Write an expression for the total number of cans collected.

Solution

Step 1 Write a verbal model.   Amount × Number of
                                of cans
                                         _____

Step 2 Translate the verbal   ___ × ___
       model into an
       algebraic expression.

An expression that represents the total number of cans is _____.

8   Lesson 1.3 • Algebra 1 Notetaking Guide

Your Notes

✓ **Checkpoint** Complete the following exercise.

> 3. In Example 2, suppose that the total number of cans collected are distributed equally to 2 food banks. Write an expression that represents the number of cans each food bank receives.

Example 3 *Find a unit rate*

Three gallons of milk cost $9.15. Find the unit rate.

Solution

$$\frac{\boxed{}}{\boxed{} \text{ gallons}} = \frac{\boxed{} \div 3}{\boxed{} \text{ gallons} \div \boxed{}}$$

$$= \frac{\boxed{}}{\boxed{} \text{ gallon}}$$

The unit rate is _____, or _____.

✓ **Checkpoint** Find the unit rate.

4. $\dfrac{420 \text{ miles}}{3 \text{ hours}}$

5. $\dfrac{\$12}{3 \text{ ft}^2}$

6. $\dfrac{20 \text{ cups}}{8 \text{ people}}$

Homework

1.4 Write Equations and Inequalities

 • Translate verbal sentences into equations or inequalities.

Your Notes

VOCABULARY

Open sentence

Equation

Inequality

Solution of an equation

Solution of an inequality

EXPRESSING OPEN SENTENCES

Symbol	Meaning	Associated Words
$a = b$	a is _____ to b	a is the _____ as b
$a < b$	a is _____ b	a is _____ than b
$a \leq b$	a is _____ than or _____ to b	a is _____ b, a is _____ than b
$a > b$	a is _____ b	a is _____ than b
$a \geq b$	a is _____ than or _____ to b	a is _____ b, a is _____ than b

Your Notes

> Sometimes two inequalities are combined. For example, the inequalities $a < b$ and $b < c$ can be combined to form the inequality $a < b < c$.

Example 1 Write equations and inequalities

Write an equation or an inequality.

Verbal Sentence	Equation or Inequality
a. The sum of three times a number a and 4 is 25.	_____
b. The quotient of a number x and 4 is fewer than 10.	_____
c. A number n is greater than 6 and less than 12.	_____

Example 2 Check possible solutions

Check whether 2 is a solution of the equation or inequality.

Equation or Inequality	Substitute	Conclusion
a. $7x - 8 = 9$	$7(2) - 8 \stackrel{?}{=} 9$	_____ _____ a solution.
b. $4 + 5y < 18$	$4 + 5(2) \stackrel{?}{<} 18$	_____ _____ a solution.
c. $6n - 9 \geq 2$	$6(2) - 9 \stackrel{?}{\geq} 2$	_____ _____ a solution.

✓ **Checkpoint** Check whether the given number is a solution of the equation or inequality.

1. $6r + 1 = 25$ $r = 4$	2. $x^2 - 5 > 10$ $x = 5$	3. $7a \leq 21$ $a = 6$

Your Notes

Example 3 Use mental math to solve an equation

Solve the equation using mental math.
a. $n + 6 = 11$
b. $18 - x = 10$
c. $7a = 56$
d. $\dfrac{b}{11} = 3$

Solution

Equation	Think	Solution	Check
a. $n + 6 = 11$	What number plus 6 equals 11?	___	___ $+ 6 = 11$
b. $18 - x = 10$	_____	___	$18 -$ ___ $= 10$
c. $7a = 56$	_____	___	$7(\_\_) = 56$
d. $\dfrac{b}{11} = 3$	_____	___	$\dfrac{\Box}{11} = 3$

> Think of an equation as a question when solving using mental math.

✓ **Checkpoint** Solve the equation using mental math.

4. $x + 9 = 14$	5. $5t - 4 = 11$	6. $\dfrac{y}{4} = 15$

Homework

12 Lesson 1.4 • Algebra 1 Notetaking Guide

1.5 Use a Problem Solving Plan

Goal • Use a problem solving plan to solve problems.

Your Notes

VOCABULARY

Formula

A PROBLEM SOLVING PLAN

Use the following four-step plan to solve a problem.

Step 1 _____ Read the problem carefully. Identify what you want to know and what you want to find out.

Step 2 _____ Decide on an approach to solving the problem.

Step 3 _____ Carry out your plan. Try a new approach if the first one isn't successful.

Step 4 _____ Check that your answer is reasonable.

Example 1 *Read a problem and make a plan*

You have $7 to buy orange juice and bagels at the store. A container of juice costs $1.25 and a bagel costs $.75. If you buy two containers of juice, how many bagels can you buy?

Solution

Step 1 _____ *What do you know?* You know how much money you have and the price of a _____ and a container of juice.

What do you want to find out? You want to find out the number of _____ you can buy.

Step 2 _____ Use what you know to write a _____ that represents what you want to find out. Then write an _____ and solve it.

Your Notes

| Example 2 | *Solve a problem and look back* |

Solve the problem in Example 1 by carrying out the plan. Then check your answer.

Solution

Step 3 _____ Write a verbal model. Then write an equation. Let *b* be the number of bagels you buy.

| Price of juice (in dollars) | Number of containers | Price of bagel (in dollars) | Number of bagels | Cost (in dollars) |

____ • ____ + ____ • *b* = ____

The equation is ____ + ____ *b* = ____. One way to solve the equation is to use the strategy *guess*, *check*, and *revise*.

Guess an even number that is easily multiplied by ____. Try 4.

____ + ____ *b* = ____   Write equation.
____ + ____ (4) $\stackrel{?}{=}$ ____   Substitute 4 for *b*.
_____   Simplify; 4 _____ check.

Because _____, try an even number _____ 4. Try 6.

____ + ____ *b* = ____   Write equation.
____ + ____ (6) $\stackrel{?}{=}$ ____   Substitute 6 for *b*.
_____   Simplify.

For ____ you can buy ____ bagels and ____ containers of juice.

Step 4 _____ Each additional bagel you buy adds ____ to the _____ you pay for the juice. Make a table.

Bagels	0	1	2	3	4	5	6
Total Cost							

The total cost is ____ when you buy ____ bagels and ____ containers of juice. The answer in step 3 is _____.

Your Notes

✓ **Checkpoint** Complete the following exercise.

1. Suppose in Example 1 that you have $12 and you decide to buy three containers of juice. How many bagels can you buy?

FORMULA REVIEW

Temperature

$C = \frac{5}{9}(F - 32)$, where $F =$ _____

and $C =$ _____

Simple interest

$I = Prt$, where $I =$ _____, $P =$ _____,
$r =$ _____ (as a decimal), and $t =$ _____

Distance traveled

$d = rt$, where $d =$ _____, $r =$ _____,
and $t =$ _____

Profit

$P = I - E$, where $P =$ _____, $I =$ _____, and
$E =$ _____

✓ **Checkpoint** Complete the following exercise.

2. In Example 1, the store where you bought the juice and bagels had an income of $7 from your purchase. The profit the store made from your purchase is $2.50. Find the store's expense for the juice and bagels.

Homework

Lesson 1.5 • Algebra 1 Notetaking Guide

1.6 Represent Functions as Rules and Tables

Goal • Represent functions as rules and as tables.

Your Notes

VOCABULARY

Function

Domain

Range

Independent variable

Dependent variable

Example 1 Identify the domain and range of a function

The input-output table shows temperatures over various increments of time. Identify the domain and range of the function.

Input (hours)	0	2	4	6
Output (°C)	24	27	30	33

Solution

Domain: _____

Range: _____

Your Notes

✓ **Checkpoint** Identify the domain and range of the function.

1.
Input	4	7	11	13
Output	10	20	35	45

Example 2 Identify a function

Tell whether the pairing is a function. Explain your reasoning.

Solution

a. Input   Output

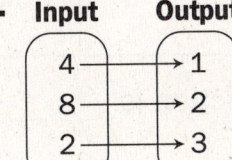

Mapping diagrams are often used to represent functions. Take note of the pairings to make your decision.

b.
Input	Output
2	2
2	4
3	6
4	8

✓ **Checkpoint** Tell whether the pairing is a function.

2.
Input	5	5	10	15
Output	3	4	6	8

3.
Input	0	4	12	20
Output	3	5	9	13

Your Notes

A function may be represented using a rule that relates one variable to another.

FUNCTIONS

Verbal Rule	Equation	Table

The output is 2 less than the input.

Equation: _____

Input	2	4	6	8	10
Output					

Example 3 *Make a table for a function*

The domain of the function $y = 3x$ is 0, 1, 2, and 3. Make a table for the function, then identify the range of the function.

Solution

x				
$y = 3x$				

The range of the function is _____.

Example 4 *Write a function rule*

Write a rule for the function.

Input	3	5	7	9	11
Output	6	10	14	18	22

Solution

Let x be the input and let y be the output. Notice that each output is _____ the corresponding input. So, a rule for the function is _____.

✓ **Checkpoint** Write a rule for the function. Identify the domain and the range.

4.

Yarn (yd)	1	2	3	4
Total Cost ($)	1.5	3	4.5	6

Homework

1.7 Represent Functions as Graphs

Goal • Represent functions as graphs.

Your Notes

GRAPHING A FUNCTION

- You can use a graph to represent a _____.
- In a given table, each corresponding pair of input and output values forms an _____.
- An ordered pair of numbers can be plotted as a _____.
- The x-coordinate is the _____.
- The y-coordinate is the _____.
- The horizontal axis of the graph is labeled with the _____.
- The vertical axis is labeled with the the _____ _____.

Example 1 Graph a function

Graph the function y = x + 1 with domain 1, 2, 3, 4, and 5.

Solution

Step 1 Make an _____ table.

x					
y					

Step 2 Plot a point for each _____ (x, y).

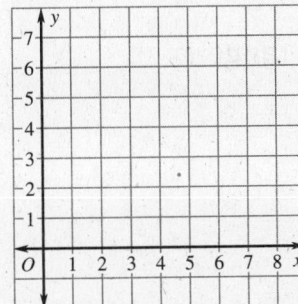

Lesson 1.7 • Algebra 1 Notetaking Guide   19

Your Notes

Example 2 — *Write a function rule for a graph*

Write a function rule for the function represented by the graph. Identify the domain and the range of the funtion.

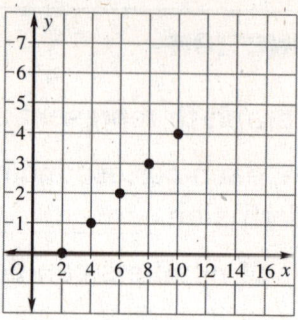

Solution

Step 1 Make a _____ for the graph.

x					
y					

Step 2 Find a _____ between the input and output values.

Step 3 Write a _____ that describes the relationship.

y = _____

A rule for the function is y = _____ . The

domain of the function is _____.

The range is _____.

Your Notes

✓ **Checkpoint** Complete the following exercise.

1. Graph the function $y = \frac{1}{3}x + 1$ with domain 0, 3, 6, 9, and 12.

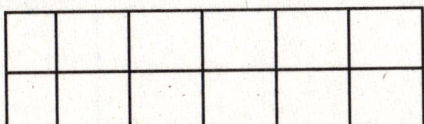

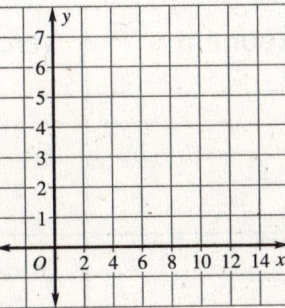

✓ **Checkpoint** Write a rule for the function represented by the graph. Identify the domain and the range of the function.

2.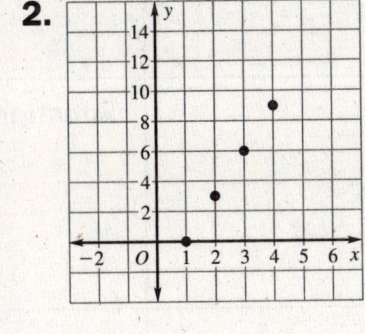

3.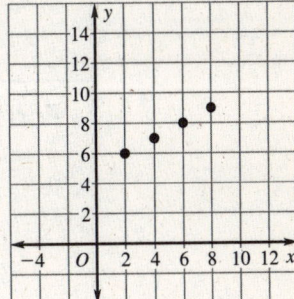

Homework

Words to Review

Give an example of the vocabulary word.

Variable	Algebraic expression
Power, Base, Exponent	Verbal model
Rate	Unit rate
Equation	Inequality
Formula	Function
Domain	Range

Review your notes and Chapter 1 by using the Chapter Review on pages 53–56 of your textbook.

2.1 Use Integers and Rational Numbers

Goal • Graph and compare positive and negative numbers.

Your Notes

VOCABULARY

Whole number

Integer

Rational number

Opposite

Absolute value

Conditional statement

Example 1 Graph and compare integers

Graph −2 and −5 on a number line. Then tell which number is less.

Solution

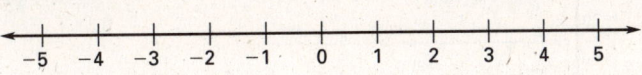

On the number line, _____ is to the left of _____.

So, _____ < _____.

> Negative integers are integers less than 0 and positive integers are integers greater than 0. The integer 0 is neither negative nor positive.

Your Notes

Example 2: Classify numbers

Tell whether each of the following numbers is a whole number, an integer, or a rational number: 3, 1.7, −14, and $-\frac{1}{2}$.

Solution

Number	Whole Number?	Integer?	Rational Number?
3			
1.7			
−14			
$-\frac{1}{2}$			

Example 3: Order rational numbers

Temperature The table shows the low daily temperatures for a town over a five-day period. Order the days from warmest to coldest.

Day	1	2	3	4	5
Temperature	0°C	10°C	−2°C	5°C	−7°C

Solution

Step 1

Graph the numbers on a number line.

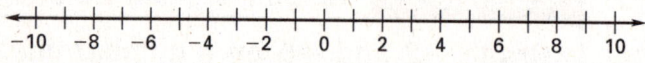

Step 2

Read the numbers from left to right:

_____.

From warmest to coldest the days are _____.

Your Notes

✓ **Checkpoint** Complete the following exercise.

1. Tell whether each of the following numbers is a whole number, an integer, or a rational number: 0.8, −17, −5$\frac{3}{4}$, and 2. Then order the numbers from least to greatest.

Example 4 Find opposites of numbers

a. If $a = -4.8$, then $-a =$ _____ = _____.

b. If $a = \frac{5}{6}$, then $-a =$ _____.

ABSOLUTE VALUE OF A NUMBER

Words

If x is a positive number, then $|x| =$ ___.

If x is 0, then $|x| =$ ___.

If x is a _____ number, then $|x| = -x$.

Numbers

$|5| =$ _____

$|0| =$ _____

$|-4| =$ _____

= _____

Example 5 Find absoute values of numbers

a. If $a = -\frac{3}{7}$, then $|a| =$ _____ = _____ = ___.

b. If $a = 2.9$, then $|a| =$ _____ = ___.

Your Notes

Example 6 — Analyze a conditional statement

Identify the hypothesis and the conclusion of the statement "If a number is an integer, then the number is positive." Tell whether the statement is *true* or *false*. If it is false, give a counterexample.

Solution

Hypothesis: _____

Conclusion: _____

The statement is _____ _____.

✓ **Checkpoint** For the given value of a, find $-a$ and $|a|$.

2. $a = 6$	3. $a = -9.5$	4. $a = -\dfrac{3}{8}$

✓ **Checkpoint** Identify the hypothesis and conclusion of the statement. Tell whether the statement is *true* or *false*. If it is false, give a counterexample.

5. If a number is negative, then the absolute value of the number is negative.

Homework

2.2 Add Real Numbers

Goal • Add positive and negative numbers.

VOCABULARY

Additive identity

Additive inverse

Example 1 — Add two integers using a number line

Use the number line to find the sum.

a. $-5 + 7$

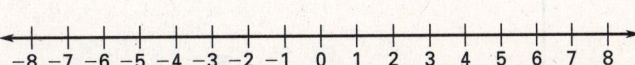

Start at ____.

To add, move ____ units to the ____.

End at ____.

Answer: $-5 + 7 =$ ____.

b. $-3 + (-4)$

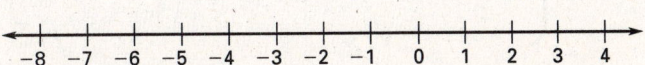

Start at ____.

To add, move ____ units to the ____.

End at ____.

Answer: $-3 + (-4) =$ ____.

Remember: To add a positive number, move to the right on a number line. To add a negative number, move to the left.

Your Notes

> **RULES OF ADDITION**
>
> **To add two numbers with the *same sign*:**
> 1. Add their _____.
> 2. The sum has the _____ as the numbers added.
>
> Example: $-5 + (-7) =$ _____
>
> **To add two numbers with *different signs*:**
> 1. Subtract the _____ absolute value.
> 2. The sum has the _____ as the number with the _____ absolute value.
>
> Example: $-10 + 4 =$ _____

Example 2   **Add real numbers**

> **Find the sum.**
>
> a. $-2.5 + (-4.2) = -(\_\_\_\_ + \_\_\_\_)$ Rule of same signs
>
> $= -(\_\_\_ + \_\_\_)$ Take absolute values.
>
> $= \_\_\_\_$ Add.
>
> b. $10.5 + (-15.0) = \_\_\_\_ - \_\_\_\_$ Rule of different signs
>
> $= \_\_\_\_ - \_\_\_\_$ Take absolute values.
>
> $= \_\_\_\_$ Subtract and take sign from greater absolute value.

✓ **Checkpoint** Find the sum.

1. $-7 + (-3)$	2. $9.6 + (-2.1)$

Your Notes

PROPERTIES OF ADDITION

Commutative Property The order in which you add two numbers does not change the sum.

$a + b = \underline{} + \underline{}$

Example: $-1 + 3 = \underline{} + \underline{}$

Associative Property The way you group three numbers in a sum does not change the sum.

$(a + b) + c = \underline{} + (\underline{} + \underline{})$

Example: $(1 + 2) + 3 = \underline{} + (\underline{} + \underline{})$

Identity Property The sum of a number and 0 is the number.

$a + 0 = \underline{} + \underline{} = \underline{}$

Example: $4 + 0 = \underline{}$

Inverse Property The sum of a number and its opposite is 0.

$a + (-a) = \underline{} + \underline{} = \underline{}$

Example: $-9 + \underline{} = 0$

Example 3 Identify properties of addition

Identify the property illustrated by the statement.

Statement   **Property Illustrated**

a. $x + 5 = 5 + x$

_____ of addition

b. $y + 0 = y$

_____ of addition

Homework

✓ **Checkpoint** Identify the property being illustrated.

3. $-5 + 5 = 0$

_____

4. $(-5 + 2) + 3 = -5 + (2 + 3)$

2.3 Subtract Real Numbers

Goal • Subtract real numbers.

Your Notes

SUBTRACTION RULE

Words: To subtract b from a, add the _____ of b to a.

Algebra: $a - b =$ ___ $+$ _____

Numbers: $15 - 7 =$ ___ $+$ _____

Example 1 Subtract real numbers

Find the difference.

a. $-10 - 4 = -10 +$ _____ $=$ _____

b. $13 - (-11) = 13 +$ ___ $=$ ___

Example 2 Evaluate a variable expression

Evaluate the expression $a - b + 5.3$ when $a = 6.5$ and $b = -3$.

Solution

$a - b + 5.3 =$ _____ $-$ _____ $+ 5.3$ Substitute values.

$=$ _____ $+$ ___ $+ 5.3$ Add the opposite of _____.

$=$ _____   Add.

✓ **Checkpoint** Find the difference.

1. $-4 - 8$	2. $9 - 18$

Your Notes

✓ **Checkpoint** Evaluate the expression when $m = 3.2$ and $t = -4$.

3. $m - t + 2$	4. $(m - 3) - t$

Example 3   Evaluate change

Hiking Trail A sign at the start of a hiking trail states you are 320 feet below sea level. At the end of the trail another sign states you are 880 feet above sea level. Find the change in elevation of the trail.

Solution

Step 1 Write a verbal model of the situation.

Change in elevation = Elevation at _____ of trail − Elevation at _____ of trail

Step 2 Find the change in elevation.

Change in elevation = _____ − _____   Substitute values.

= _____ + _____   Add the opposite of _____.

= _____   Add _____ and _____.

The change in elevation is _____ feet.

✓ **Checkpoint** Complete the following exercise.

5. In the morning, the temperature was −3°F. In the afternoon, the temperature was 21°F. What was the change in temperature?

Homework

2.4 Multiply Real Numbers

Goal • Multiply real numbers.

Your Notes

VOCABULARY

Multiplicative identity _____

THE SIGN OF A PRODUCT

The product of two real numbers with the **same sign** is _____.

Examples: 5(2) = ____

   −4(−5) = ____

The product of two real numbers with **different signs** is _____.

Examples: 5(−3) = ____

   −8(4) = ____

Example 1 *Multiply real numbers*

Find the product.

Solution

a. −7(−3) = ____   Same signs: product is _____.

b. 3(4)(−2) = ____(−2)   Multiply 3 and 4.

   = ____   Different signs: product is _____.

c. $\frac{1}{4}$(−16)(−3) = ____(−3)   Multiply $\frac{1}{4}$ and −16.

   = ____   Same signs: product is _____.

32 Lesson 2.4 • Algebra 1 Notetaking Guide   Copyright © McDougal Littell/Houghton Mifflin Company

Your Notes

✓ **Checkpoint** Find the product.

1. −4(−6)	2. −3(−2)(−7)

PROPERTIES OF MULTIPLICATION

Commutative Property The order in which two numbers are multiplied does not change the product.

$a \cdot b =$ ___ · ___

Example: $3 \cdot 4 =$ ___ · ___

Associative Property The way you group three numbers when multiplying does not change the product.

$(a \cdot b) \cdot c =$ ___ · (___ · ___)

Example: $(2 \cdot 3) \cdot 4 =$ ___ · (___ · ___)

Identity Property The product of a number and 1 is that number.

$a \cdot 1 =$ ___ · ___ = ___

Example: $(-2) \cdot 1 =$ ___

Property of Zero The product of a number and 0 is 0.

$a \cdot 0 =$ ___ · ___ = ___

Example: $4 \cdot$ ___ $= 0$

Property of −1 The product of a number and −1 is the opposite of the number.

$a \cdot (-1) =$ ___ · ___ = ___

Example: $-5 \cdot (-1) =$ ___

Your Notes

> **Example 2** *Identify properties of multiplication*
>
> Identify the property illustrated by each expression.
>
> **Solution**
>
> | Statement | Property Illustrated |
> |---|---|
> | a. $3 \cdot 0 = 0$ | _____ |
> | b. $t \cdot 1 = t$ | _____ of multiplication |
> | c. $a \cdot 3 = 3 \cdot a$ | _____ of multiplication |
> | d. $n \cdot (3 \cdot 5) = (n \cdot 3) \cdot 5$ | _____ of multiplication |
> | e. $-7(-1) = 7$ | _____ |

✓ **Checkpoint** Identify the property illustrated.

3. $-4 \cdot 0 = 0$

4. $6 \cdot 2 = 2 \cdot 6$

5. $(4 \cdot 5) \cdot 6 = 4 \cdot (5 \cdot 6)$

6. $4 \cdot (-1) = -4$

Your Notes

Example 3 *Use properties of multiplication*

Find the product $(0.5)(-2x)(6)$. Justify your steps.

Solution

$(0.5)(-2x)(6) = (-2x)(0.5)(6)$ _____

$ = (-2x)(0.5 \cdot 6)$ _____

$ = (-2x)(3)$ _____

$ = 3 \cdot (-2x)$ _____

$ = [3 \cdot (-2)]x$ _____

$ = -6x$

✓ **Checkpoint** Find the product. Justify your steps.

7. $-\frac{1}{2}(2)(3y)$

8. $(-2)(a)(-5)$

Homework

Lesson 2.4 • Algebra 1 Notetaking Guide 35

2.5 Apply the Distributive Property

Goal • Apply the distributive property.

Your Notes

VOCABULARY

Equivalent expressions

_____

Distributive property

_____

Terms

_____

Coefficient

_____

Constant term

_____

Like terms

THE DISTRIBUTIVE PROPERTY

Let a, b, and c be real numbers.

Algebra

$a(b + c) = ab + $ ____

$(b + c)a = ba + $ ____

$a(b - c) = ab - $ ____

$(b - c)a = ba - $ ____

Numbers

$4(2 + 3) = $ ____ $+$ ____

$(3 + 5)2 = $ ____ $+$ ____

$7(5 - 3) = $ ____ $-$ ____

$(6 - 4)9 = $ ____ $-$ ____

Your Notes

> Be sure to distribute the factor outside of the parentheses to *all* of the numbers inside the parentheses.

Example 1 Apply the distributive property

Use the distributive property to write an equivalent equation.

Solution

a. $4(a + 3) =$ _____

b. $(a + 5)6 =$ _____

c. $3(x - 8) =$ _____

d. $(4 - x)(x) =$ _____

> Use the distributive property to combine like terms with variable parts. Your expression is *simplified* if there are no grouping symbols and all like terms are combined.

Example 2 Distribute a negative number

Use the distributive property to write an equivalent equation.

Solution

a. $-3(7 + x)$

   $=$ ____(7) + _____(x)   Distribute _____.

   $=$ _____   _____.

b. $(6 - a)(-2a)$

   $= 6($____$) - a($_____$)$ Distribute _____.

   $=$ _____   _____.

✓ Checkpoint Use the distributive property to write an equivalent equation.

1. $5(n + 4)$	2. $-a(3 + a)$

Lesson 2.5 • Algebra 1 Notetaking Guide

Your Notes

> **Example 3** *Identify parts of an expression*
>
> Identify the terms, like terms, coefficients, and constant terms of the expression $2x - 5 + 8x - 3$.
>
> **Solution**
>
> _____   Write the expression as a sum.
>
> **Terms:**   **Like terms:**
>
> _____   _____
>
> **Coefficients:**   **Constant terms:**
>
> _____   _____

✓ **Checkpoint** Identify the terms, like terms, coefficients, and constant terms of the expressions.

3. $10 + 3a - 4 - 6a$

4. $7y - 11 - 4y - 1$

Homework

2.6 Divide Real Numbers

Goal • Divide real numbers.

Your Notes

VOCABULARY

Multiplicative inverse

INVERSE PROPERTY OF MULTIPLICATION

Words

The _____ of a nonzero number and its multiplicative inverse is ___.

Algebra

$a \cdot \frac{1}{a} =$ ___, $a \neq$ ___

Numbers

$4 \cdot \frac{1}{4} =$ ___

Example 1 Find multiplicative inverses of numbers

Identify the multiplicative inverse and justify your answer.

Solution

Number	Multiplicative inverse	Reason
a. 9	_____	_____
b. $-\frac{5}{6}$	_____	_____

Lesson 2.6 • **Algebra 1 Notetaking Guide** 39

Your Notes

✓ **Checkpoint** Find the multiplicative inverse.

1. $-\dfrac{2}{3}$	2. 3

DIVISION RULE

Words

To divide a number a by a nonzero number b, multiply ___ by the multiplicative inverse of ___.

Algebra

$a \div b = a \cdot \underline{}$, $b \neq \underline{}$

Numbers

$7 \div 3 = \underline{}$

> You cannot divide a real number by 0, because 0 does not have a multiplicative inverse.

THE SIGN OF A QUOTIENT

The quotient of two real numbers with the same sign is _____.

The quotient of two real numbers with different signs is _____.

The quotient of 0 and any nonzero real number is ___.

Example 2 *Divide real numbers*

Find the quotient.

Solution

a. $25 \div 5 = 25 \cdot \underline{} = \underline{}$

b. $-40 \div \dfrac{2}{3} = -40 \cdot \underline{} = \underline{}$

Your Notes

✓ **Checkpoint** Find the quotient.

3. $\frac{1}{2} \div \frac{3}{4}$	4. $16 \div \left(-\frac{1}{4}\right)$

Example 3 Simplify an expression

Simplify the expression $\frac{48y - 32}{8}$.

Solution

$\frac{48y - 32}{8} = (48y - 32) \div \underline{}$ Rewrite fraction as division.

$= (48y - 32) \cdot \underline{}$ Division rule

$= 48y \cdot \underline{} - 32 \cdot \underline{}$ Distributive property

$= \underline{}$ Simplify.

✓ **Checkpoint** Simplify the expression.

5. $\frac{3a + 4}{2}$	6. $\frac{12x - 8}{4}$

Homework

2.7 Find Square Roots and Compare Real Numbers

Goal • Find square roots and compare real numbers.

Your Notes

VOCABULARY

Square root

Radicand

Perfect square

Irrational number

Real number

SQUARE ROOT OF A NUMBER

Words

If $b^2 = a$, then ___ is a square root of ___.

Numbers

$5^2 = 25$ and $(-5)^2 = 25$, so ___ and ___ are square roots of 25.

Your Notes

> All positive real numbers have two square roots, a positive and a negative square root. The positive square root is called the *principal* square root.

Example 1 — Find square roots

Evaluate the expression.

Solution

a. $-\sqrt{36} =$ _____   The negative square root of 36 is _____ .

b. $\sqrt{16} =$ _____   The positive square root of 16 is _____ .

c. $\pm\sqrt{64} =$ _____   The positive and negative square roots of 64 are _____ and _____ .

✓ **Checkpoint** Evaluate the expression.

1. $\sqrt{100}$	2. $-\sqrt{1}$

Example 2 — Classify numbers

Tell whether each of the following numbers is a real number, a rational number, an irrational number, an integer, or a whole number: $\sqrt{144}$, $-\sqrt{49}$, $\sqrt{32}$.

Solution

Number	Real Number?	Rational Number?	Irrational Number?	Integer?	Whole Number?
$\sqrt{144}$					
$-\sqrt{49}$					
$\sqrt{32}$					

Lesson 2.7 • Algebra 1 Notetaking Guide

Your Notes

> **Example 3** *Graph and order real numbers*
>
> Order the numbers from least to greatest:
>
> $\sqrt{16}, \frac{5}{2}, \sqrt{4}, -3, -\sqrt{6}.$
>
> **Solution**
>
> Graph the numbers on a number line.
>
>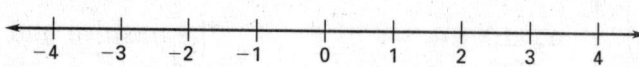
>
> Read the numbers from left to right:
>
> _____ .

✓ **Checkpoint** Complete the following exercises.

3. Tell whether each of the following numbers is a real number, rational number, irrational number, integer, or whole number: $\sqrt{49}, 0, -\frac{6}{4}, -2, \sqrt{17}.$

4. Order the numbers from Exercise 3 from least to greatest.

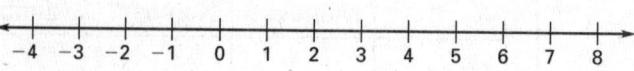

Homework

Words to Review

Give an example of the vocabulary word.

Whole number	Integer
Rational number	Opposite
Absolute Value	Conditional Statement
Additive identity/ Additive inverse	Multiplicative identity
Equivalent expressions	Distributive property
Terms	Coefficient
Constant term	Like terms

Multiplicative inverse	Square root
Radicand	Perfect square
Irrational number	Real number

Review your notes and Chapter 2 by using the Chapter Review on pages 121–124 of your textbook.

3.1 Solve One-Step Equations

Goal • Solve one-step equations using algebra.

Your Notes

VOCABULARY

Inverse operations

Equivalent equations

ADDITION PROPERTY OF EQUALITY

Words Adding the same number to each side of an equation produces an _____.

Algebra If $x - a = b$, then $x - a + a = $ ___ $+$ ___
or $x = $ ___ $+$ ___.

SUBTRACTION PROPERTY OF EQUALITY

Words Subtracting the same number from each side of an equation produces an _____ _____.

Algebra If $x + a = b$, then $x + a - a = $ ___ $-$ ___
or $x = $ ___ $-$ ___.

Your Notes

> Remember to check your solution in the original equation for accuracy.

Example 1 — Solve an equation using subtraction

Solve $y + 3 = 10$.

Solution

$y + 3 = 10$ Write original equation.

$y + 3 - \underline{} = 10 - \underline{}$ Use subtraction property of equality: Subtract ___ from each side.

$y = \underline{}$ Simplify.

The solution is ___.

CHECK

$y + 3 = 10$ Write original equation.

$\underline{} + 3 \stackrel{?}{=} 10$ Substitute ___ for y.

$\underline{} = 10$ ✓   Solution checks.

Example 2 — Solve an equation using addition

Solve $t - 9 = 11$.

Solution

$t - 9 = 11$ Write original equation.

$t - 9 + \underline{} = 11 + \underline{}$ Use addition property of equality: Add ___ to each side.

$t = \underline{}$ Simplify.

The solution is ___.

CHECK

$t - 9 = 11$ Write original equation.

$\underline{} - 9 \stackrel{?}{=} 11$ Substitute ___ for t.

$\underline{} = 11$ ✓   Solution checks.

Your Notes

✓ **Checkpoint** Solve each equation. Check your solution.

1. $a + 6 = 17$	2. $b - 17 = 12$
3. $-3 = x + 2$	4. $y - 4 = -6$

MULTIPLICATION PROPERTY OF EQUALITY

Words Multiplying each side of an equation by the same non-zero number produces an _____.

Algebra If $\frac{x}{a} = b$ and $a \neq 0$, then $a \cdot \frac{x}{a} =$ ___ · ___ or $x =$ ___.

DIVISION PROPERTY OF EQUALITY

Words Dividing each side of an equation by the same non-zero number produces an _____.

Algebra If $ax = b$, and $a \neq 0$, then $\frac{ax}{a} = \frac{\Box}{\Box}$ or $x = \frac{\Box}{\Box}$.

Your Notes

> The *division property of equality* can be used to solve equations involving multiplication.

Example 3 Solve an equation using division

Solve $8x = 56$.

Solution

$8x = 56$ Write original equation.

$\dfrac{8x}{\Box} = \dfrac{56}{\Box}$ Use division property of equality: Divide each side by ___.

$x =$ ___ Simplify.

The solution is ___.

CHECK

$8x = 56$ Write original equation.

$8(\underline{}) \stackrel{?}{=} 56$ Substitute ___ for x.

___ $= 56$ ✓ Solution checks.

> The *multiplication property of equality* can be used to solve equations involving division.

Example 4 Solve an equation using multiplication

Solve $\dfrac{a}{5} = 12$.

Solution

$\dfrac{a}{5} = 12$ Write original equation.

___ $\cdot \dfrac{a}{5} =$ ___ $\cdot 12$ Use multiplication property of equality: Multiply each side by ___.

$a =$ ___ Simplify.

The solution is ___.

CHECK

$\dfrac{a}{5} = 12$ Write original equation.

$\dfrac{\Box}{5} \stackrel{?}{=} 12$ Substitute ___ for a.

___ $= 12$ ✓ Solution checks.

Your Notes

Example 5 *Solve an equation by multiplying by a reciprocal*

Solve $\frac{3}{5}t = 6$.

Solution

The coefficient of t is $\frac{3}{5}$. The reciprocal of $\frac{3}{5}$ is ___.

$\frac{3}{5}t = 6$ Write original equation.

___ · $\frac{3}{5}t =$ ___ · 6   Multiply each side by the reciprocal ___.

$t =$ ___   Simplify.

The solution is ___.

CHECK

$\frac{3}{5}t = 6$ Write original equation.

$\frac{3}{5}($ ___ $) \stackrel{?}{=} 6$ Substitute ___ for t.

___ $= 6$ ✓   Solution checks.

✓ **Checkpoint** Solve each equation. Check your solution.

5. $3x = 39$	6. $\frac{b}{4} = 13$
7. $-24 = 4x$	8. $-\frac{3}{8}m = 21$

Homework

3.2 Solve Two-Step Equations

Goal • Solve two-step equations.

Your Notes

IDENTIFYING OPERATIONS

Identify the operations involved in the equation $3x + 7 = 19$.

Operations performed on x	Operations to isolate x
1. Multiply by ___.	1. Subtract ___.
2. Add ___.	2. Divide by ___.

Example 1 Solve a two-step equation

Solve $3x + 7 = 19$.

Solution

> When solving a two-step equation, apply the inverse operations in the reverse order of the order of operations.

$3x + 7 = 19$ Write original equation.

$3x + 7 - \underline{} = 19 - \underline{}$ Subtract ___ from each side.

$3x = \underline{}$ Simplify.

$\dfrac{3x}{\boxed{}} = \dfrac{12}{\boxed{}}$ Divide each side by ___.

$x = \underline{}$ Simplify.

The solution is ___.

CHECK

$3x + 7 = 19$ Write original equation.

$3(\underline{}) + 7 \stackrel{?}{=} 19$ Substitute ___ for x.

$\underline{} + 7 \stackrel{?}{=} 19$ Multiply 3 by ___.

$\underline{} = 19 \checkmark$ Simplify. Solution checks.

Your Notes

✓ **Checkpoint** Solve the two-step equation. Check your solution.

1. $\frac{r}{4} - 12 = -5$	2. $7k - 14 = 42$

Example 2 Solve a two-step equation by combining like terms

Solve $4a + 3a = 63$.

Solution

$4a + 3a = 63$ Write original equation.

$\underline{} = 63$ Combine like terms.

$\dfrac{\boxed{}}{\boxed{}} = \dfrac{63}{\boxed{}}$ Divide each side by ___.

$a = \underline{}$ Simplify.

The solution is ___.

CHECK

$4a + 3a = 63$ Write original equation.

$4(\underline{}) + 3(\underline{}) \stackrel{?}{=} 63$ Substitute ___ for a.

$\underline{} + \underline{} \stackrel{?}{=} 63$ Multiply 4 by ___ and 3 by ___.

$\underline{} = 63$ ✓   Add. Solution checks.

✓ **Checkpoint** Solve the equation. Check your solution.

3. $5z + 4z = 36$	4. $5b - 2b = 9$

Lesson 3.2 • Algebra 1 Notetaking Guide

Your Notes

Example 3 — Find an input of a function

The output of a function is 2 more than 4 times the input. Find the input when the output is 14.

Solution

Step 1 Write an equation for the function. Let x be the input and y be the output.

$y =$ _____ y is 2 more than 4 times x.

Step 2 Solve the equation when $y = 14$.

$y =$ _____	Write original function.
_____ $=$ _____	Substitute ____ for y.
_____ $=$ _____	Subtract ___ from each side.
_____ $=$ _____	Simplify.
$\dfrac{\Box}{\Box} = \dfrac{\Box}{\Box}$	Divide each side by ___.
_____ $= x$	Simplify.

An input of ___ produces an output of ____.

CHECK

$y =$ _____	Write original function.
_____ $\stackrel{?}{=}$ _____	Substitute ___ for y and ___ for x.
_____ $\stackrel{?}{=}$ _____	Multiply ___ and ___.
_____ $=$ _____ ✓	Simplify. Solution checks.

✅ **Checkpoint** Solve the equation. Check your solution.

Homework

5. The output of a function is 3 less than 6 times the input. Find the input when the output is 15.

3.3 Solve Multi-Step Equations

Goal • Solve multi-step equations.

Your Notes

Example 1 — Solve an equation by combining like terms

Solve $3t + 5t - 5 = 11$.

Solution

$3t + 5t - 5 = 11$	Write original equation.
$\underline{} - 5 = 11$	Combine like terms.
$\underline{} - 5 + \underline{} = 11 + \underline{}$	Add ___ to each side.
$\underline{} = \underline{}$	Simplify.
$\dfrac{\Box}{\Box} = \dfrac{\Box}{\Box}$	Divide each side by ___.
$t = \underline{}$	Simplify.

The solution is ___.

Example 2 — Solve an equation using the distributive property

Solve $5a + 3(a + 2) = 22$.

Solution

Method 1
Show All Steps

$5a + 3(a + 2) = 22$
$5a + \underline{} + \underline{} = 22$
$\underline{} + \underline{} = 22$
$\underline{} = 22 - \underline{}$
$\underline{} = 16$
$\dfrac{\Box}{\Box} = \dfrac{16}{\Box}$
$a = \underline{}$

Method 2
Do Some Steps Mentally

$5a + 3(a + 2) = 22$
$5a + \underline{} + \underline{} = 22$
$\underline{} + \underline{} = 22$
$\underline{} = 16$
$a = \underline{}$

Your Notes

✓ **Checkpoint** Solve the equation. Check your solution.

1. $9d - 4d - 2 = 18$	2. $2x + 7(x - 3) = 6$
3. $3w + 4 + w = 36$	4. $40 = 2(10 + 4k) + 2k$

Example 3 Multiply by a reciprocal to solve an equation

Solve $\frac{3}{4}(a - 5) = 9$.

Solution

$\frac{3}{4}(a - 5) = 9$ Write original equation.

___ • $\frac{3}{4}(a - 5) =$ ___ • 9 Multiply each side by ___.

$a - 5 =$ ___ Simplify.

$a - 5 +$ ___ $= 12 +$ ___ Add ___ to each side.

$a =$ ___ Simplify.

✓ **Checkpoint** Solve the equation. Check your solution.

5. $\frac{1}{2}(4x - 2) = 7$	6. $\frac{5}{6}(2y + 4) = 10$

Homework

3.4 Solve Equations with Variables on Both Sides

Goal • Solve equations with variables on both sides.

Your Notes

VOCABULARY

Identity

Example 1 *Solve an equation with variables on both sides*

Solve $15 + 4a = 9a - 5$.

Solution

> Collect variables on one side of the equation and constant terms on the other to solve equations with variables on both sides.

$15 + 4a = 9a - 5$	Write original equation.
$15 + 4a - \_\_\_ = 9a - \_\_\_ - 5$	Subtract ___ from each side.
$15 = \_\_\_ - 5$	Simplify.
$15 + \_\_\_ = \_\_\_ - 5 + \_\_\_$	Add ___ to each side.
$\_\_\_ = \_\_\_$	Simplify.
$\dfrac{\Box}{\Box} = \dfrac{\Box}{\Box}$	Divide each side by ___.
$\_\_\_ = a$	Simplify.

The solution is ___.

CHECK

$15 + 4a = 9a - 5$	Write original equation.
$15 + 4(\_\_\_) \stackrel{?}{=} 9(\_\_\_) - 5$	Substitute ___ for a.
$15 + \_\_\_ \stackrel{?}{=} \_\_\_ - 5$	Multiply.
$\_\_\_ = \_\_\_$ ✓	Solution checks.

Lesson 3.4 • Algebra 1 Notetaking Guide 57

Your Notes

Example 2 — Solve an equation with grouping symbols

Solve $4t - 12 = 6(t + 3)$.

Solution

$4t - 12 = 6(t + 3)$	Write original equation.
$4t - 12 = \underline{} + \underline{}$	Distributive property
$-12 = \underline{} + \underline{}$	Subtract ____ from each side.
$\underline{} = \underline{}$	Subtract ____ from each side.
$\underline{} = t$	Divide each side by ____.

✓ **Checkpoint** Solve the equation. Check your solution.

1. $3b + 7 = 8b + 2$	2. $6d - 6 = \frac{3}{4}(4d + 8)$

Example 3 — Identify the number of solutions of an equation

Solve the equation, if possible.

a. $4x + 5 = 4(x + 5)$ b. $6x - 3 = 3(2x - 1)$

Solution

a.
$4x + 5 = 4(x + 5)$	Original equation
$4x + 5 = \underline{}$	Distributive property

The equation $4x + 5 = \underline{}$ is _____ because the number $4x$ _____ equal to 5 more than itself and ____ more than itself. So, the equation has ____ solution.

b.
$6x - 3 = 3(2x - 1)$	Original equation
$6x - 3 = \underline{}$	Distributive property

The statement $6x - 3 = \underline{}$ is _____ for all values of x. So, the equation is an _____.

Your Notes

✓ **Checkpoint** Solve the equation, if possible.

3. $\frac{1}{2}(4t - 6) = 2t$

4. $10m - 4 = -2(2 - 5m)$

STEPS FOR SOLVING LINEAR EQUATIONS

Step 1 Use the _____ to remove any grouping symbols.

Step 2 _____ the expression on each side of the equation.

Step 3 Use the properties of equality to collect the _____ terms on one side of the equation and the _____ terms on the other side of the equation.

Step 4 Use the properties of equality to solve for the _____.

Step 5 Check your _____ in the original equation.

Homework

3.5 Write Ratios and Proportions

Goals • Find ratios and write and solve proportions.

Your Notes

VOCABULARY

Ratio
_____

Proportion
_____

RATIOS

1. A ratio uses _____ to compare two quantities.

2. The ratio of two quantities, *a* and *b*, where *b* is not equal to 0, can be written in three ways:

    _____   _____   ____

3. Each ratio is read "the _____ of *a* to *b*".

4. Ratios should be written in _____ form.

Example 1 *Write a ratio*

Cell Phone Use A person makes 6 long distance calls and 15 local calls in 1 month.

a. Find the ratio of long distance calls to local calls.
b. Find the ratio of long distance calls to all calls.

Solution

a. $\dfrac{\text{long distance calls}}{\text{local calls}} = \dfrac{\square}{\square} = \dfrac{\square}{\square}$

b. $\dfrac{\text{long distance calls}}{\text{all calls}} = \dfrac{\square}{\square} = \dfrac{\square}{\square}$

Your Notes

✓ **Checkpoint** Shawn and Myra are selling tickets to their school's talent show. Shawn sold 36 tickets, and Myra sold 44 tickets. Find the specified ratio.

1. The number of tickets Shawn sold to the number of tickets Myra sold

2. The number of tickets Myra sold to the number of tickets Shawn and Myra sold

Example 2 *Solve a proportion*

Solve the proportion $\frac{y}{15} = \frac{3}{5}$.

Solution

$\frac{y}{15} = \frac{3}{5}$ Write original proportion.

$\underline{} \cdot \frac{y}{15} = \underline{} \cdot \frac{3}{5}$ Multiply each side by $\underline{}$.

$y = \frac{\square}{\square}$ Simplify.

$y = \underline{}$ Divide.

Use the same methods for solving equations to solve proportions with a variable in the numerator.

✓ **Checkpoint** Solve the proportion. Check your solution.

3. $\frac{9}{4} = \frac{c}{28}$

4. $\frac{a}{32} = \frac{7}{8}$

Your Notes

Example 3 Solve a multi-step problem

Swimming Pool A empty swimming pool is being filled with water. After 5 minutes the pool has 400 gallons of water. If the pool has a volume of 11,200 gallons, how long does it take to fill the empty pool?

Solution

Step 1 Write a proportion involving two ratios that compare the amount of water in the pool to the amount of time.

$$\frac{400}{5} = \frac{\boxed{}}{x} \quad \begin{array}{l}\leftarrow \text{gallons} \\ \leftarrow \text{minutes}\end{array}$$

Step 2 Solve the proportion.

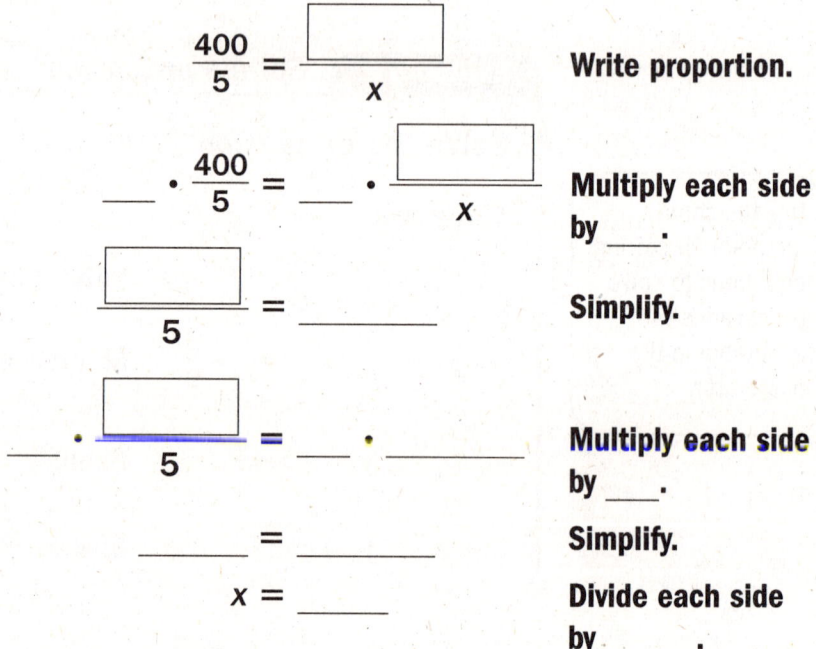

The pool is full after _____ minutes.

✓ Checkpoint Complete the following exercise.

Homework

5. An Olympic sized pool has a volume of 810,000 gallons. If it is filled at the same rate as the pool in Example 3, how long will it take to fill the pool?

3.6 Solve Proportions Using Cross Products

Goal • Solve proportions using cross products.

Your Notes

VOCABULARY

Cross product

Scale drawing

Scale model

Scale

CROSS PRODUCTS PROPERTY

Words The cross products of a proportion are _____.

Example $\dfrac{5}{6} = \dfrac{10}{12}$ ___ • 10 = 60
                                        ___ • 12 = 60

Algebra If $\dfrac{a}{b} = \dfrac{c}{d}$ where $b \neq 0$ and $d \neq 0$, then $ad =$ _____.

Your Notes

Example 1 — Solve a proportion using cross products

Solve the proportion $\dfrac{5}{y} = \dfrac{15}{75}$.

Solution

$\dfrac{5}{y} = \dfrac{15}{75}$ Write original proportion.

___ · 75 = ___ · 15   Cross products property

___ = ___   Simplify.

___ = y   Divide each side by ___.

The solution is ___.

Example 2 — Write and solve a proportion

Plant Food To feed your plants, you need to mix 3 tablespoons of plant food with 16 ounces of water. If it takes 80 ounces of water to feed all of your plants, how many tablespoons of plant food are needed?

Solution

Step 1 Write a proportion involving two ratios that compare the amount of plant food with the amount of water.

$\dfrac{3}{16} = \dfrac{x}{\boxed{}}$ ← amount of plant food
← amount of water

Step 2 Solve the proportion.

$\dfrac{3}{16} = \dfrac{x}{\boxed{}}$ Write proportion.

3 · ___ = ___ · x   Cross product property

___ = ___   Simplify.

___ = x   Divide each side by ___.

You need ___ tablespoons of plant food for 80 ounces of water.

Your Notes

✓ **Checkpoint** Solve the proportion. Check your solution.

1. $\dfrac{5}{n} = \dfrac{25}{45}$

2. $\dfrac{6}{b} = \dfrac{3}{b-2}$

3. In Example 2, suppose it takes 120 ounces to feed all of the plants. How many tablespoons of plant food are needed?

Example 3 Use a scale model

Scale Model An architect creates a scale model of a school. The school is 50 feet high. The ratio of the model to the actual school is 1 foot to 75 feet. Estimate the height of the model.

Solution

Write and solve a proportion to find the height h of the scale model.

$\dfrac{1}{\boxed{}} = \dfrac{h}{\boxed{}}$ ← height of model (feet)
  ← actual height (feet)

$1 \cdot \underline{} = \underline{} \cdot h$ Cross products property

$\underline{} = h$ Simplify.

The height of the scale model is ___ foot, or ___ inches.

✓ **Checkpoint** Complete the following exercise.

4. In Example 3, suppose the ratio of the model to the actual school is 1 foot to 100 feet. Estimate the height of the model.

Homework

3.7 Solve Percent Problems

Goal • Solve percent problems.

Your Notes

SOLVING PERCENT PROBLEMS USING PROPORTIONS

You can represent "*a* is *p* percent of *b*" by using the proportion

$$\frac{a}{b} = \frac{p}{\boxed{}}$$

where *a* is a part of the base ___ and $\frac{p}{\boxed{}}$, or *p*%, is the _____.

Example 1   *Find a percent using a proportion*

What percent of 50 is 33?

Solution

Write a proportion when 50 is the base and 33 is part of the base.

$\dfrac{a}{b} = \dfrac{p}{100}$ Write proportion.

$\dfrac{\boxed{}}{\boxed{}} = \dfrac{p}{100}$ Substitute ___ for *a* and ___ for *b*.

_____ = 50*p*   Cross products property

_____ = *p*   Divide each side by ___.

33 is _____ of 50.

66   Lesson 3.7 • Algebra 1 Notetaking Guide

Your Notes

✓ **Checkpoint** Use a proportion to answer the question.

1. What percent of 80 is 28?

_____

2. What percent of 90 is 36?

THE PERCENT EQUATION

You can represent "*a* is *p* percent of *b*" by using the equation:

$a = $ _____ $\cdot\ b$

where *a* is a part of the base _____ and *p*% is the _____.

> The percent equation, $a = p\% \cdot b$, is derived from the proportion, $\dfrac{a}{b} = \dfrac{p}{100}$.

Example 2 *Find a percent using the percent equation*

What percent of 224 is 98?

Solution

$a = p\% \cdot b$	Write percent equation.
_____ $= p\% \cdot$ _____	Substitute _____ for *a* and _____ for *b*.
_____ $= p\%$	Divide each side by _____.
_____ $= p\%$	Write decimal as a percent.

98 is _____ of 224.

CHECK

_____ $= p\% \cdot$ _____	Write original equation.
_____ $\overset{?}{=}$ _____ $\cdot$ _____	Substitute _____ for *p*%.
_____ $=$ _____ ✓	Multiply. Solution checks.

Your Notes

Example 3 Find a part of a base using the percent equation

What number is 75% of 164?

Solution

$a = p\% \cdot b$ Write percent equation.

= ____ · ____   Substitute ____ for p and ____ for b.

= ____ · ____   Write percent as a decimal.

= ____   Multiply.

____ is 75% of 164.

✓ **Checkpoint** Use the percent equation to answer the question.

3. What percent of 76 is 57?

4. What number is 35% of 80?

Example 4 Find a base using the percent equation

21 is 37.5% of what number?

Solution

$a = p\% \cdot b$ Write percent equation.

____ = ____ · b Substitute ____ for a and ____ for p.

____ = ____ · b Write percent as a decimal.

____ = b Divide each side by ____.

21 is 75% of ____.

68 Lesson 3.7 • Algebra 1 Notetaking Guide

Your Notes

✓ **Checkpoint** Use the percent equation to answer the question.

5. 27 is 25% of what number?

6. 78 is 150% of what number?

Homework

TYPES OF PERCENT PROBLEMS

Percent Problem	Example	Equation
Find a percent.	What percent of 252 is 84?	____ = p% · ____
Find part of a base.	What number is 30% of 90?	a = ____ · ____
Find a base.	16 is 20% of what number?	16 = ____ · b

Lesson 3.7 • Algebra 1 Notetaking Guide

3.8 Rewrite Equations and Formulas

Goal • Write equations in function form and rewrite formulas.

Your Notes

VOCABULARY

Function form

Literal equation

Example 1 *Rewrite an equation in function form*

Write $2x + 2y = 10$ in function form.

Solution

Solve the equation for y.

$2x + 2y = 10$	Write original equation.
$2y = $ _____	Subtract _____ from each side.
$y = $ _____	Divide each side by ____.

The equation $y = $ _____ is written in function form.

Example 2 *Solve a literal equation*

Solve $a + by = c$ for a.

Solution

$a + by = c$	Write original equation.
$a = $ _____	Subtract _____ from each side.

The solution is $a = $ _____.

Your Notes

Example 3: Solve and use a formula

The interest I on an investment of P dollars at an interest rate r for t years is given by the formula $I = Prt$.

a. Solve the formula for the time t.

b. Use the rewritten formula to find the time it takes to earn $100 interest on $1000 at a rate of 5.0%.

Solution

a. $I = Prt$ Write original formula.

$\dfrac{I}{\boxed{}} = t$ Divide each side by ____.

b. Substitute ____ for I, ____ for P, and ____ for r in the rewritten formula.

$t = \dfrac{I}{\boxed{}}$ Write rewritten formula.

$= \dfrac{\boxed{}}{\boxed{} \cdot \boxed{}}$ Substitute.

$= \underline{}$ Simplify.

It will take ____ years to earn $100 in interest.

✓ Checkpoint Write the equation in function form.

1. $2x + y = 5$	2. $3 + 3y = 9 - 6x$

✓ Checkpoint Complete the following exercises.

3. Solve $a + by = c$ for b.

4. In Example 3, solve the equation for P. Find the investment P if $I = \$400$, $r = 4\%$, and $t = 4$ years.

Homework

Words to Review

Give an example of the vocabulary word.

Inverse operations	Equivalent equations
Identity	Ratio
Proportion	Cross product
Scale drawing	Scale model
Scale	Function form
Literal equation	

Review your notes and Chapter 3 by using the Chapter Review on pages 192–196 of your textbook.

4.1 Plot Points in a Coordinate Plane

Goal • Identify and plot points in a coordinate plane.

Your Notes

VOCABULARY

Quadrant

Example 1 Name points in a coordinate plane

Give the coordinates of the point.

a. A   b. B

Solution

a. Point A is ___ units to the _____ of the origin and ___ units _____.
The x-coordinate is ___.
The y-coordinate is ___.
The coordinates are _____.

b. Point B is ___ units to the _____ of the origin and ___ units _____.
The x-coordinate is ___.
The y-coordinate is ___.
The coordinates are _____.

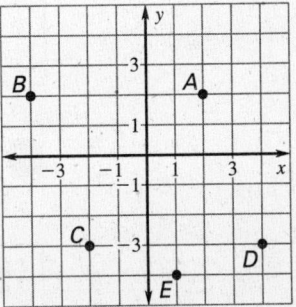

> Points in Quadrant I have two positive coordinates. Points in the other three quadrants have at least one negative coordinate.

✓ **Checkpoint** Complete the following exercise.

1. Use the coordinate plane in Example 1 to give the coordinates of points C, D, and E.

Lesson 4.1 • Algebra 1 Notetaking Guide 73

Your Notes

Example 2 Plot points in a coordinate plane

Plot the point in a coordinate plane. Describe the location of the point.

a. A(0, 3)   b. B(1, −2)   c. C(−3, −4)

Solution

a. Begin at the _____.
   Move ___ units _____.
   Point A is on the _____.

b. Begin at the _____.
   Move ___ unit to the _____.
   Move ___ units _____.
   Point B is in Quadrant ___.

c. Begin at the _____.
   Move ___ units to the _____.
   Move ___ units _____.
   Point C is in Quadrant ___.

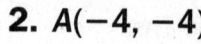

✓ **Checkpoint** Plot the point in a coordinate plane. Describe the location of the point.

2. A(−4, −4)	3. B(2, 0)
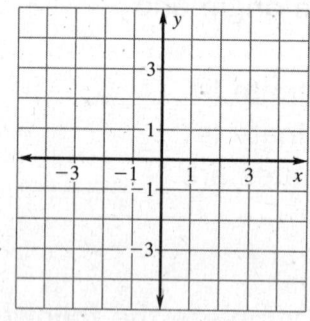	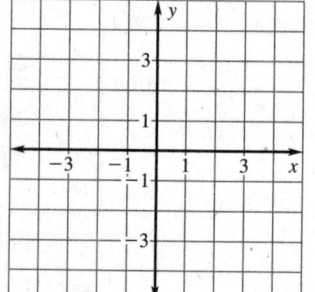

Your Notes

Example 3 Graph a function

Graph the function y = x + 1 with domain −2, −1, 0, 1, 2. Then identify the range of the function.

Solution

Step 1 Make a table.

x	y = x + 1
−2	y = −2 + 1 = _____
−1	y = −1 + 1 = _____
0	y = 0 + 1 = _____
1	y = 1 + 1 = _____
2	y = 2 + 1 = _____

Step 2 List the ordered pairs:

(−2, ____), (−1, ____), (0, ____), (1, ____), (2, ____).

Then graph the function.

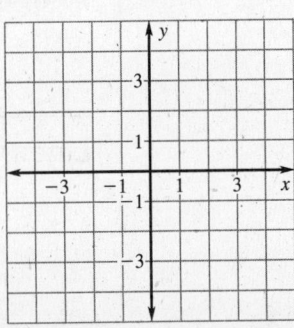

Step 3 Identify the range: _____.

✓ **Checkpoint** Complete the following exercise.

4. Graph the function $y = -\frac{1}{2}x + 3$ with domain −4, −2, 0, 2, and 4. Then identify the range.

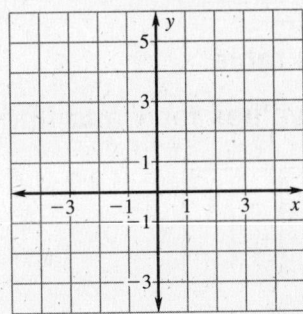

Homework

4.2 Graph Linear Equations

Goal • Graph linear equations in a coordinate plane.

Your Notes

VOCABULARY

Solution of an equation in two variables

Graph of an equation in two variables

Linear equation

Standard form of a linear equation

Linear function

Example 1 *Graph an equation*

Graph the equation $x + y = 4$.

Solution

Step 1 Solve the equation for y.

$x + y = 4$

$y =$ _____

Step 2 Make a table.

Choose a few values for x and find the values for y.

x	−2	−1	0	1	2
y					

Use convenient values for x when making a table. These should include a combination of negative values, zero, and positive values.

Your Notes

Step 3 Plot the points.

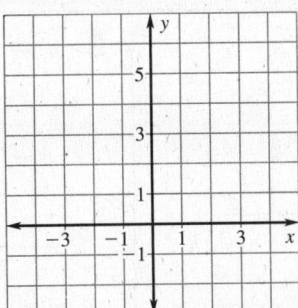

Step 4 **Connect** the points by drawing a line through them. Use arrows to indicate that the graph goes on without end.

Example 2 Graph y = b and x = a

Graph (a) y = −3 and (b) x = 2.

Solution

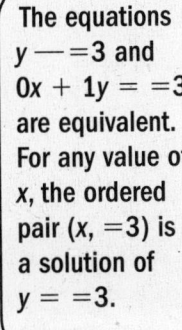

The equations y —=3 and 0x + 1y = =3 are equivalent. For any value of x, the ordered pair (x, =3) is a solution of y = =3.

a. Regardless of the value of x, the value of y is always _____. The graph of y = −3 is a _____ line 3 units _____ the x-axis.

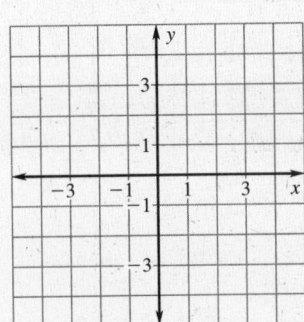

b. Regardless of the value of y, the value of x is always _____. The graph of x = 2 is a _____ line 2 units to the _____ of the y-axis.

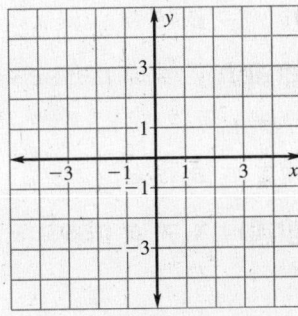

Your Notes

✓ **Checkpoint** Graph the equation.

1. $y = 2x - 1$

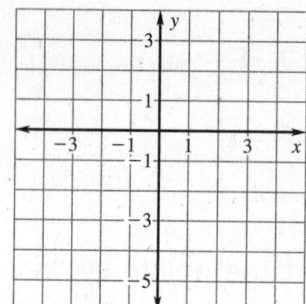

2. $x = 0.5$

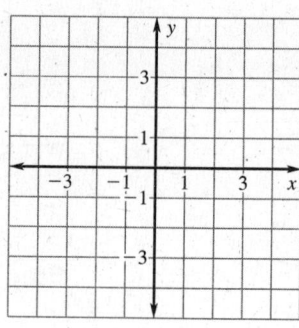

3. $y = -4x + 1$

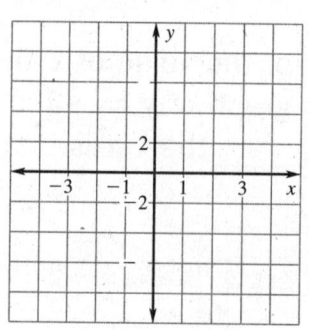

4. $y = -1.5$

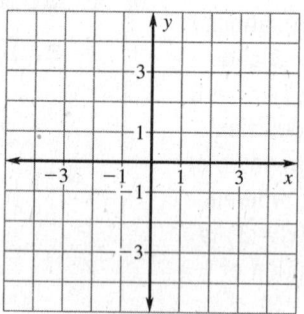

EQUATIONS OF HORIZONTAL AND VERTICAL LINES

1. The graph of $y = b$ is a _____ line.
2. The line of graph $y = b$ passes through the point _____.
3. The graph of $x = a$ is a _____ line.
4. The line of graph $x = a$ passes through the point _____.

Your Notes

Example 3 Graph a linear function

Graph the function y = 2x + 2 with domain x ≥ 0. Then identify the range of the function.

Solution

Step 1 Make a _____.

x	0	1	2	3	4
y					

Step 2 Plot the _____.

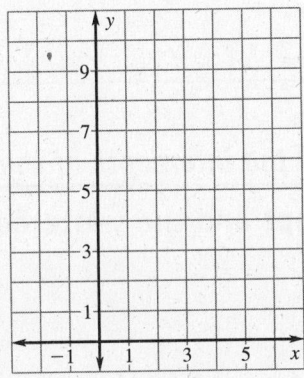

Step 3 Connect the points with a _____ because the domain is _____.

Step 4 Identify the range. From the graph, you can see that all points have a y-coordinate of _____, so the range of the function is _____.

✓ **Checkpoint** Complete the following exercise.

5. Graph the function y = −x + 4 with domain x ≥ 0. Then identify the range of the function.

Homework

4.3 Graph Using Intercepts

Goal • Graph a linear equation using intercepts.

Your Notes

VOCABULARY

x-intercept

_____

y-intercept

_____

Example 1 *Find the intercepts of the graph of an equation*

Find the *x*-intercept and the *y*-intercept of the graph of $8x - 2y = 32$.

Solution

1. Substitute ___ for *y* and solve for *x*.

   $8x - 2y = 32$ Write original equation.

   $8x - 2(\_\_) = 32$ Substitute ___ for *y*.

   $x = \dfrac{\boxed{}}{\boxed{}} = \_\_$ Solve for ___.

2. Substitute ___ for *x* and solve for *y*.

   $8x - 2y = 32$ Write original equation.

   $8(\_\_) - 2y = 32$ Substitute ___ for *x*.

   $y = \dfrac{\boxed{}}{\boxed{}} = \_\_\_\_$ Solve for ___.

The *x*-intercept is ___. The *y*-intercept is _____.

Your Notes

✓ **Checkpoint** Find the x-intercept and y-intercept of the graph of the equation.

1. $2x + 3y = 18$	2. $-12x - 4y = 36$

Example 2 Use intercepts to graph an equation

Graph $3.5x + 2y = 14$. Label the points where the line crosses the axis.

Solution

Step 1 Find the _____.

$3.5x + 2y = 14$ | $3.5x + 2y = 14$
$3.5x + 2(\_\_) = 14$ | $3.5(\_\_) + 2y = 14$
$x = \dfrac{\boxed{}}{\boxed{}} = \_\_$ | $y = \dfrac{\boxed{}}{\boxed{}} = \_\_$

Step 2 Plot the points that correspond to the intercepts.

The x-intercept is ___, so plot the point _____.

The y-intercept is ___, so plot the point _____.

Step 3 _____ the points by drawing a line through them.

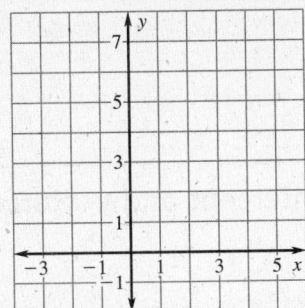

CHECK

You can check the graph of the equation by using a third point. When $x = 2$, $y = $ _____, so the ordered pair _____ is a third solution of the equation. You can see that _____ lies on the graph, so the graph is correct.

Your Notes

Example 3   *Use a graph to find the intercepts*

Identify the x-intercept and y-intercept of the graph.

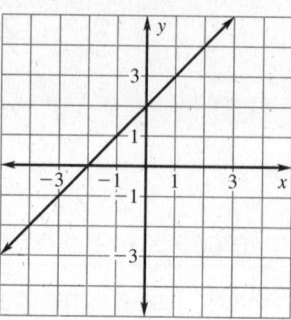

Solution

To find the x-intercept, look to see where the graph crosses the _____. The x-intercept is ____. To find the y-intercept, look to see where the graph crosses the _____. The y-intercept is ___.

✓ **Checkpoint** Complete the following exercises.

3. Graph $2x - 7y = 14$. Label the points where the line crosses the axes.

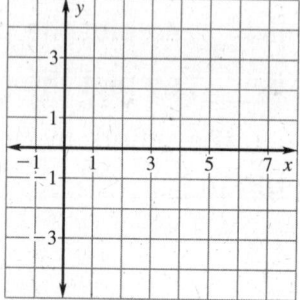

4. Identify the x-intercept and y-intercept of the graph.

Homework

4.4 Find Slope and Rate of Change

Goal • Find the slope of a line and interpret slope as a rate of change.

Your Notes

VOCABULARY

Slope

Rate of change

FINDING THE SLOPE OF A LINE

Words

The slope of the nonvertical line passing through the two points (x_1, y_1) and (x_2, y_2) is the ratio of the _____ (change in y) to the _____ (change in x).

$$\text{slope} = \frac{\boxed{}}{\boxed{}} = \frac{\text{change in } y}{\text{change in } x}$$

Symbols

$$m = \frac{y_2 - y_1}{x_2 - x_1}$$

Graph

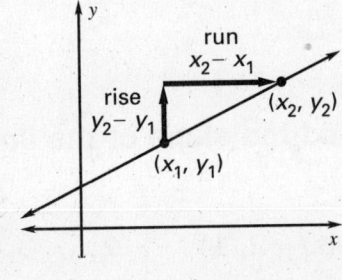

Lesson 4.4 • Algebra 1 Notetaking Guide 83

Your Notes

Example 1 Find a slope

Find the slope of the line shown.

a. Let $(x_1, y_1) = (-1, 2)$ and $(x_2, y_2) = (3, 5)$.

b. Let $(x_1, y_1) = (1, 4)$ and $(x_2, y_2) = (3, -2)$.

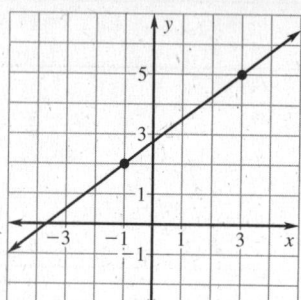
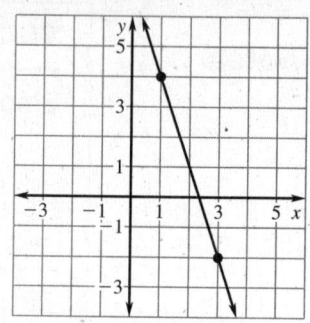

> Keep the x- and y-coordinates in the same order in the numerator and denominator when calculating slope. This will help avoid error.

Solution

a. $m = \dfrac{y_2 - y_1}{x_2 - x_1}$ Write formula for slope.

$= \dfrac{\Box - 2}{\Box - (-1)}$ Substitute.

$= \underline{}$ Simplify.

The line _____ from left to right. The slope is _____.

b. $m = \dfrac{y_2 - y_1}{x_2 - x_1}$ Write formula for slope.

$= \dfrac{\Box - 4}{\Box - 1}$ Substitute.

$= \underline{} = \underline{}$ Simplify.

The line _____ from left to right. The slope is _____.

✓ **Checkpoint** Find the slope of the line passing through the points.

1. $(-3, -1)$ and $(-2, 1)$	2. $(-6, 3)$ and $(5, -2)$

84 Lesson 4.4 • **Algebra 1 Notetaking Guide**

Your Notes

Example 2 Find the slope of a line

Find the slope of the line shown.

a. Let $(x_1, y_1) = (2, 5)$ and $(x_2, y_2) = (-4, 5)$.

b. Let $(x_1, y_1) = (4, -2)$ and $(x_2, y_2) = (4, 3)$.

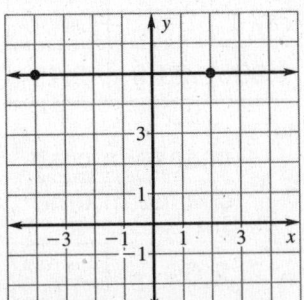
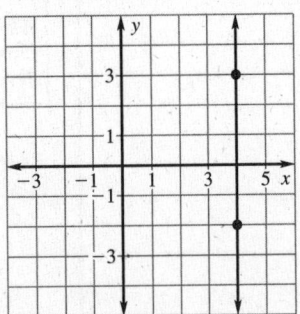

Solution

a. $m = \dfrac{y_2 - y_1}{x_2 - x_1}$ Write formula for slope.

$= \dfrac{5 - \boxed{}}{4 - \boxed{}}$ Substitute.

$= \underline{}$ Simplify.

The line is _____. The slope is _____.

b. $m = \dfrac{y_2 - y_1}{x_2 - x_1}$ Write formula for slope.

$= \dfrac{3 - \boxed{}}{4 - \boxed{}}$ Substitute.

$= \underline{}$ Simplify.

The line is _____. The slope is _____.

✓ **Checkpoint** Find the slope of the line passing through the points. Then classify the line by its slope.

3. $(1, -2)$ and $(1, 3)$	4. $(-3, 7)$ and $(4, 7)$

Lesson 4.4 • Algebra 1 Notetaking Guide

Your Notes

Example 3 **Find a rate of change**

Gas Prices The table shows the cost of a gallon of gas for a number of days. Find the rate of change with respect to time.

Time (days)	Day 1	Day 3	Day 5
Price/gal ($)	1.99	2.09	2.19

Rate of change = $\dfrac{\text{change in cost}}{\text{change in time}}$ Write formula.

= $\dfrac{2.09 - \boxed{}}{3 - \boxed{}}$ Substitute.

= $\dfrac{\boxed{}}{\boxed{}}$ = _____   Simplify.

The rate of change in price is _____ per day.

✓ **Checkpoint**

5. The table shows the change in temperature over time. Find the rate of change in degrees Fahrenheit with respect to time.

Temperature (°F)	Time (hours)
38	0
43	2
48	4
53	6

Homework

4.5 Graph Using Slope-Intercept Form

Goal • Graph linear equations using slope-intercept form.

Your Notes

VOCABULARY

Slope-intercept form

_____

_____

Parallel

FINDING THE SLOPE AND Y-INTERCEPT OF A LINE

Words	Symbols
A linear equation of the form $y = mx + b$ is written in _____ where ____ is the slope and ____ is the y-intercept of the equation's graph.	$y = mx + b$ $y = 2x + 1$

Graph

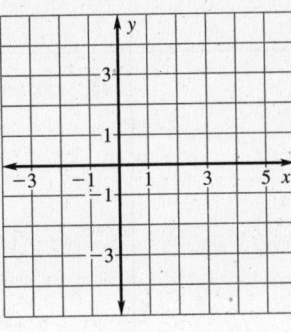

Your Notes

Example 1   *Identify slope and y-intercept*

Identify the slope and *y*-intercept of the line with the given equation.

a. $y = x + 3$ b. $-2x + y = 5$

Solution

a. The equation is in the form _____. So, the slope of the line is ___, and the *y*-intercept is ___.

b. Rewrite the equation in slope-intercept form by solving for ___.

$-2x + y = 5$ Write original equation.

$y = $ _____   Subtract _____ from each side.

The line has a slope of ___ and a *y*-intercept of ___.

✓ **Checkpoint** Identify the slope and *y*-intercept of the line with the given equation.

1. $y = 4x - 1$	2. $4x - 2y = 8$
3. $4y = 3x + 16$	4. $6x + 3y = -21$

Your Notes

Example 2 Graph an equation using slope-intercept form

Graph the equation 4x + y = 2.

Solution

Step 1 Rewrite the equation in slope-intercept form.

_____

Step 2 _____ the slope and the y-intercept.

m = ____   b = ____

Step 3 _____ the point that corresponds to the y-intercept, (____).

Step 4 Use the slope to locate a second point on the line. Draw a line through the two points.

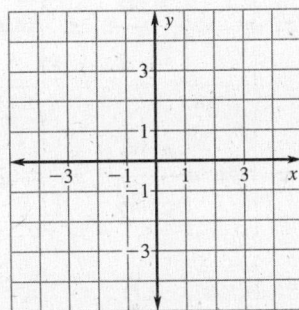

✓ **Checkpoint** Complete the following exercise.

5. Graph the equation $-\frac{1}{2}x + y = 1$.

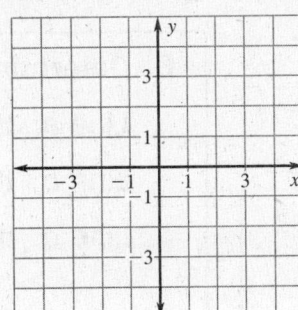

Lesson 4.5 • Algebra 1 Notetaking Guide 89

Your Notes

Example 3 Identify parallel lines

Determine which of the lines are parallel.

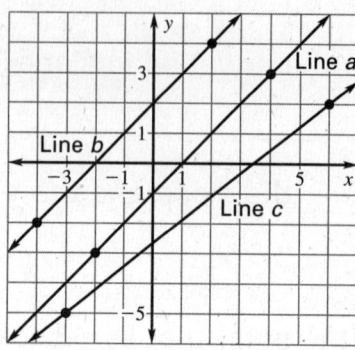

Solution

Find the slope of each line.

Line a: $m = \dfrac{\boxed{} - 3}{\boxed{} - 4} = \dfrac{\boxed{}}{\boxed{}} = \underline{}$

Line b: $m = \dfrac{\boxed{} - 4}{\boxed{} - 2} = \dfrac{\boxed{}}{\boxed{}} = \underline{}$

Line c: $m = \dfrac{\boxed{} - 2}{\boxed{} - 6} = \dfrac{\boxed{}}{\boxed{}} = \underline{}$

Lines ___ and ___ have the same slope. They are parallel.

✓ **Checkpoint** Complete the following exercise.

6. Determine which lines are parallel.

   Line a: through (2, 5) and (−2, 2)

   Line b: through (4, 1) and (−3, −4)

   Line c: through (2, 3) and (−2, 0)

Homework

4.6 Model Direct Variation

Goal • Write and graph direct variation equations.

Your Notes

VOCABULARY

Direct variation

Constant of variation

Example 1 Identify direct variation equations

Tell whether the equation represents direct variation. If so, identify the constant of variation.

a. $4x + 2y = 0$ b. $-2x + y = 3$

Solution

To tell whether an equation represents direct variation, try to rewrite the equation in the form $y = ax$.

a. $4x + 2y = 0$ Write original equation.

   $2y =$ _____   Subtract _____ from each side.

   $y =$ _____   Simplify.

Because the equation $4x + 2y = 0$ _____ be rewritten in the form $y = ax$, it _____ direct variation. The constant of variation is _____.

b. $-2x + y = 3$ Write original equation.

   $y =$ ____ $+ 3$ Add ____ to each side.

Because the equation $-2x + y = 3$ _____ be rewritten in the form $y = ax$, it _____ direct variation.

Your Notes

✓ **Checkpoint** Tell whether the equation represents direct variation. If so, identify the constant of variation.

1. $3x + 4y = 0$	2. $5x + y = 1$

Example 2 *Graph direct variation equations*

Graph the direct variation equation.

a. $y = -5x$ b. $y = \frac{3}{5}x$

Solution

> The graph of a direct variation equation is a line with a slope of *a* and a *y*-intercept of 0. This line passes through the origin.

a. Plot a point at the origin. The slope is equal to the constant of variation, or _____. Find and plot a second point, then draw a line through the points.

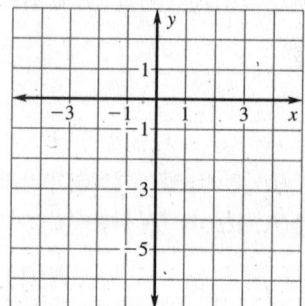

b. Plot a point at the origin. The slope is equal to the constant of variation, or _____. Find and plot a second point, then draw a line through the points.

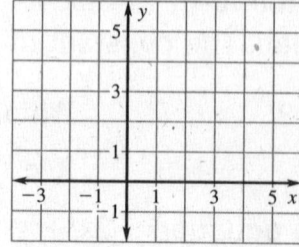

Your Notes

Example 3 Write and use a direct variation equation

The graph of a direct variation equation is shown.

a. Write the direct variation equation.

b. Find the value of y when $x = 80$.

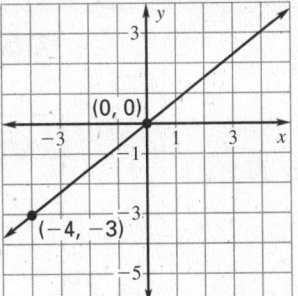

Solution

a. Because y varies directly with x, the equation has the form $y = ax$. Use the fact that $y = -3$ when $x = -4$ to find a.

$y = ax$ Write direct variation equation.

___ = a(___)   Substitute.

___ = a   Solve for a.

A direct variation equation that relates x and y is $y =$ ___.

b. When $x = 80$, $y =$ ___ = ___.

✓ Checkpoint Complete the following exercises.

3. Graph the direct variation equation $y = \frac{1}{2}x$.

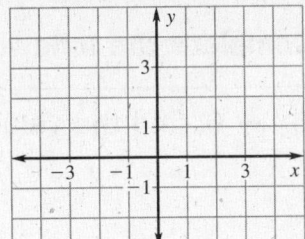

4. The graph of a direct variation equation passes through the point $(3, -4)$. Write the direct variation equation and find the value of y when $x = 15$.

Homework

4.7 Graph Linear Functions

Goal • Use function notation.

Your Notes

VOCABULARY

Function notation

Family of functions

Parent linear function

Example 1 Find an x-value

For the function $f(x) = 3x + 1$, find the value of x so that $f(x) = 10$.

Solution

$f(x) = 3x + 1$	Write original equation.
___ $= 3x + 1$	Substitute ___ for $f(x)$.
___ $= x$	Solve for x.

When $x =$ ___, $f(x) = 10$.

✔ **Checkpoint** Complete the following exercises.

1. For $f(x) = 6x - 6$, find the value of x so that $f(x) = 24$.

2. For $f(x) = 7x + 3$, find the value of x so that $f(x) = 17$.

Your Notes

Example 2 *Graph a function*

Text Messages A wireless communication provider estimates that the number of text messages m (in millions) sent over several years can be modeled by the function $m = 120t + 95$ where t represents the number of years since 2002. Graph the function and identify its domain and range.

t	m
0	___
1	___
2	___
3	___

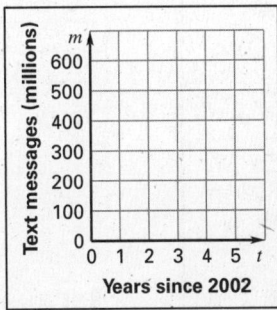

The domain of the function is $t \geq$ ___. From the graph or table, you can see that the range of the function is $m \geq$ ___.

✓ **Checkpoint** Complete the following exercise.

3. Use the model from Example 2 to find the value of t so that $m = 1055$. Explain what the solution means in this situation.

PARENT FUNCTION FOR LINEAR FUNCTIONS

1. The _____ is the most basic linear function.

2. _____ is the form of the parent linear function.

Your Notes

Example 3 Compare graphs with the graph $f(x) = x$

Graph the function. Compare the graph with the graph of $f(x) = x$.

a. $p(x) = x - 4$ b. $q(x) = -2x$

Solution

a.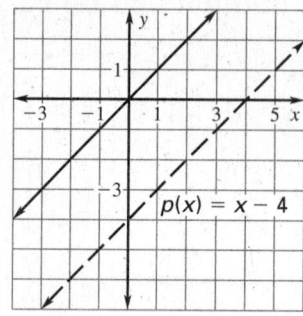

b.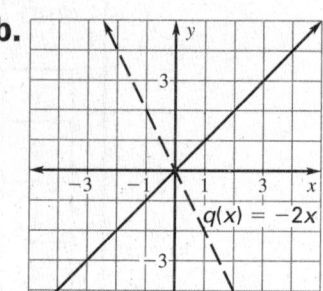

Because the graphs of p and f have the same slope, $m = 1$, the lines are _____. Also, the y-intercept of the graph of p is ___ less than the y-intercept of the graph of f.

Because the slope of the graph of q _____ from left to right and the slope of the graph of f _____ from left to right, the slope of q is _____. The y-intercept of both graphs is ___.

✓ **Checkpoint** Complete the following exercise.

4. Graph $r(x) = \frac{1}{2}x$. Compare the graph with the graph of $f(x) = x$.

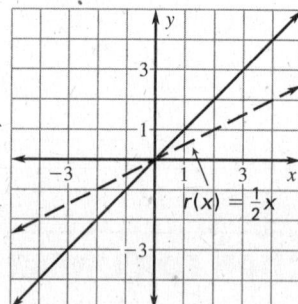

Your Notes

COMPARING GRAPHS OF LINEAR FUNCTIONS WITH THE GRAPH OF f(x) = x

$g(x) = x + b$

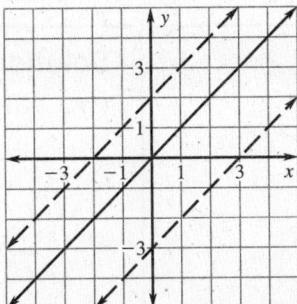

The graphs have the same _____.

The graphs have different _____.

Graphs of this family are _____ of the graph of f(x) = x.

$g(x) = mx$ where $m > 0$

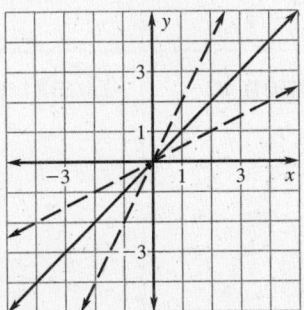

The graphs have different (positive) _____.

The graphs have the same _____.

Graphs of this family are vertical _____ or _____ of the graph of f(x) = x.

$g(x) = mx$ where $m < 0$

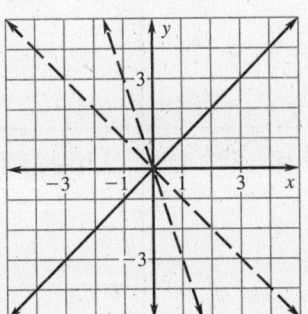

The graphs have different (negative) _____.

The graphs have the same _____.

Graphs of this family are vertical _____ or _____ or _____ of the graph of f(x) = x.

Homework

Words to Review

Give an example of the vocabulary word.

Quadrant	Solution of an equation in two variables.
Graph of an equation in two variables	Linear equation
Standard form of a linear equation	Linear function
x-intercept	y-intercept
Slope	Rate of change

Slope-intercept form	Parallel
Direct variation	Constant of variation
Function notation	Family of functions
Parent linear function	

Review your notes and Chapter 4 by using the Chapter Review on pages 271–274 of your textbook.

5.1 Write Linear Equations in Slope-Intercept Form

Goal • Write equations of lines.

Your Notes

> Use the slope-intercept form ($y = mx + b$) to write an equation of a line if slope and y-intercept are given.

Example 1 *Use slope and y-intercept to write an equation*

Write an equation of the line with a slope of −4 and a y-intercept of 6.

Solution

$y = mx + b$ Write slope-intercept form.

$y = $ ____ $x + $ ____   Substitute ____ for m and ____ for b.

✓ **Checkpoint** Write an equation of the line with the given slope and y-intercept.

1. Slope is 8; y-intercept is −5.	2. Slope is $\frac{2}{3}$; y-intercept is −2.
3. Slope is −3; y-intercept is 7.	4. Slope is $-\frac{5}{2}$; y-intercept is 9.

Your Notes

Example 2 — Write an equation of a line given two points

Write an equation of the line shown.

Solution

Step 1 Calculate the slope.

$$m = \frac{y_2 - y_1}{x_2 - x_1}$$

$$= \frac{\boxed{} - \boxed{}}{\boxed{} - \boxed{}}$$

$$= \frac{\boxed{}}{\boxed{}} = \underline{}$$

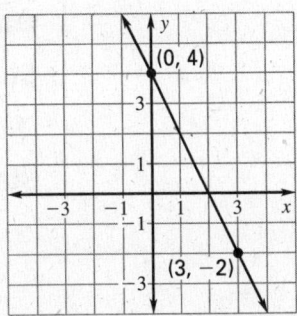

> You can write an equation of a line if you know the y-intercept and any other point on the line.

Step 2 Write an equation of the line. The line crosses the y-axis at _____. So, the y-intercept is ___.

$y = mx + b$ Write slope-intercept form.

$y = $ ___ $x + $ ___   Substitute ___ for m and ___ for b.

✔ **Checkpoint** Complete the following exercise.

5. Write an equation of the line shown.

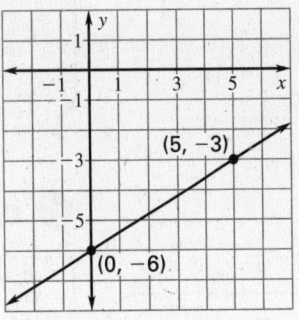

Your Notes

Example 3   Write a linear function

Write an equation for the linear function f with the values $f(0) = 4$ and $f(2) = 12$.

Solution

Step 1 Write $f(0) = 4$ as _____ and $f(2) = 12$ as _____.

Step 2 Calculate the slope of the line that passes through _____ and _____.

$$m = \frac{y_2 - y_1}{x_2 - x_1}$$

$$= \frac{\Box - \Box}{\Box - \Box}$$

$$= \frac{\Box}{\Box}$$

$$= \_\_$$

Step 3 Write an equation of the line. The line crosses the y-axis at $(0, \_\_)$. So, the y-intercept is ___.

$y = mx + b$ Write slope-intercept form.

$y = $ _____   Substitute ___ for m and ___ for b.

The function is _____.

✓ Checkpoint Complete the following exercise.

6. Write an equation for the linear function with the values $f(0) = 3$ and $f(3) = 15$.

Homework

5.2 Use Linear Equations in Slope-Intercept Form

Goal • Write an equation of a line using points on the line.

Your Notes

WRITING AN EQUATION OF A LINE IN SLOPE-INTERCEPT FORM

Step 1 Identify the slope ____. You can use the _____ _____ to calculate the slope if you know two points on the line.

Step 2 Find the _____. You can substitute the _____ and the _____ of a point (x, y) on the line into $y = mx + b$. Then solve for ___.

Step 3 Write an equation using _____.

Example 1   Write an equation given the slope and a point

Write an equation of the line that passes through the point (1, 2) and has a slope of 3.

Solution

Step 1 Identify the slope. The slope is ___.

Step 2 Find the y-intercept. Substitute the slope and the coordinates of the given point into $y = mx + b$. Solve for b.

Be careful not to mix up the x- and y-values when you substitute.

$y = mx + b$	Write slope-intercept form.
___ = ___(___) + b	Substitute ___ for m, ___ for x, and ___ for y.
____ = b	Solve for ___.

Step 3 Write an equation of the line.

$y = mx + b$	Write slope-intercept form.
y = _____	Substitute ___ for m and ____ for b.

Your Notes

✓ **Checkpoint** Complete the following exercise.

> 1. Write an equation of the line that passes through the point (2, 2) and has a slope of 4.

Example 2   *Write an equation given two points*

Write an equation of the line that passes through (2, −3) and (−2, 1).

Solution

Step 1 Calculate the slope.

$$m = \frac{y_2 - y_1}{x_2 - x_1}$$

$$= \frac{\boxed{} - \boxed{}}{\boxed{} - \boxed{}}$$

$$= \frac{\boxed{}}{\boxed{}} = \underline{}$$

> You can also find the y-intercept using the coordinates of the other given point.

Step 2 Find the y-intercept. Use the slope and the point (2, −3).

$y = mx + b$ Write slope-intercept form.

$-3 = \underline{}(\underline{}) + b$ Substitute _____ for m, _____ for x, and _____ for y.

$\underline{} = b$ Solve for b.

Step 3 Write an equation of the line.

$y = mx + b$ Write slope-intercept form.

$y = \underline{}$ Substitute _____ for m and _____ for b.

Your Notes

✓ **Checkpoint** Complete the following exercise.

2. Write an equation for the line that passes through (−8, −13) and (4, 2).

3. Write an equation for the line that passes through (−3, 4) and (1, −2).

HOW TO WRITE EQUATIONS IN SLOPE-INTERCEPT FORM

1. Given slope m and y-intercept b.
   Substitute ____ and ____ in the equation _____.

2. Given slope m and one point.
   Substitute ____ and the _____ of the point in _____. Solve for ____. Write the _____.

3. Given two points.
   Use the points to find the slope ____. Then substitute ____ and the _____ of ____ ____ in _____. Solve for ____. Write the _____.

Homework

5.3 Write Linear Equations in Point-Slope Form

Goal • Write linear equations in point-slope form.

Your Notes

VOCABULARY

Point-slope form

POINT-SLOPE FORM

The **point-slope form** of the equation of the nonvertical line through a given point (x_1, y_1) with a slope of m is

_____ .

Example 1 *Write an equation in point-slope form*

Write an equation in point-slope form on the line that passes through the point (3, 2) and has a slope of 2.

Solution

$y - y_1 = m(x - x_1)$ Write point-slope form.

$y - \underline{} = \underline{}(x - \underline{})$ Substitute ___ for m, ___ for x_1, and ___ for y_1.

Your Notes

> **Example 2** **Graph an equation in point-slope form**
>
> Graph the equation $y - 2 = \frac{1}{2}(x - 2)$.
>
> **Solution**
> Because the equation is in point-slope form, you know that the line has a slope of ____ and passes through the point _____.
>
> Plot the point _____ Find a second point on the line using the _____. Draw a line through the points.

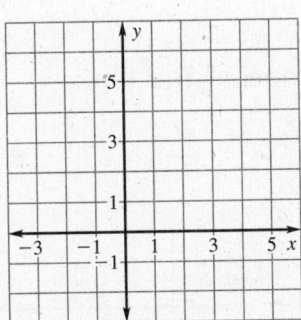

✓ **Checkpoint** Complete the following exercises.

1. Write an equation in point-slope form of the line that passes through the point (−3, 5) and has a slope of 4.

2. Graph the equation $y + 1 = 2(x - 1)$.

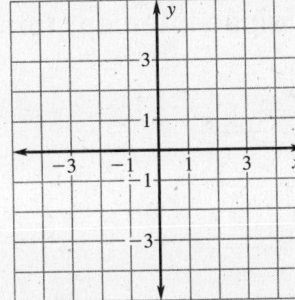

Your Notes

Example 3   *Use point-slope form to write an equation*

Write an equation in point-slope form of the line shown.

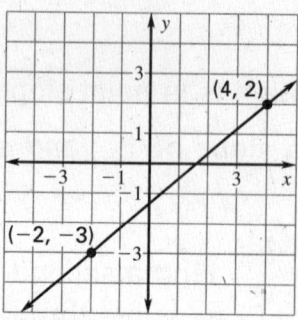

Solution

Step 1 Find the slope of the line.

$$m = \frac{y_2 - y_1}{x_2 - x_1}$$

$$= \frac{\boxed{} - \boxed{}}{\boxed{} - \boxed{}}$$

$$= \frac{\boxed{}}{\boxed{}} = \underline{}$$

Step 2 Write the equation in point-slope form.
You can use either given point.

Method 1 Use $(-2, -3)$.   **Method 2** Use $(4, 2)$.

$y - y_1 = m(x - x_1)$ $y - y_1 = m(x - x_1)$

_____   _____

CHECK Check that the equations are equivalent by writing them in slope-intercept form.

y _____ = x _____ y _____ = x _____

$y =$ _____ $y =$ _____

Homework

5.4 Write Linear Equations in Standard Form

Goal • Write equations in standard form.

Your Notes

Example 1 *Write equivalent equations in standard form*

Write two equations in standard form that are equivalent to $4x + 2y = 12$.

Solution

To write one equivalent equation, multiply each side by ____ .

_____

To write one equivalent equation, multiply each side by ___ .

_____

✓ **Checkpoint** Complete the following exercises.

1. Write two equations in standard form that are equivalent to $6x - 4y = 6$.

2. Write two equations in standard form that are equivalent to $-12x + 6y = -9$.

Your Notes

Example 2 *Write an equation from a graph*

Write an equation in standard form of the line shown.

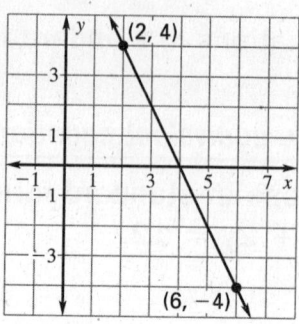

> All linear equations can be written in standard form, $Ax + By = C$.

Solution

Step 1 Calculate the slope.

$$m = \frac{y_2 - y_1}{x_2 - x_1}$$

$$= \frac{\boxed{} - \boxed{}}{\boxed{} - \boxed{}}$$

$$= \frac{\boxed{}}{\boxed{}}$$

$$= -\underline{}$$

Step 2 Write an equation in point-slope form. Use (2, 4).

$y - y_1 = m(x - x_1)$ Write point-slope form.

$y - \underline{} = \underline{}(x - \underline{})$ Substitute ___ for y_1, ___ for m, and ___ for x_1.

Step 3 Rewrite the equation in standard form.

$y - \underline{} = \underline{}x + \underline{}$ Distributive property

$y + \underline{}x = \underline{}$ Collect variable terms on one side, constants on the other.

Lesson 5.4 • Algebra 1 Notetaking Guide

Your Notes

✓ **Checkpoint** Complete the following exercise.

3. Write an equation in standard form of the line through (3, −1) and (2, −4).

Example 3 *Write an equation of a line*

Write an equation of the specified line.

a. Line A

b. Line B

Solution

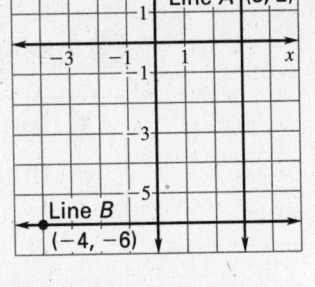

a. The x-coordinate of the given point on Line A is ___. This means that all points on the line have an x-coordinate of ___. An equation of the line is _____.

b. The y-coordinate of the given point on Line B is ___. This means that all points on the line have a y-coordinate of ___. An equation of the line is _____.

Lesson 5.4 • Algebra 1 Notetaking Guide

Your Notes

Example 4 — Complete an equation in standard form

Find the missing coefficient in the equation of the line shown. Write the completed equation.

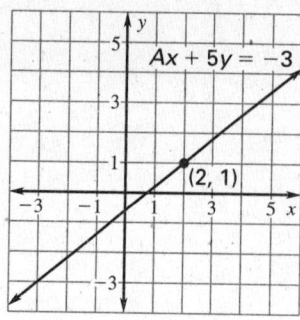

Solution

Step 1 Find the value of A. Substitute the coordinates of the given point for x and y in the equation.

$Ax + 5y = -3$	Write equation.
$A(\_\_) + 5(\_\_) = -3$	Substitute ___ for x and ___ for y.
$\_\_A + \_\_ = -3$	Simplify.
$\_\_A = \_\_$	Subtract ___ from each side.
$A = \_\_$	Divide by ___.

Step 2 Complete the equation.

$\_\_x + 5y = -3$ Substitute ___ for A.

✓ **Checkpoint** Complete the following exercises.

4. Write equations of the horizontal and vertical lines that pass through $(-10, 5)$.

Homework

5. Find the missing coefficient in the equation of the line that passes through $(-2, 2)$. Write the completed equation.

    $6x + By = 4$

5.5 Write Equations of Parallel and Perpendicular Lines

Goal • Write equations of parallel and perpendicular lines.

Your Notes

VOCABULARY

Converse

Perpendicular lines

PARALLEL LINES

If two nonvertical lines have the same _____, then they are _____.

If two nonvertical lines are _____, then they have the same _____.

Example 1 Write an equation of a parallel line

Write an equation of the line that passes through (2, 4) and is parallel to the line $y = 4x + 1$.

Solution

Step 1 Identify the slope. The graph of the given equation has a slope of ___. So, the parallel line through (2, 4) has a slope of ___.

Step 2 Find the y-intercept. Use the slope and the given point.

$y = mx + b$ Write slope-intercept form.

___ = ___(___) + b   Substitute ___ for m, ___ for x, and ___ for y.

___ = b   Solve for b.

Step 3 Write an equation. Use $y = mx + b$.

$y = $ _____   Substitute ___ for m and ___ for b.

Your Notes

PERPENDICULAR LINES

If two nonvertical lines have the slopes that are _____, then the lines are _____.

If two nonvertical lines are _____, then their slopes are _____.

Example 2 *Determine parallel or perpendicular lines*

Determine which of the following lines, if any, are parallel or perpendicular:

Line a: $12x - 3y = 3$

Line b: $y = 4x + 2$

Line c: $4y + x = 8$

Solution

Find the slopes of the lines.

Line b: The equation is in slope-intercept form. The slope is ___.

Write the equations for lines a and c in slope-intercept form.

Line a: $12x - 3y = 3$

$-3y = $ _____ $ + 3$

$y = $ _____

Line c: $4y + x = 8$

$4y = $ _____ $ + 8$

$y = $ _____

Lines a and b have a slope of ___, so they are _____.

Line c has a slope of ___, the negative reciprocal of ___, so it is _____ to lines a and b.

Your Notes

✓ **Checkpoint** Complete the following exercises.

1. Write an equation of the line that passes through (−4, 6) and is parallel to the line y = −3x + 2.

2. Determine which of the following lines, if any, are parallel or perpendicular.
   Line a: 4x + y = 2
   Line b: 5y + 20x = 10
   Line c: 8y = 2x + 8

Example 3 *Determine whether lines are perpendicular*

Determine if the following lines are perpendicular.

Line a: 6y = 5x + 8
Line b: −10y = 12x + 10

Solution

Find the slopes of the lines. Write the equations in slope-intercept form.

Line a: 6y = 5x + 8

   y = _____

Line b: −10y = 12x + 10

   y = _____

The slope of line a is _____. The slope of line b is _____.

The two slopes _____ negative reciprocals, so lines a and b _____ perpendicular.

Your Notes

Example 4   **Write an equation of a perpendicular line**

Write an equation of the line that passes through $(-3, 4)$ and is perpendicular to the line $y = \frac{1}{3}x + 2$.

Solution

Step 1 Identify the slope. The graph of the given equation has a slope of ___. Because the slopes of perpendicular lines are negative reciprocals, the slope of the perpendicular line through $(-3, 4)$ is ___.

Step 2 Find the y-intercept. Use the slope and the given point.

$y = mx + b$ Write slope-intercept form.

___ = ___ (___) + b   Substitute ___ for m, ___ for x, and ___ for y.

___ = b   Solve for b.

Step 3 Write an equation.

$y = mx + b$ Write slope-intercept form.

$y = $ _____   Substitute ___ for m and ___ for b.

✓ **Checkpoint** Complete the following exercises.

3. Determine whether line a through $(1, 3)$ and $(3, 4)$ is perpendicular to line b through $(1, -3)$ and $(2, -5)$. Justify your answer using slopes.

Homework

4. Write an equation of the line that passes through $(4, -2)$ and is perpendicular to the line $y = 5x + 2$.

5.6 Fit a Line to Data

Goal • Make scatter plots and write equations to model data.

Your Notes

VOCABULARY

Scatter plot

___

Correlation

___

Line of fit

___

CORRELATION

- If y tends to increase as x increases, the paired data are said to have a _____ correlation.

- If y tends to decrease as x increases, the paired data are said to have a _____ correlation.

- If x and y have no apparent relationship, the paired data are said to have _____ correlation.

Example 1 Describe the correlation of data

Describe the correlation of data graphed in the scatter plot.

a. 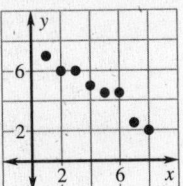   b.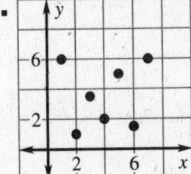

Solution

a. _____   b. _____
   correlation   correlation

Lesson 5.6 • Algebra 1 Notetaking Guide 117

Your Notes

Example 2 Make a scatter plot

a. Make a scatter plot of the data in the table.

x	1	1.5	2	2	3	3.5	4
y	3	1	1	−0.5	−1	−0.5	−2

b. Describe the correlation of the data.

Solution

a. Treat the data as ordered pairs. Plot the ordered pairs as _____ in a coordinate plane.

b. The scatter plot shows a _____ correlation.

USING A LINE OF FIT TO MODEL DATA

Step 1 Make a _____ of the data.

Step 2 Decide whether the data can be modeled by a _____.

Step 3 Draw a line that appears to ____ the data closely. There should be approximately as many points _____ the line as _____ it.

Step 4 Write an equation using _____ points on the line. The points do not have to represent actual data pairs, but they must lie on the line of fit.

Your Notes

Example 3 *Write an equation to model data*

Game Attendance The table shows the average attendance at a school's varsity basketball games for various years. Write an equation that models the average attendance at varsity basketball games as a function of the number of years since 2000.

Year	2000	2001	2002	2003	2004	2005	2006
Avg. Game Attendance	488	497	525	567	583	621	688

Solution

Step 1 Make a _____ of the data. Let x represent the number of years since 2000. Let y represent average game attendance.

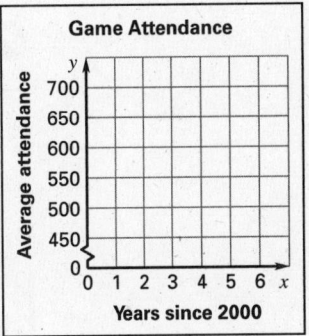

Step 2 Decide whether the data can be modeled by a line. Because the scatter plot shows a _____ correlation, you can fit a line to the data.

Step 3 Draw a line that appears to fit the points in the scatter plot _____.

Step 4 Write an equation using two points on the line. Use (1, 493) and (5, 621).

Find the _____ of the line.

$$m = \frac{y_2 - y_1}{x_2 - x_1} = \frac{\boxed{} - \boxed{}}{\boxed{} - \boxed{}}$$

$$= \frac{\boxed{}}{\boxed{}}$$

$$= \boxed{}$$

Your Notes

Find the *y*-intercept of the line. Use the point (5, 621).

$y = mx + b$ Write slope-intercept form.

____ = ____ (____) + b   Substitute ____ for *m*, ____ for *x*, and ____ for *y*.

____ = b   Solve for *b*.

An equation of the line of fit is _____.

The average attendance *y* of varsity basketball games can be modeled by the function _____ where *x* is the number of years since 2000.

✓ **Checkpoint** Complete the following exercises.

1. Make a scatter plot of the data in the table. Describe the correlation of the data.

x	1	2	2	3	4	5
y	5	5	6	7	8	8

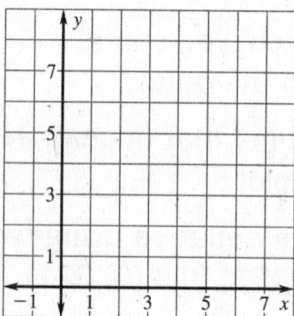

2. Use the data in the table to write an equation that models *y* as a function of *x*.

x	1	2	3	4	5	6
y	65	76	82	86	92	97

Homework

5.7 Predict with Linear Models

Goal • Make predictions using best-fitting lines.

Your Notes

VOCABULARY

Best-fitting line

Interpolation

Extrapolation

Zero of a function

Your Notes

Example 1 Interpolate using an equation

NFL Salaries The table shows the average National Football League (NFL) player's salary (in thousands of dollars) from 1997 to 2001.

Year	1997	1999	2000	2001
Average Player's Salary (in thousands of dollars)	585	708	787	986

a. Make a scatter plot of the data.

b. Find an equation that models the average NFL player's salary (in thousands of dollars) as a function of the number of years since 1997.

c. Approximate the average NFL player's salary in 1998.

Solution

a. Enter the data into lists on a graphing calculator. Make a scatter plot, letting the number of years since 1997 be the _____ (0, 2, 3, 4) and the average player's salary be the _____.

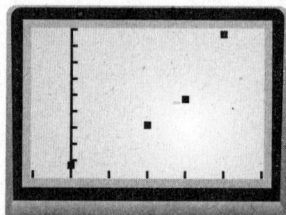

b. Perform _____ using the paired data. The equation of the best-fitting line is $y =$ _____.

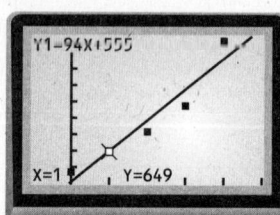

c. Graph the best-fitting line. Use the trace feature and the arrow keys to find the value of the equation when $x =$ ___.

The average NFL player's salary in 1998 was _____ thousand dollars.

Example 2 Extrapolate using an equation

NFL Salaries Look back at Example 1.

a. Use the equation from Example 1 to approximate the average NFL player's salary in 2002 and 2003.

b. In 2002, the average NFL player's salary was actually 1180 thousand dollars. In 2003, the average NFL player's salary was actually 1259 thousand dollars. Describe the accuracy of the extrapolations made in part (a).

Solution

a. Evaluate the equation of the best-fitting line from Example 1 for $x =$ ___ and $x =$ ___.

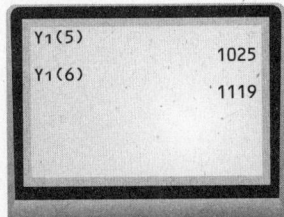

The model predicts the average NFL player's salary as _____ thousand dollars in 2002 and _____ thousand dollars in 2003.

b. The differences between the predicted average NFL player's salary and the actual average NFL player's salary in 2002 and 2003 are _____ thousand dollars and _____ thousand dollars, respectively. The equation of the best-fitting line gives a less accurate prediction for the years outside of the given years.

RELATING SOLUTIONS OF EQUATIONS, ZEROS OF FUNCTIONS, AND x-INTERCEPTS OF GRAPHS

In Chapter 3, you learned to solve an equation like $4x - 4 = 0$:	In Chapter 4, you found the _____ of the graph of a function like $y = 4x - 4$:	Now you are finding the zero of a function like $f(x) = 4x - 4$:
$4x - 4 = 0$ $4x =$ 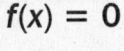 $x =$ 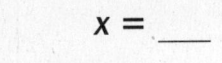 The solution of $4x - 4 = 0$ is ___.		$f(x) = 0$ _____ $= 0$ $x =$ ___ The zero of $f(x) = 4x - 4$ is ___.

Lesson 5.7 • Algebra 1 Notetaking Guide

Your Notes

Example 3 — Find the zero of a function

Public Transit The percentage y of people in the U.S. that use public transit to commute to work can be modeled by the function $y = -0.045x + 5.7$ where x is the number of years since 1983. Find the zero of the function. Explain what the zero means in this situation.

Solution

Substitute ___ for y in the equation of the _____ ____ and solve for x.

$y = -0.045x + 5.7$ Write the equation.

___ $= -0.045x + 5.7$ Substitute ___ for y.

_____   Solve for x.

The zero of the function is about _____. The function has a _____ slope, which means that the percentage of people using public transit to commute to work is _____. According to the model there will be no people who use public transit to commute to work _____ years after _____, or in _____.

✓ **Checkpoint** Complete the following exercise.

1. **Baseball Salaries** The table shows the average major league baseball player's salary (in thousands of dollars) from 1997 to 2001.

Year	1997	1999	2000	2001
Average Player's Salary (in thousands of dollars)	1337	1607	1896	2139

Find an equation that models the average major league baseball player's salary (in thousands of dollars) as a function of the number of years since 1997. Approximate the average major league baseball player's salary is 1998, 2002, and 2003.

Homework

Words to Review

Give an example of the vocabulary word.

Point-slope form	Converse
Perpendicular lines	**Scatter plot**
Correlation	**Line of fit**
Best-fitting line	**Interpolation**

Extrapolation	Zero of a function

Review your notes and Chapter 5 by using the Chapter Review on pages 345–348 of your textbook.

6.1 Solve Inequalities Using Addition and Subtraction

Goal • Solve inequalities using addition and subtraction.

Your Notes

VOCABULARY

Graph of a linear inequality in one variable

_____

Equivalent inequalities

Example 1 *Write and graph an inequality*

Food Drive Your school wants to collect at least 5000 pounds of food for a food drive. Write and graph an inequality to describe the amount of food that your school hopes to collect.

Solution

Let p represent the _____

_____. The value of p must

be _____ 5000 pounds. So, an

inequality is _____.

> Remember to use an open circle for < or > and a closed circle for ≤ or ≥.

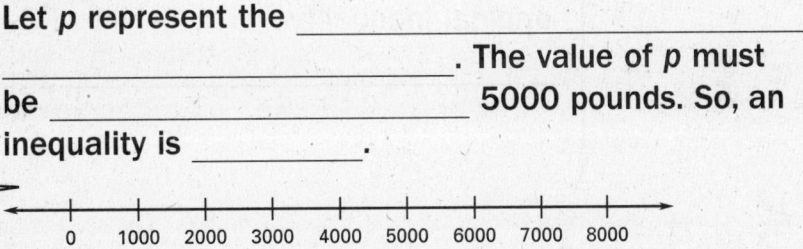

✓ **Checkpoint** Complete the following exercise.

1. You must be 16 years old or older to get your driver's license. Write and graph an inequality to describe the ages of people who may get their driver's license.

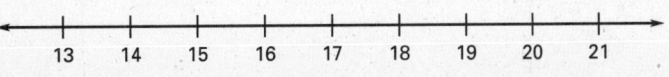

Lesson 6.1 • Algebra 1 Notetaking Guide **127**

Your Notes

ADDITION PROPERTY OF INEQUALITY

Words Adding the same number to each side of an inequality produces an _____ _____.

Algebra If $a > b$, then $a + c >$ _____.

If $a < b$, then $a + c <$ _____.

If $a \geq b$, then $a + c \geq$ _____.

If $a \leq b$, then $a + c \leq$ _____.

Example 2 *Solve an inequality using addition*

Solve $n - 3.5 < 2.5$. Graph your solution.

Solution

$n - 3.5 < 2.5$ Write original inequality.

$n - 3.5 +$ _____ $< 2.5 +$ _____   Add _____ to each side.

_____   Simplify.

The solutions are all real numbers _____. Check by substituting a number _____ for n in the original inequality.

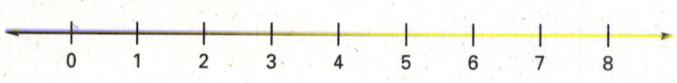

✓ Checkpoint Solve the inequality. Graph your solution.

2. $6 > y - 3.3$	3. $z - 7 \geq 4$
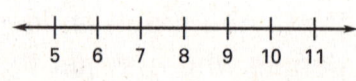	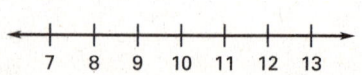

Your Notes

SUBTRACTION PROPERTY OF INEQUALITY

Words Subtracting the same number from each side of an inequality produces an _____ _____.

Algebra If $a > b$, then $a - c >$ _____.

If $a < b$, then $a - c <$ _____.

If $a \geq b$, then $a - c \geq$ _____.

If $a \leq b$, then $a - c \leq$ _____.

Example 3 *Solve an inequality using subtraction*

Solve $3 \leq y + 8$. Graph your solution.

Solution

$3 \leq y + 8$ Write original inequality.

$3 -$ ___ $\leq y + 8 -$ ___   Subtract ___ from each side.

_____   Simplify.

You can rewrite _____ as _____. The solutions are all real numbers _____.

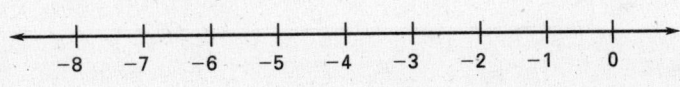

✓ **Checkpoint** Solve the inequality. Graph your solution.

4. $r + 3\frac{1}{4} < 5$

5. $3 + m \geq 7.2$

Homework

6.2 Solve Inequalities Using Multiplication and Division

Goal • Solve inequalities using multiplication and division.

Your Notes

MULTIPLICATION PROPERTY OF INEQUALITY

Words Multiplying each side of an inequality by a _____ number produces an _____.

Multiplying each side of an inequality by a _____ number and _____ produces an equivalent inequality.

Algebra If $a < b$ and $c > 0$, then _____.

If $a < b$ and $c < 0$, then _____.

If $a > b$ and $c > 0$, then _____.

If $a > b$ and $c < 0$, then _____.

This property is also true for inequalities involving $\leq$ and $\geq$.

Example 1 Solve an inequality using multiplication

Solve $\dfrac{y}{9} > 3$. Graph your solution.

Solution

$\dfrac{y}{9} > 3$ Write original inequality.

_____ · $\dfrac{y}{9}$ > _____ · 3   Multiply each side by _____.

_____   Simplify.

The solutions are all real numbers _____.

```
+----+----+----+----+----+----+----+----+----+
24   25   26   27   28   29   30   31   32
```

Your Notes

Example 2 *Solve an inequality using multiplication*

Solve $\dfrac{m}{-2} < 5$. Graph your solution.

Solution

$\dfrac{m}{-2} < 5$ Write original inequality.

____ $\cdot \dfrac{m}{-2}$ > ____ $\cdot 5$ Multiply each side by ____ and ____ the inequality symbol.

____   Simplify.

The solutions are all real numbers _____.

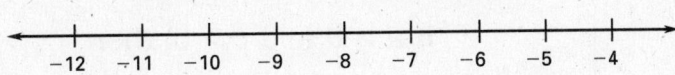

✓ Checkpoint Solve the inequality. Graph your solution.

1. $\dfrac{r}{7} \le 6$

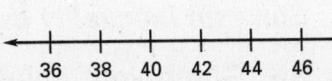

2. $\dfrac{s}{-4} > 0.4$

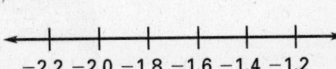

3. $\dfrac{n}{-5} \ge -2$

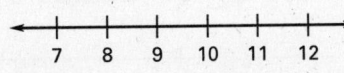

4. $\dfrac{w}{6} < -0.8$

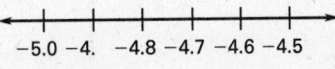

Your Notes

DIVISION PROPERTY OF INEQUALITY

Words Dividing each side of an inequality by a _____ number produces an _____.

Dividing each side of an inequality by a _____ number and _____ _____ produces an equivalent inequality.

Algebra If $a < b$ and $c > 0$, then _____.

If $a < b$ and $c < 0$, then _____.

If $a > b$ and $c > 0$, then _____.

If $a > b$ and $c < 0$, then _____.

This property is also true for inequalities involving $\leq$ and $\geq$.

Example 3 Solve an inequality using division

Solve $-4x < 36$. Graph your solution.

Solution

$-4x < 36$ Write original inequality.

$\dfrac{-4x}{\Box} > \dfrac{36}{\Box}$ Divide each side by _____ and _____ the inequality symbol.

_____   Simplify.

The solutions are all real numbers _____.

-13 -12 -11 -10 -9 -8 -7 -6 -5

Your Notes

Example 4 Solve a real-world problem

Pizza Party You have a budget of $45 to buy pizza for a student council meeting. Pizzas cost $7.50 each. Write and solve an inequality to find the possible numbers of pizzas that you can buy.

Solution

| Price per pizza (dollars per pizza) | • | Number of pizzas (pizzas) | ≤ | Budget amount (dollars) |

_____ • p ≤ _____

_____ Write inequality.

p ≤ _____ Divide each side by _____.

You can buy at most ___ pizzas.

Checkpoint Solve the inequality. Graph your solution.

5. $-9k < 36$

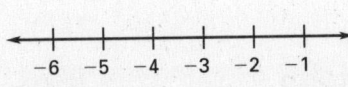

6. $10n \geq 140$

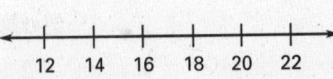

7. In Example 4, suppose that you had a budget of $50 and each pizza costs $8. Write and solve an inequality to find the possible numbers of pizzas that you can buy.

Homework

6.3 Solve Multi-Step Inequalities

Goal • Solve multi-step inequalities.

Your Notes

Example 1 Solve a two-step inequality

Solve $4x + 6 \geq 54$. Graph your solution.

Solution

$4x + 6 \geq 54$ Write original inequality.

$4x \geq 48$ Subtract ___ from each side.

_____   Divide each side by ___.

The solutions are all real numbers  _____.

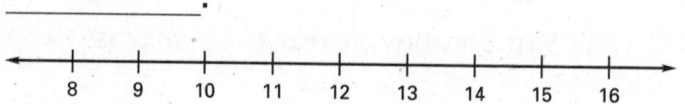

Example 2 Solve a multi-step inequality

Solve $-\frac{1}{3}(x + 21) < 2$.

Solution

$-\frac{1}{3}(x + 21) < 2$ Write original inequality.

$-\frac{1}{3}x - $ ___ < 2 Distributive property.

$-\frac{1}{3}x < $ ___   Add ___ to each side.

_____   Multiply each side by ___.
_____ the inequality symbol.

The solutions are all real numbers _____.

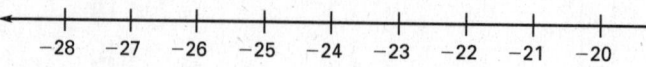

Your Notes

✓ **Checkpoint** Solve the inequality. Graph your solution.

1. $-5w - 2 \geq 23$	2. $2(y - 2.2) > 0$
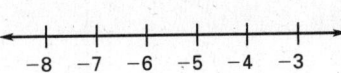	

Example 3 *Identify the number of solutions of an inequality*

Solve the inequality, if possible.

a. $8x + 3 > 2(4x + 1)$

b. $3(8b - 1) \leq 24b - 4$

Solution

a. $8x + 3 > 2(4x + 1)$ Write original inequality.

   $8x + 3 > $ _____   Distributive property

   _____   Subtract ____ from each side.

   _____ are solutions because _____ is _____.

b. $3(8b - 1) \leq 24b - 4$ Write original inequality.

   _____ $\leq 24b - 4$ Distributive property

   _____   Subtract ____ from each side.

   There are _____ because _____ is _____.

Your Notes

✓ **Checkpoint** Solve the inequality, if possible.

3. $18 + 4w \geq \frac{1}{2}(8w + 36)$	4. $-2(3z - 1) < 1 - 6z$

Example 4 *Solve a multi-step problem*

Cell Phone Your cell phone plan is $35 a month for 1000 minutes. You are charged $.25 per minute for any additional minutes. What are the possible numbers of additional minutes you can use if you want to spend no more than $50 on your monthly cell phone bill?

Solution

The amount spent on the monthly plan plus additional minutes must be less than or equal to your monthly budget. Let m be the number of additional minutes that you use.

| Price per minute (dollars/min) | • | Number of minutes (minutes) | + | Monthly fee (dollars) | ≤ | Monthly budget (dollars) |

_____ • m + _____ ≤ _____

_____ ≤ _____   Write inequality.

_____ $m \leq$ _____   Subtract _____ from each side.

$m \leq$ _____   Divide each side by _____.

You can use an additional _____ per month to keep within your monthly cell phone budget.

Homework

6.4 Solve Compound Inequalities

Goal • Solve and graph compound inequalities.

Your Notes

VOCABULARY

Compound inequality

Example 1 *Write and graph compound inequalities*

Translate the verbal phrase into an inequality. Then graph the inequality.

a. All real numbers that are greater than or equal to −2 *and* less than 2.

b. All real numbers that are less than or equal to 3 *or* greater than 6.

c. All real numbers that are greater than −8 *and* less than or equal to −3.

Solution

a. −2 ___ x ___ 2

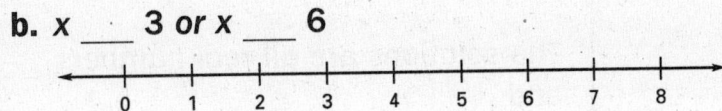

b. x ___ 3 or x ___ 6

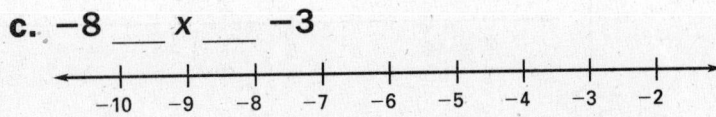

c. −8 ___ x ___ −3

Your Notes

Example 2 — Solve a compound inequality with and

Solve $15 \leq 3x - 3 < 24$. Graph your solution.

Solution

Separate the compound inequality into two inequalities. Then solve each inequality separately.

$15 \leq 3x - 3$ and $3x - 3 < 24$		Write two inequalities.
___ $\leq 3x$ and $3x <$ ___		Add ___ to each expression.
___ $\leq x$ and $x <$ ___		Divide each expression by ___.

The compound inequality can be written as _____.
The solutions are all real numbers _____ _____ and _____.

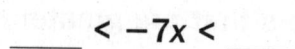

Example 3 — Solve a compound inequality with and

Solve $15 < -7x + 1 < 50$. Graph your solution.

Solution

$15 < -7x + 1 < 50$	Write original inequality.
___ $< -7x <$ ___	Subtract ___ from each expression.
___ $> x >$ ___	Divide each expression by ___ and _____ _____.

The solutions are all real numbers _____ and _____.

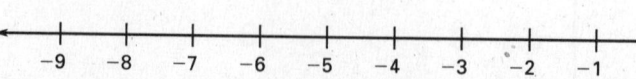

138 Lesson 6.4 • Algebra 1 Notetaking Guide

Your Notes

Example 4 *Solve a compound inequality with or*

Solve $5x + 6 \leq -9$ or $2x - 8 > 12$. Graph your solution.

Solution

$5x + 6 \leq -9$	or	$2x - 8 > 12$	Write original inequality.
$5x \leq$ _____	or	$2x >$ _____	Use addition or subtraction property of inequality.
$x \leq$ _____	or	$x >$ _____	Use division property of inequality.

The solutions are all real numbers _____ or _____.

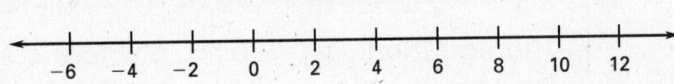

✓ **Checkpoint** Solve the inequality. Graph your solution.

1. $-3 \leq -2x + 1 < 11$

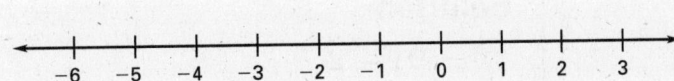

2. $9x + 1 < -17$ or $7x - 12 > 9$

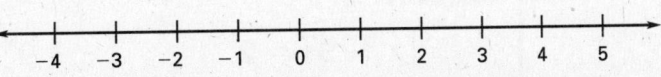

Homework

6.5 Solve Absolute Value Equations

Goal • Solve absolute value equations.

Your Notes

VOCABULARY

Absolute value equation

Absolute deviation

SOLVING AN ABSOLUTE VALUE EQUATION

The equation $|ax + b| = c$ where $c \geq 0$ is equivalent to the statement _____ or _____.

Example 1 Solve an absolute value equation

Solve $|x - 9| = 2$.

Solution

$\|x - 9\| = 2$		Write original equation.
$x - 9 = 2$ or $x - 9 = -2$		Rewrite as two equations.
$x = $ ___ or $x = $ ___		Add ___ to each side.

The solutions are ___ and ___. Check your solution.

CHECK

$\|x - 9\| = 2$	$\|x - 9\| = 2$	Write original equation.
$\|\underline{} - 9\| = 2$	$\|\underline{} - 9\| = 2$	Substitute for x.
$\|\underline{}\| = 2$	$\|\underline{}\| = 2$	Subtract.
_____ ✓	_____ ✓	Simplify. Solution checks.

Your Notes

Example 2 Rewrite an absolute value equation

Solve $4|2x + 8| + 6 = 30$.

Solution

First, rewrite the equation in the form _____.

$4|2x + 8| + 6 = 30$ Write original equation.

$4|2x + 8| =$ ____   Subtract ____ from each side.

$|2x + 8| =$ ____   Divide each side by ____.

Next, solve the absolute value equation.

$|2x + 8| =$ ____   Write absolute value equation.

$2x + 8 =$ ____   or $2x + 8 =$ ____   Rewrite as two equations.

$2x =$ ____   or $2x =$ ____   Subtract ____ from each side.

$x =$ ____   or $x =$ ____   Divide each side by ____.

> Remember to check your solutions in the original equation for accuracy.

✓ **Checkpoint** Solve the equation.

1. $|x + 6| = 11$	2. $3|5x - 10| + 6 = 21$

Lesson 6.5 • Algebra 1 Notetaking Guide

Your Notes

Example 3 *Decide if an equation has no solutions*

Solve $|7x - 3| + 8 = 5$, if possible.

Solution

$|7x - 3| + 8 = 5$ Write original equation.

$|7x - 3| =$ _____   Subtract ____ from each side.

The absolute value of a number is never _____. So, there are no solutions.

Example 4 *Use absolute deviation*

The absolute deviation of x from 10 is 1.8. Find the values of x that satisfy this requirement.

Solution

Absolute deviation = |x − given value|

____ = |x − ____|

_____   Write original equation.

____ = x − ____ or ____ = x − ____   Rewrite as two equations.

____ = x or ____ = x   Add ____ to each side.

So, x is ____ or ____.

✓ **Checkpoint** Complete the following exercise.

3. Find the values of x that satisfy the definition of absolute value for a given value of −13.6 and an absolute deviation of 2.8.

Homework

6.6 Solve Absolute Value Inequalities

Goal • Solve absolute value inequalities.

Your Notes

Example 1   Solve an absolute value inequality

Solve the inequality. Graph your solution.

a. $|x| \leq 9$ b. $|x| > \dfrac{1}{4}$

Solution

a. The distance between x and 0 is less than or equal to 9. So, ____ $\leq x \leq$ ____. The solutions are all real numbers _____ and _____.

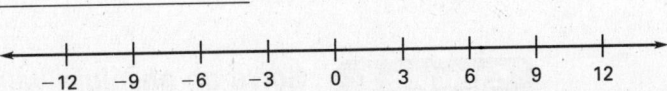

b. The distance between x and 0 is greater than $\dfrac{1}{4}$.

So, $x >$ ____ or $x <$ ____. The solutions are all real

numbers _____ or _____.

SOLVING ABSOLUTE VALUE INEQUALITIES

• The inequality $|ax + b| < c$ where $c > 0$ is equivalent to the compound inequality _____.

• The inequality $|ax + b| > c$ where $c > 0$ is equivalent to the compound inequality _____ or _____.

Note that < can be replaced by ≤ and > can be replaced by ≥.

Your Notes

Example 2 Solve an absolute value inequality

Solve $|2x - 7| < 9$. Graph your solution.

Solution

$|2x - 7| < 9$ Write original inequality.

____ $< 2x - 7 <$ ____   Rewrite as compound inequality.

_____   Add ____ to each expression.

_____   Divide each expression by ____.

The solutions are all real numbers _____ and _____. Check several solutions in the original inequality.

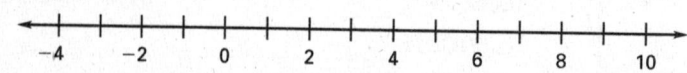

Example 3 Solve an absolute value inequality

Solve $|x + 8| - 4 \geq 2$. Graph your solution.

Solution

$|x + 8| - 4 \geq 2$ Write original inequality.

$|x + 8| \geq$ ____   Add ____ to each side.

$x + 8 \geq$ ____ or $x + 8 \leq$ ____   Rewrite as compound inequality.

$x \geq$ ____ or $x \leq$ ____   Subtract ____ from each side.

The solutions are all real numbers _____ or _____.

Your Notes

✓ **Checkpoint** Solve the inequality. Graph your solution.

1. $3|x - 6| > 9$

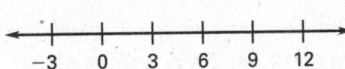

2. $|6x - 11| \leq 7$

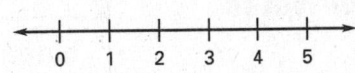

3. $-2|6x - 1| + 5 < 3$

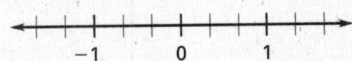

SOLVING INEQUALITIES

One-Step and Multi-Step Inequalities

• Follow the steps for solving an equation, but _____ the inequality symbol when _____ _____.

Compound Inequalities

• If necessary, rewrite the inequality as two separate inequalities. Then solve each inequality separately. Include _____ or _____ in the solution.

Absolute Value Inequalities

• If necessary, isolate the absolute value expression on one side of the inequality. Rewrite the absolute value inequality as a _____. Then solve the compound inequality.

Homework

6.7 Graph Linear Inequalities in Two Variables

Goal • Graph linear inequalities in two variables.

Your Notes

VOCABULARY

Linear inequality in two variables

Graph of an inequality in two variables

Example 1 *Check solutions of a linear inequality*

Tell whether the ordered pair is a solution of $3x - 4y > 9$.

a. (2, 0)   b. (2, −1)

Solution

a. Test (2, 0):

$3x - 4y > 9$ Write inequality.

$3(\_\_) - 4(\_\_) > 9$ Substitute ___ for x and ___ for y.

$\_\_ > 9$ Simplify.

(2, 0) _____ a solution.

b. Test (2, −1):

$3x - 4y > 9$ Write inequality.

$3(\_\_) - 4(\_\_) > 9$ Substitute ___ for x and ___ for y.

$\_\_ > 9$ Simplify.

(2, −1) _____ a solution.

Your Notes

GRAPHING A LINEAR INEQUALITY IN TWO VARIABLES

Step 1 Graph the boundary line. Use a _____ line for < or >, and use a _____ line for ≤ or ≥.

Step 2 Test a point not on _____ by checking whether the ordered pair is a solution of the inequality.

Step 3 Shade the _____ containing the point if the ordered pair _____ a solution of the inequality. Shade the _____ if the ordered pair _____ a solution.

Example 2 *Graph a linear inequality in two variables*

Graph the inequality $y < -\frac{1}{2}x + 4$.

Solution

1. Graph the equation $y = -\frac{1}{2}x + 4$. The inequality is <, so use a _____ line.

2. Test (0, 0) in $y < -\frac{1}{2}x + 4$.

   $\underline{} < -\frac{1}{2}(\underline{}) + 4$

   $\underline{} < \underline{}$

3. _____ the half-plane that _____ (0, 0) because (0, 0) _____ a solution of the inequality.

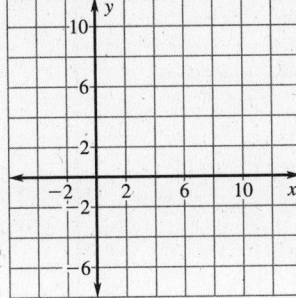

Your Notes

Example 3 — *Graph a linear inequality in one variable*

Graph the inequality $x \geq 4$.

Solution

1. Graph the equation $x = 4$. The inequality is $\geq$, so use a _____ line.

2. Test $(0, 3)$ in $x \geq 4$. You only substitute the _____ because the inequality does not have the variable ___.
   ___ ≥ 4

3. _____ the half-plane that _____ $(0, 3)$, because $(0, 3)$ _____ a solution of the inequality.

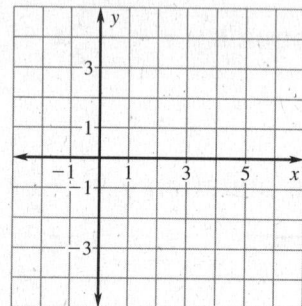

✓ **Checkpoint** Graph the inequality.

1. $2y + 4x > 8$	2. $y < 2$
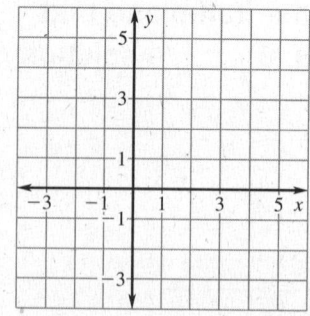	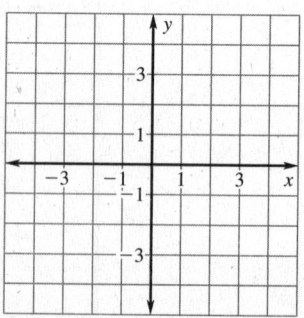

Homework

Words to Review

Give an example of the vocabulary word.

Graph of an inequality	Equivalent inequalities
Compound inequality	Absolute value equation
Absolute deviation	Linear inequality in two variables
Graph of a linear inequality in two variables	

Review your notes and Chapter 6 by using the Chapter Review on pages 415–418 of your textbook.

7.1 Solve Linear Systems by Graphing

Goal • Graph and solve systems of linear equations.

Your Notes

VOCABULARY

Systems of linear equations

Solution of a system of linear equations

Consistent independent system

SOLVING A LINEAR SYSTEM USING THE GRAPH-AND-CHECK METHOD

Step 1 _____ both equations in the same coordinate plane. For ease of graphing, you may want to write each equation in _____.

Step 2 **Estimate** the coordinates of the _____ _____.

Step 3 _____ the coordinates algebraically by substituting into each equation of the original linear system.

Your Notes

Example 1 Use the graph-and-check method

Solve the linear system: $3x + y = 9$ Equation 1
$x - y = 1$ Equation 2

Solution

1. _____ both equations.

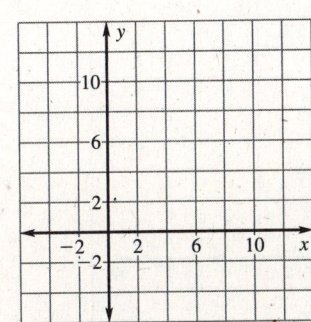

> To ease graphing, write each equation in slope intercept form.

2. **Estimate** the point of intersection. The two lines appear to intersect at (___, ___).

3. **Check** whether (___, ___) is a solution by substituting ___ for x and ___ for y in each of the original equations.

Equation 1
$3x + y = 9$
_____ $\stackrel{?}{=} 9$
___ $= 9$ ✓

Equation 2
$x - y = -1$
_____ $\stackrel{?}{=} -1$
___ $= -1$ ✓

Because (___, ___) is a solution of each equation in the linear system, it is a _____.

Your Notes

✓ **Checkpoint** Solve the linear system by graphing.

1. $2y + 4x = 12$
   $2x - y = -10$

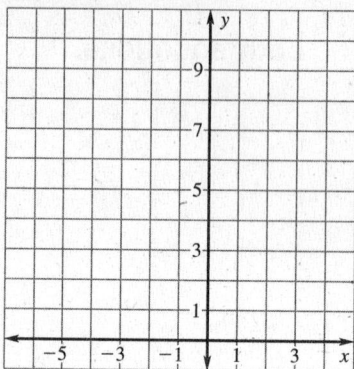

2. $4x + 2y = 6$
   $3x - 3y = 9$

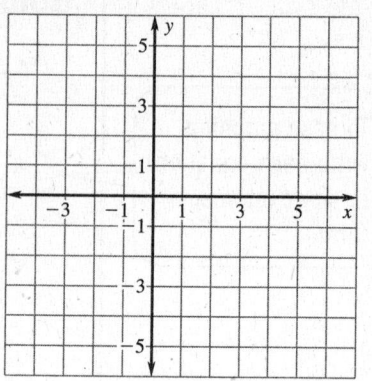

3. $2y = 6x + 8$
   $4x + y = -3$

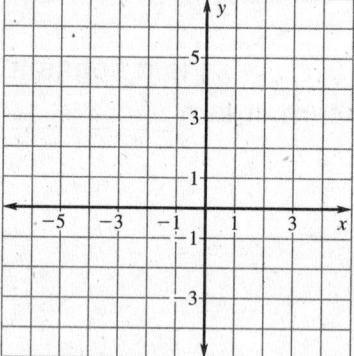

4. $y = 4x + 4$
   $2y = -3x - 14$

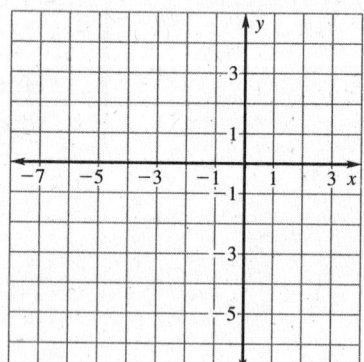

Homework

7.2 Solve Linear Systems by Substitution

Goal • Solve systems of linear equations by substitution.

Your Notes

SOLVING A LINEAR SYSTEM USING THE SUBSTITUTION METHOD

Step 1 _____ one of the equations for one of its variables. When possible, solve for a variable that has a coefficient of ___ or ___.

Step 2 _____ the expression from Step 1 into the other equation and solve for the other variable.

Step 3 _____ the value from Step 2 into the revised equation from Step 1 and solve.

Example 1 Use the substitution method

Solve the linear system: $x = -2y + 2$ Equation 1
$3x + y = 16$ Equation 2

1. _____ for x. Equation 1 is already solved for x.

2. Substitute _____ for x in Equation 2 and solve for y.

   $3x + y = 16$ Write Equation 2.
   $3(\_\_\_) + y = 16$ Substitute _____ for x.
   $\_\_\_ + y = 16$ Distributive property
   $\_\_\_ = 16$ Simplify.
   $\_\_\_ = \_\_\_$ Subtract ___ from each side.
   $y = \_\_\_$ Divide each side by ___.

3. Substitute ___ for y in the original Equation 1 to find the value of x.

   $x = -2y + 2 = -2(\_\_\_) + 2 = 4 + 2 = \_\_\_$

The solution is (___, ___).

> Remember to check your solution in each of the original equations.

Your Notes

Example 2 *Use the substitution method*

Solve the linear system: $4x - 2y = 14$ Equation 1
$2x + y = -3$ Equation 2

Solution

1. **Solve** Equation 2 for y.

   $2x + y = -3$ Write original Equation 2.

   $y = $ _____   Revised Equation 2

2. **Substitute** _____ for y in Equation 1 and solve for x.

   $4x - 2y = 14$ Write Equation 1.
   $4x - 2($ _____ $) = 14$ Substitute _____ for y.
   $4x + $ _____ $= 14$ Distributive property
   _____ $= 14$ Simplify.
   ___ $=$ ___   Subtract ___ from each side.
   $x = $ ___   Divide each side by ___.

3. **Substitute** ___ for x in the revised Equation 2 to find the value of y.

   $y = $ _____ $= $ _____ $= $ _____ $= $ ___

The solution is (___ , _____).

✓ **Checkpoint** Solve the linear system using the substitution method.

1. $5x - 4y = -1$	2. $x + y = 5$
$y = 6x + 5$	$7x - 9y = 3$

Homework

154   Lesson 7.2 • Algebra 1 Notetaking Guide

7.3 Solve Linear Systems by Adding or Subtracting

Goal • Solve linear systems using elimination.

Your Notes

> **SOLVING A LINEAR SYSTEM USING THE ELIMINATION METHOD**
>
> **Step 1** _____ the equations to _____ one variable.
>
> **Step 2** _____ the resulting equation for the other variable.
>
> **Step 3 Substitute** in either original equation to _____.

Example 1   Use addition to eliminate a variable

Solve the linear system: $x + 5y = 9$ Equation 1
$4x - 5y = -14$ Equation 2

Solution

1. _____ the equations to eliminate one variable.

   $x + 5y = 9$
   $4x - 5y = -14$
   _____ = _____

2. Solve for x. $x = $ _____

3. Substitute _____ for x in either equation and _____.

   $x + 5y = 9$ Write Equation 1.
   _____ $+ 5y = 9$ Substitute _____ for x.
   $y = $ ___   Solve for y.

The solution is (___, ___).

Make sure to check your solution by substituting it into each of the original equations.

Your Notes

Example 2 *Use subtraction to eliminate a variable*

Solve the linear system: $3x - 4y = 2$ Equation 1
$3x + 2y = 26$ Equation 2

Solution

1. _____ the equations to eliminate one variable.

   $3x - 4y = 2$
   $3x + 2y = 26$
   _____ = _____

2. **Solve** for y. $y =$ ___

3. **Substitute** ___ for y in either equation and _____.

   $3x + 2y = 26$ Write Equation 2.
   $3x + 2(\_\_) = 26$ Substitute ___ for y.
   $x =$ ___   Solve for x.

The solution is (__, __).

✓ **Checkpoint** Solve the linear system.

1. $-8x + 3y = 12$ $8x - 9y = 12$	2. $x + 6y = 13$ $-2x + 6y = -8$

156 Lesson 7.3 • Algebra 1 Notetaking Guide

Your Notes

Example 3 — Arrange like terms

Solve the linear system: $6x + 7y = 16$ Equation 1
$y = 6x - 32$ Equation 2

Solution

1. _____ Equation 2 so that the like terms are arranged in columns.

   $6x + 7y = 16$ $6x + 7y = 16$
   $y = 6x - 32$ _____

2. _____ the equations.   _____ = _____
3. Solve for y. $y = $ _____
4. Substitute _____ for y in either equation and _____.

   $6x + 7y = 16$ Write Equation 1.
   $6x + 7(\_\_) = 16$ Substitute _____ for y.
   $x = \_\_$ _____.

The solution is (___, ___).

✓ **Checkpoint** Solve the linear system.

3. $4x - 5y = 5$ $5y = x + 10$	4. $7y = 4 - 2x$ $2x + y = -8$

Homework

7.4 Solve Linear Systems by Multiplying First

Goal • Solve linear systems by multiplying first.

Your Notes

Example 1 Multiply one equation, then add

Solve the linear system: $3x - 3y = 21$ Equation 1
$\qquad\qquad\qquad\qquad\qquad\;\; 8x + 6y = -14$ Equation 2

Solution

1. **Multiply** Equation 1 by ___ so that the coefficients of y are _____.

   $3x - 3y = 21$ ×___   _____
   $8x + 6y = -14$ $\underline{8x + 6y = -14}$

2. **Add** the equations.   _____ = ____

3. **Solve** for x. $x =$ ___

4. **Substitute** ___ for x in either of the original equations and _____.

   $3x - 3y = 21$ Write Equation 1.
   $3(\underline{\quad}) - 3y = 21$ Substitute ___ for x.
   $y =$ _____   Solve for y.

The solution is (____, ____).

CHECK Substitute _____ for x and _____ for y in the original equations.

   Equation 1   Equation 2
   $3x - 3y = 21$ $8x + 6y = -14$
$3(\underline{\quad}) - 3(\underline{\quad}) \stackrel{?}{=} 21$ $8(\underline{\quad}) + 6(\underline{\quad}) \stackrel{?}{=} -14$
   ____ = 21 ✓   ____ = -14 ✓

Your Notes

Example 2 — Multiply both equations, then subtract

Solve the linear system: $3y = -2x + 17$ Equation 1
$3x + 5y = 27$ Equation 2

Solution

1. **Arrange** the equations so that like terms are in columns.

   $2x + 3y = 17$ Rewrite Equation 1.
   $3x + 5y = 27$ Write Equation 2.

2. **Multiply** Equation 1 by ___ and Equation 2 by ___ so that the coefficient of x in each equation is the _____ _____ of 2 and 3, or ___.

   $2x + 3y = 17$ ×___ ⟶   ___$x +$ ___$y =$ ___

   $3x + 5y = 27$ ×___ ⟶   ___$x +$ ___$y =$ ___

3. _____ the equations.   _____ = ___

4. **Solve** for y. $y =$ ___

5. **Substitute** ___ for y in either of the original equations and solve for x.

   $3x + 5y = 27$ Write Equation 2.
   $3x + 5(\_\_) = 27$ Substitute ___ for x.
   $x =$ ___   Solve for x.

The solution is (___, ___).

✓ **Checkpoint** Solve the linear system using elimination.

1. $7x + 2y = 26$	2. $5y = 9x - 8$
$10x - 5y = -10$	$-20x + 10y = -10$

Homework

7.5 Solve Special Types of Linear Systems

Goal • Identify the number of solutions of a linear system.

Your Notes

VOCABULARY

Inconsistent system

Consistent dependent system

Example 1 **A linear system with no solutions**

Show that the linear system has no solution.

$-2x + y = 1$ Equation 1
$-2x + y = -3$ Equation 2

Solution

Method 1 Graphing

Graph the linear system.

The lines are _____ because they have the same slope but different y-intercepts. Parallel lines do _____, so the system has _____.

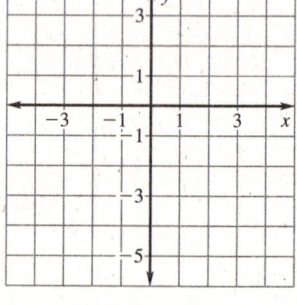

To ease graphing, write each equation in slope intercept form.

Method 2 Elimination

Subtract the equations.

$-2x + y = 1$
$-2x + y = -3$
___ = ___

The variables are _____ and you are left with a _____ regardless of the values of x and y. This tells you that the system has _____.

Your Notes

> **Example 2** *A linear system with infinitely many solutions*
>
> Show that the linear system has infinitely many solutions.
>
> $x + 3y = -3$ Equation 1
> $3x + 9y = -9$ Equation 2
>
> **Solution**
>
> **Method 1 Graphing**
>
> Graph the linear system. The equations represent the _____, so any point on the line is a solution. So, the linear system has _____.
>
>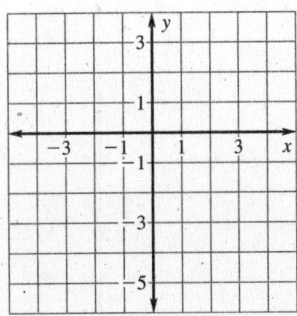
>
> **Method 2 Substitution**
>
> $x =$ _____   Solve Equation 1 for x.
>
> $3x + 9y = -9$ Write Equation 2.
>
> $3(\_\_\_\_) + 9y = -9$ Substitute _____ for x.
>
> _____ $+ 9y = -9$ Distributive property
>
> ____ $= -9$ Simplify.
>
> The variables are _____ and you are left with a statement that is _____ regardless of the values of x and y. This tells you that the system has _____.

Your Notes

✓ **Checkpoint** Tell whether the linear system has no solution or infinitely many solutions.

1. $y = 2x - 7$	2. $2y = 8x + 4$
$4x - 2y = 14$	$-4x + y = 4$

NUMBER OF SOLUTIONS OF A LINEAR SYSTEM

One solution   No solution   Infinitely many solutions

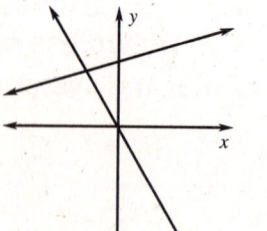 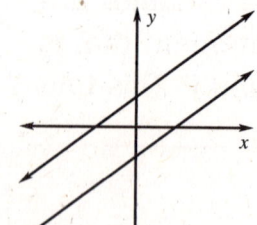 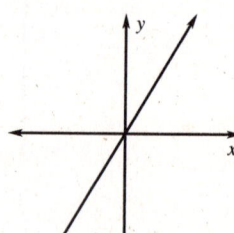

The lines _____.
The lines have _____ slopes.

The lines are _____.
The lines have the same slope and _____ y-intercepts.

The lines _____.
The lines have the same slope and the _____ _____.

Homework

7.6 Solve Linear Systems of Linear Inequalities

Goal • Solve systems of linear inequalities in two variables.

Your Notes

VOCABULARY

System of linear inequalities

Solution of a system of linear inequalities

Graph of a system of linear inequalities

GRAPHING A SYSTEM OF LINEAR INEQUALITIES

Step 1 _____ each inequality.

Step 2 Find the _____ of the graphs. The graph of the system is this intersection.

Your Notes

Example 1 **Graph a system of three linear inequalities**

Graph the system of inequalities.

y > 1   Inequality 1
x ≤ 4   Inequality 2
3y < 6x − 6   Inequality 3

Solution

Graph all three inequalities in the same coordinate plane. The graph of the system is the _____ shown.

The region is _____ the line y = 1.

The region is _____ of the line x = 4.

The region is _____ the line 3y = 6x − 6.

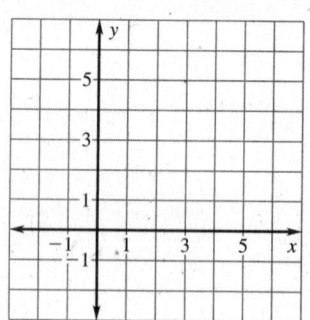

✓ **Checkpoint** Graph the system of linear equations.

1. x + y ≤ 5
   y < x + 3

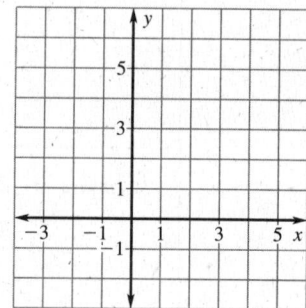

2. x > −2
   y ≤ 4
   3x + 4y ≤ 24

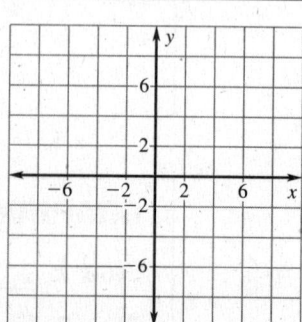

Your Notes

Example 2 Write a system of linear inequalities

Write a system of inequalities for the shaded region.

Solution

Inequality 1 One boundary line for the shaded region is _____. Because the shaded region is _____ the _____ line, the inequality is _____.

Inequality 2 Another boundary line for the shaded region has a slope of ___ and a y-intercept of ____. So, its equation is _____. Because the shaded region is _____ the _____ line, the inequality is _____.

The system of inequalities for the shaded region is:

_____ Inequality 1

_____ Inequality 2

✓ **Checkpoint** Write a system of inequalities that defines the shaded region.

3.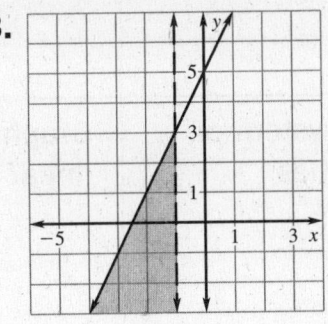

4.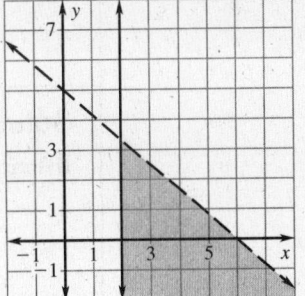

Homework

Lesson 7.6 • Algebra 1 Notetaking Guide 165

Words to Review

Give an example of the vocabulary word.

System of linear equations	Solution of a system of linear equations
Consistent independent system	Inconsistent system
Dependent system	System of linear inequalities
Solution of a system of linear inequalities	Graph of a system of linear inequalities

Review your notes and Chapter 7 by using the Chapter Review on pages 475–478 of your textbook.

8.1 Apply Exponent Properties Involving Products

Goal • Use properties of exponents involving products.

Your Notes

VOCABULARY

Order of magnitude

PRODUCT OF POWERS PROPERTY

Let a be a real number, and let m and n be positive integers.

Words: To multiply powers having the same base, _____ _____.

Algebra: $a^m \cdot a^n = a$____

Example: $5^6 \cdot 5^3 = 5$____ $= 5$____

Example 1 *Use the product of powers property*

Simplify the expression.

a. $2^2 \cdot 2^3 = 2$____
    $= 2$____

b. $w^9 \cdot w^2 \cdot w^7 = w$____
    $= w$____

c. $4^4 \cdot 4 = 4^4 \cdot 4$____
    $= 4$____
    $= 4$____

d. $(-6)(-6)^6 = (-6)$____ $\cdot (-6)^6$
    $= (-6)$____
    $= (-6)$____

> When simplifying powers with numerical bases only, write your answers using exponents.

Your Notes

POWER OF A POWER PROPERTY

Let a be a real number, and let m and n be positive integers.

Words: To find a power of a power, _____.

Algebra: $(a^m)^n = a$___

Example: $(3^4)^2 = 3$___ $= 3$___

Example 2 Use the power of a power property

Simplify the expression.

a. $(5^2)^3 = 5$___ $= 5$___

b. $(n^7)^2 = n$___ $= n$___

c. $[(-3)^5]^3 = (-3)$___
       $= (-3)$___

d. $[(z-4)^2]^5 = (z-4)$___
       $= (z-4)$___

POWER OF A PRODUCT PROPERTY

Let a and b be real numbers, and let m be a positive integer.

Words: To find a power of a product, find the _____ _____.

Algebra: $(ab)^m =$ _____

Example: $(23 \cdot 17)^5 =$ _____

Example 3 Use the power of a product property

Simplify the expression.

a. $(4 \cdot 16)^7 =$ _____

b. $(-3rs)^2 = ($_____$)^2 = ($___$)^2 \cdot$ ___$^2 \cdot$ ___^{2}
   $=$ _____

c. $-(3rs)^2 = -($_____$)^2 = -($___$^2 \cdot$ ___$^2 \cdot$ ___$^2)$
   $=$ _____

When simplifying powers with numerical and variable bases, evaluate the numerical power.

Your Notes

✓ **Checkpoint** Simplify the expression.

1. $(-7)^8(-7)^5$	2. $k^3 \cdot k \cdot k^2$	3. $(p^3)^4$
4. $[(q+8)^2]^6$	5. $(8cd)^2$	6. $-(5z)^3$

Example 4 Use all three properties

Simplify $x^2 \cdot (3x^3y)^3$.

Solution

$x^2 \cdot (3x^3y)^3 =$ _____ _____ property

$=$ _____ _____ property

$=$ _____ _____ property

✓ **Checkpoint** Simplify the expression.

7. $(2x^5)^4$	8. $(3y^3)^4 \cdot y^5$

Homework

8.2 Apply Exponent Properties Involving Quotients

Goal • Use properties of exponents involving quotients.

Your Notes

QUOTIENT OF POWERS PROPERTY

Let a be a nonzero real number, and let m and n be positive integers such that $m > n$.

Words: To divide powers having the same base, _____ the exponents.

Algebra: $\dfrac{a^m}{a^n} = a$ _____ , $a \neq 0$

Example: $\dfrac{4^7}{4^2} = 4$ _____ $= 4$ ___

Example 1   *Use the quotient of powers property*

Simplify the expression.

a. $\dfrac{6^{12}}{6^5} = 6$ _____ $= 6$ ___

b. $\dfrac{(-2)^7}{(-2)^4} = (-2)$ _____ $= (-2)$ ___

c. $\dfrac{4^2 \cdot 4^8}{4^4} = \dfrac{4\_\_\_}{4^4}$

$= 4$ _____

$=$ _____

d. $\dfrac{1}{y^9} \cdot y^{12} = \dfrac{y^{12}}{y^9}$

$= y$ _____

$=$ _____

> When simplifying powers with numerical bases only, write your answers using exponents.

Your Notes

POWER OF A QUOTIENT PROPERTY

Let a and b be real numbers with $b \neq 0$, and let m be a positive integer.

Words: To find a power of a quotient, find the power of the _____ and the power of the _____ and divide.

Algebra: $\left(\dfrac{a}{b}\right)^m = $ _____ , $b \neq 0$ **Example:** $\left(\dfrac{4}{7}\right)^3 = $ _____

Example 2 *Use the power of a quotient property*

Simplify the expression.

When simplifying powers with numerical and variable bases, evaluate the numerical power.

a. $\left(\dfrac{r}{s}\right)^5 = $ _____

b. $\left(-\dfrac{4}{w}\right)^3 = \left(\right)^3 = $ _____ $=$ _____ $=$ _____

✓ **Checkpoint** Simplify the expression.

1. $\dfrac{(-8)^8}{(-8)^5}$	2. $\dfrac{3^5 \cdot 3^4}{3^3}$
3. $\left(-\dfrac{r}{3}\right)^2$	4. $\left(\dfrac{5}{t}\right)^4$

Your Notes

Example 3 *Use properties of exponents*

Simplify $\left(\dfrac{2y^7}{y^5}\right)^3$.

Solution

$\left(\dfrac{2y^7}{y^5}\right)^3 = $ _____ _____ property

$= $ _____ _____ property

$= $ _____ _____ property

$= $ _____ _____ property

✓ **Checkpoint** Simplify the expression.

5. $\left(\dfrac{7y^3 z}{y}\right)^2$

6. $\dfrac{2s^4}{t} \cdot \left(\dfrac{2t}{s}\right)^3$

7. $\left(\dfrac{6m^3 n^2}{3mn}\right)^3$

8. $\dfrac{4a}{b^2} \cdot \left(\dfrac{2a^2 b^3}{a}\right)^4$

Homework

8.3 Define and Use Zero and Negative Exponents

Goal • Use zero and negative exponents.

Your Notes

DEFINITION OF ZERO AND NEGATIVE EXPONENTS

Words	Algebra	Example
a to the zero power is 1.	$a^0 = \underline{}$, $a \neq 0$	$5^0 = \underline{}$
a^{-n} is the reciprocal of a^n.	$a^{-n} = \underline{}$, $a \neq 0$	$2^{-1} = \underline{}$
a^n is the reciprocal of a^{-n}.	$a^n = \underline{}$, $a \neq 0$	$2 = \underline{}$

Example 1 Use definition of zero and negative exponents

Evaluate the expression.

a. $2^{-3} = \underline{}$ Definition of _____

     $= \underline{}$ Evaluate exponent.

b. $(-10)^0 = \underline{}$ Definition of _____

c. $\left(\dfrac{1}{4}\right)^{-3} = \underline{}$ Definition of _____

     $= \underline{}$ Evaluate exponent.

     $= \underline{}$ Simplify.

d. $0^{-7} = \underline{}$ a^{-n} is defined only for a _____ number a.

Your Notes

PROPERTIES OF EXPONENTS

Let a and b be real numbers, and let m and n be integers.

$a^m \cdot a^n = a\text{\_\_\_\_}$ _____ property

$(a^m)^n = a\text{\_\_\_\_}$ _____ property

$(ab)^m = \text{\_\_\_\_}$ _____ property

$\dfrac{a^m}{a^n} = a\text{\_\_\_\_}, a \neq 0$ _____ property

$\left(\dfrac{a}{b}\right)^m = \text{\_\_\_\_}, b \neq 0$ _____ property

---

Example 2 *Evaluate exponential expressions*

Evaluate the expression.

a. $(-5)^4 \cdot (-5)^{-4} = \text{_____}$ Product of powers property

              $= \text{\_\_\_}$ _____ exponents.

              $= \text{\_\_\_}$ Definition of _____

b. $(5^{-2})^{-2} = \text{_____}$ _____ property

        $= \text{\_\_\_}$ _____ exponents.

        $= \text{\_\_\_}$ Evaluate power.

c. $\dfrac{1}{4^{-2}} = \text{\_\_\_}$ Definition of _____

     $= \text{\_\_\_}$ Evaluate power.

d. $\dfrac{3^2}{3^{-1}} = \text{_____}$ _____ property

      $= \text{\_\_\_}$ _____ exponents.

      $= \text{\_\_\_}$ Evaluate power.

Your Notes

✓ **Checkpoint** Evaluate the expression.

1. $\left(\dfrac{1}{8}\right)^{-1}$	2. $\dfrac{1}{3^{-2}}$
3. $\dfrac{6^{-1}}{6}$	4. $(5^{-1})^2$

Example 3 *Use properties of exponents*

Simplify the expression $\dfrac{2w^{-3}x}{(2wx)^2}$. Write your answer using only positive exponents.

Solution

$\dfrac{2w^{-3}x}{(2wx)^2} = $ _____ Definition of negative exponents

$= $ _____ _____ property

$= $ _____ _____ property

$= $ _____ _____ property

✓ **Checkpoint** Simplify the expression.

5. $\dfrac{6fg^{-4}}{2f^2g}$	6. $(3yz^2)^{-2}$

Homework

8.4 Use Scientific Notation

Goal • Read and write numbers in scientific notation.

Your Notes

VOCABULARY

Scientific notation

SCIENTIFIC NOTATION

A number is written in scientific notation when it is of the form _____ where $1 \leq c < 10$ and n is an integer.

Number	Standard form	Scientific notation
Sixteen million		
Two hundredths		

Example 1 *Write numbers in scientific notation*

a. $7{,}820{,}000 = $ _____ $\times 10$ ___   Move decimal point ___ places to the _____. Exponent is _____.

b. $0.00401 = $ _____ $\times 10$ ___   Move decimal point ___ places to the _____. Exponent is _____.

Example 2 *Write numbers in standard form*

a. $3.89 \times 10^9 = $ _____   Exponent is _____. Move decimal point ___ places to the _____.

b. $9.097 \times 10^{-5} = $ _____   Exponent is _____. Move decimal point ___ places to the _____.

Your Notes

✓ **Checkpoint** Complete the following exercise.

> 1. Write the number 0.0899 in scientific notation. Then write the number 6.0001×10^7 in standard form.

Example 3 Order numbers in scientific notation

Order 3.2×10^{-4}, 0.0004, and 2.8×10^{-5} from least to greatest.

Solution

Step 1 Write each number in scientific notation, if necessary.

$0.0004 =$ _____

Step 2 Order the numbers. First order the numbers with different powers of 10. Then order the numbers with the same power of 10.

Because 10^{-5} ___ 10^{-4}, you know that _____ is less than both _____ and _____. Because 3.2 ___ 4, you know that _____ is less than _____.

So, _____ < _____ < _____.

Step 3 Write the original numbers in order from least to greatest.

_____

✓ **Checkpoint** Complete the following exercise.

> 2. Order 225,000, 1,740,000, and 1.75×10^5 from least to greatest.

Your Notes

Example 4 *Compute with numbers in scientific notation*

Evaluate the expression. Write your answer in scientific notation.

a. $(5.6 \times 10^{-4})(1.4 \times 10^{-5})$
   $= (5.6 \cdot 1.4) \times (10^{-4} \cdot 10^{-5})$ — Commutative property and associative property

   $= \underline{} \times \underline{}$ — Product of powers property

b. $(3.2 \times 10^2)^3$

   $= \underline{} \times \underline{}$ — Power of a product property

   $= \underline{} \times \underline{}$ — Power of a power property

   $= (\underline{}) \times \underline{}$ — Write \underline{} in scientific notation.

   $= \underline{} \times (\underline{})$ — Associative property

   $= \underline{}$ — Product of powers property

c. $\dfrac{3.5 \times 10^{-3}}{1.75 \times 10^{-5}}$

   $= \dfrac{3.5}{1.75} \times \dfrac{10^{-3}}{10^{-5}}$ — Product rule for fractions

   $= \underline{} \times \underline{}$ — Quotient of powers property

✓ **Checkpoint** Simplify the expression.

3. $(2.01 \times 10^{-7})^2$	4. $\dfrac{4.8 \times 10^{-4}}{6 \times 10^{-4}}$

Homework

8.5 Write and Graph Exponential Growth Functions

Goal • Write and graph exponential growth models.

Your Notes

VOCABULARY

Exponential function

Exponential growth

Compound interest

Example 1 Write a function rule

Write a rule for the function.

x	−2	−1	0	1	2
y	$\frac{2}{9}$	$\frac{2}{3}$	2	6	8

Solution

Step 1 Tell whether the function is exponential. Here the y-values are multiplied by ___ for each increase of 1 in x, so the table represents an exponential function of the form _____ where _____.

Step 2 Find the value of a by finding the value of y when x = 0. When x = 0, y = _____ = _____ = ___. The value of y when x = 0 is ___, so _____.

Step 3 Write the function rule. A rule for the function is y = _____.

Your Notes

Example 2 — Graph an exponential function

Graph the function $y = 3^x$. Identify its domain and range.

Solution

Step 1 Make a table by choosing a few values for x and finding the values of y. The domain is _____.

x	2	1	0	1	2
y	__	__	__	__	__

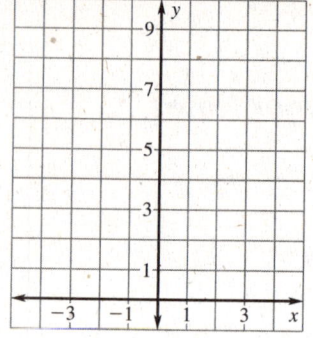

Step 2 Plot the points.

Step 3 Draw a smooth curve through the points. From either the table or the graph, you can see that the range is _____.

Example 3 — Compare graphs of exponential functions

Graph $y = 2 \cdot 3^x$. Compare the graph with the graph of $y = 3^x$.

Solution

To graph each function, make a table of values, plot the points, and draw a smooth curve through the points.

x	$y = 3^x$	$y = 2 \cdot 3^x$
2	__	__
1	__	__
0	__	__
1	__	__
2	__	__

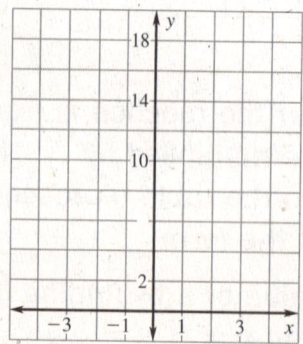

Because the y-values for $y = 2 \cdot 3^x$ are _____ the corresponding y-values for $y = 3^x$, the graph of $y = 2 \cdot 3^x$ is a _____ of the graph of $y = 3^x$.

Your Notes

✓ **Checkpoint** Complete the following exercises.

1. Write a rule for the function.

x	−2	−1	0	1	2
y	$-\frac{1}{16}$	$-\frac{1}{4}$	−1	−4	−16

2. Graph $y = 4^x$. Identify its domain and range.

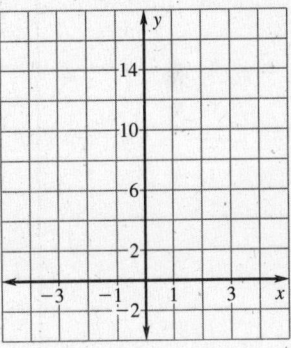

3. Graph $y = -2 \cdot 3^x$. Compare the graph with the graph of $y = 3^x$.

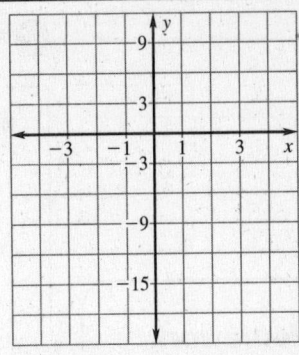

Your Notes

EXPONENTIAL GROWTH MODEL

$y = a(1 + r)^t$

a is the _____.   r is the _____.

1 + r is the _____.   t is the _____.

Example 4   Solve a compound interest problem

Investment You put $250 in a savings account that earns 4% annual interest compounded yearly. You do not make any deposits or withdrawals. How much will your investment be worth in 10 years?

Solution

The initial amount is _____, the interest rate is _____, or _____, and the time period is _____.

$y = a(1 + r)t$ Write exponential growth model.

= _____ (1 + _____) ___   Substitute _____ for a, _____ for r, and _____ for t.

= 250(_____)^{10} Simplify.

≈ _____   Use a calculator.

You will have _____ in 10 years.

✓ **Checkpoint** Complete the following exercise.

4. In Example 4, suppose the annual interest rate is 5%. How much will your investment be worth in 10 years?

Homework

8.6 Write and Graph Exponential Decay Functions

Goal • Write and graph exponential decay functions.

Your Notes

VOCABULARY

Exponential decay

Example 1 *Graph an exponential function*

Graph the function $y = \left(\dfrac{1}{3}\right)^x$ and identify its domain and range.

Solution

Step 1 Make a table of values. The domain is _____ _____.

x	−2	−1	0	1	2
y	__	__	__	__	__

Step 2 Plot the points.

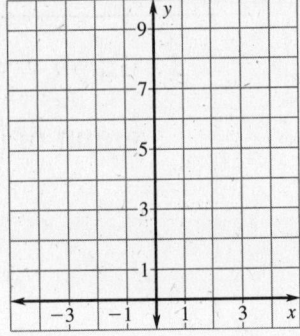

Step 3 Draw a smooth curve through the points. From either the table or the graph, you can see that the range is _____.

Your Notes

Example 2 *Compare graphs of exponential functions*

Graph $y = 2 \cdot \left(\frac{1}{3}\right)^x$. Compare the graph with the graph of $y = \left(\frac{1}{3}\right)^x$.

Solution

x	$y = \left(\frac{1}{3}\right)^x$	$y = 2 \cdot \left(\frac{1}{3}\right)^x$
−2	___	___
−1	___	___
0	___	___
1	___	___
2	___	___

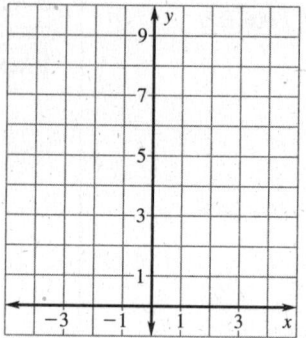

Because the y-values for $y = 2 \cdot \left(\frac{1}{3}\right)^x$ are _____ the corresponding y-values for $y = \left(\frac{1}{3}\right)^x$, the graph of $y = 2 \cdot \left(\frac{1}{3}\right)^x$ is a _____ of the graph of $y = \left(\frac{1}{3}\right)^x$.

✓ **Checkpoint** Complete the following exercise.

1. Graph $y = -2 \cdot \left(\frac{1}{3}\right)^x$. Compare the graph with the graph of $\left(\frac{1}{3}\right)^x$.

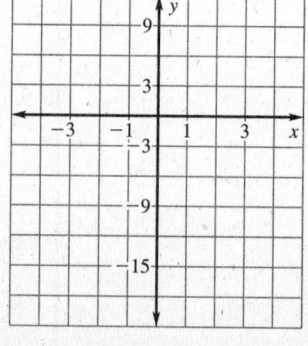

Your Notes

Example 3 *Classify and write rules for functions*

Tell whether the graph represents *exponential growth* or *exponential decay*. Then write a rule for the function.

Solution

The graph represents _____ ($y = ab^x$ where $0 < b < 1$). The y-intercept is ___, so $a =$ ___. Find the value of b by using the point $(1, 1)$ and $a =$ ___.

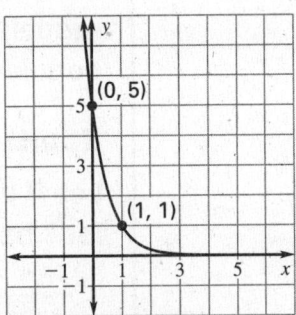

$y = ab^x$ Write function.

___ = ___ · b___   Substitute.

___ = b Solve.

A function rule is _____.

EXPONENTIAL GROWTH AND DECAY

Exponential Growth
$y = ab^x$, $a > 0$
and $b > 1$

Exponential Decay
$y = ab^x$, $a > 0$
and $0 < b < 1$

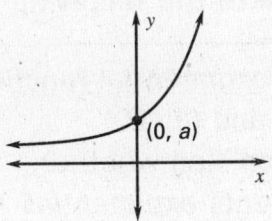   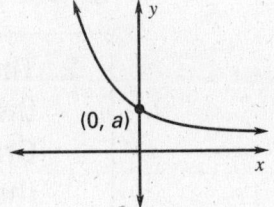

EXPONENTIAL DECAY MODEL

$y = a(1 + r)^t$

a is the _____. r is the _____.

$1 - r$ is the _____. t is the _____.

Your Notes

Example 4   *Use the exponential decay model*

Population The population of a city decreased from 1995 to 2003 by 1.5% annually. In 1995 there were about 357,000 people living in the city. Write a function that models the city's population since 1995. Then find the population in 2003.

Solution

Let P be the population of the city (in thousands), and let t be the time (in years) since 1995. The initial value is _____, and the decay rate is _____.

$P = a(1 - r)^t$ Write exponential decay model.

$= \underline{\quad}(1 - \underline{\quad})^t$ Substitute ____ for a, and ____ for r.

$= \underline{\qquad\qquad}$ Simplify.

To find the population in 2003, ____ years after 1995, substitute ____ for t.

$P = \underline{\qquad\qquad}$ Substitute ____ for t.

$\approx \underline{\qquad}$ Use a calculator.

The city's population was about _____ in 2003.

✓ Checkpoint Complete the following exercises.

2. The graph of an exponential function passes through the points (0, 4) and (1, 10). Graph the function. Tell whether the graph represents *exponential growth* or *exponential decay*. Then write a rule for the function.

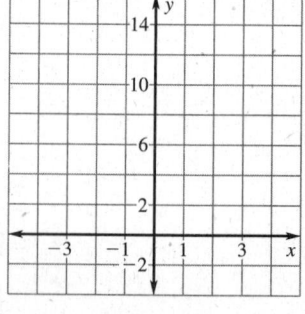

Homework

3. In Example 4, suppose that the decay rate of the city's population remains the same beyond 2003. What will be the population in 2020?

Words to Review

Give an example of the vocabulary word.

Order of magnitude	Scientific notation
Exponential function	**Exponential growth**
Compound interest	**Exponential decay**

Review your notes and Chapter 8 by using the Chapter Review on pages 543–546 of your textbook.

9.1 Add and Subtract Polynomials

Goal • Add and subtract polynomials.

Your Notes

VOCABULARY

Monomial

Degree of a monomial

Polynomial

Degree of a polynomial

Leading coefficient

Binomial

Trinomial

Example 1 *Rewrite a polynomial*

Write $7 + 2x^4 - 4x$ so that the exponents decrease from left to right. Identify the degree and leading coefficient of the polynomial.

Solution

Consider the degree of each of the polynomial's terms.

Degree is ___.   Degree is ___.   Degree is ___.

$$7 + 2x^4 - 4x$$

The polynomial can be written as _____. The greatest degree is ___, so the degree of the polynomial is ___, and the leading coefficient is ___.

Your Notes

✓ **Checkpoint** Write the polynomial so that the exponents decrease from left to right. Identify the degree and leading coefficient of the polynomial.

1. $5x + 13 + 8x^3$

2. $4y^4 - 7y^5 + 2y$

Example 2 Identify and classify polynomials

Tell whether the expression is a polynomial. If it is a polynomial, find its degree and classify it by the number of terms. Otherwise, tell why it is not a polynomial.

	Expression	Is it a polynomial?	Classify by degree and number of terms
a.	-6	_____	0 degree monomial
b.	$m^{-3} + 4$	_____	
c.	$-h^3 + 4h^2$	Yes	_____
d.	$9 - 5x^4 + 3x$	Yes	_____
e.	$2w^3 + 4^w$	_____	

✓ **Checkpoint** Tell whether the expression is a polynomial. If it is a polynomial, find its degree and classify it by the number of terms. Otherwise, tell why it is not a polynomial.

3. $4x - x^7 + 5x^3$

4. $v^3 + v^{-2} + 2v$

Your Notes

Example 3 Add polynomials

Find the sum (a) $(4x^3 + x^2 - 5) + (7x + x^3 - 3x^2)$ and (b) $(x^2 + x + 8) + (x^2 - x - 1)$.

Solution

a. Vertical format: Align like terms in vertical columns.

$$\begin{array}{r} 4x^3 + x^2 - 5 \\ + x^3 - 3x^2 + 7x \\ \hline \end{array}$$

> If a particular power of the variable appears in one polynomial but not the other, leave a space in that column, or write the term with a coefficient of 0.

b. Horizontal format: Group like terms and simplify.

$(x^2 + x + 8) + (x^2 - x - 1)$
= (_____) + (_____) + (_____)
= _____

Example 4 Subtract polynomials

Find the difference (a) $(4z^2 - 3) - (-2z^2 + 5z - 1)$ and (b) $(3x^2 + 6x - 4) - (x^2 - x - 7)$.

Solution

a. $\begin{array}{r}(4z^2 - 3) \\ -(-2z^2 + 5z - 1) \\ \hline \end{array}$ ⟶ $\begin{array}{r} 4z^2 - 3 \\ \underline{2z^2 \underline{} 5z \underline{} 1} \\ \end{array}$

> Remember to multiply *each* term in the polynomial by −1 when you write the subtraction as addition.

b. $(3x^2 + 6x - 4) - (x^2 - x - 7)$
= $3x^2 + 6x - 4$ _____
= _____
= _____

✓ **Checkpoint** Find the sum or difference.

Homework

5. $(3x^4 - 2x^2 - 1) + (5x^3 - x^2 + 9x^4)$

6. $(3t^2 - 5t + t^4) - (11t^4 - 3t^2)$

9.2 Multiply Polynomials

Goal • Multiply polynomials.

Your Notes

Example 1 — Multiply a monomial and a polynomial

Find the product $3x^3(2x^3 - x^2 - 7x - 3)$.

Solution

$3x^3(2x^3 - x^2 - 7x - 3)$
$= 3x^3(\underline{}) - 3x^3(\underline{}) - 3x^3(\underline{}) - 3x^3(\underline{})$
$= \underline{} - \underline{} - \underline{} - \underline{}$

Example 2 — Multiply polynomials vertically and horizontally

Find the product.

a. $(a^2 - 6a - 3)(2a - 5)$ b. $(3b^2 - 2b + 5)(5b - 6)$

Solution

a. Vertical format:

$$\begin{array}{r} a^2 - 6a - 3 \\ \times 2a - 5 \\ \hline -\underline{}a^2 + \underline{}a + \underline{} \\ \underline{}a^3 - \underline{}a^2 - \underline{}a \\ \hline \end{array}$$

Write the product in vertical format.

Multiply by ____.

Multiply by ____.

Add products.

> Remember that the terms of $(2a - 5)$ are $2a$ and -5. They are *not* $2a$ and 5.

b. Horizontal format:

$(3b^2 - 2b + 5)(5b - 6)$
$= \underline{}(5b - 6) - \underline{}(5b - 6)$
$ + \underline{}(5b - 6)$
$= \underline{}$
$= \underline{}$

Your Notes

Checkpoint Find the product.

1. $2x^2(x^3 - 5x^2 + 3x - 7)$

2. $(a^2 + 5a - 4)(2a + 3)$

Example 3 *Multiply binomials using the FOIL pattern*

Find the product $(2c + 7)(c - 9)$.

Solution

$(2c + 7)(c - 9)$

$= 2c(\underline{}) + 2c(\underline{}) + 7(\underline{}) + 7(\underline{})$

$= \underline{}$

$= \underline{}$

Checkpoint Complete the following exercise.

3. Find the product $(m + 3)(5m - 4)$.

Your Notes

> **Example 4** *Multiply ponynomials to find an area*
>
> **Area** The dimensions of a rectangle are $x + 4$ and $x + 5$. Write an expression that represents the area of the rectangle.
>
> **Solution**
>
> Area = length • width   Formula for area of a rectangle
>
> = (_____)(_____)   Substitute for length and width.
>
> = _____   Multiply binomials.
>
> = _____   Combine like terms.
>
> **CHECK** Use a graphing calculator to check your answer. Graph
> $y_1 = $ _____ and
> $y_2 = $ _____ in the same viewing window. The graphs _____, so the product of $x + 4$ and $x + 5$ is _____.

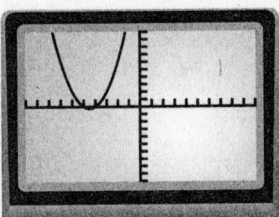

✓ **Checkpoint** Complete the following exercise.

> 4. The dimensions of a rectangle are $x + 3$ and $x + 11$. Write an expression that represents the area of the rectangle.

Your Notes

> **Example 5** — *Solve a multi-step problem*
>
> **Walkway** You are making a a walkway around part of your swimming pool. The dimensions of the swimming pool and walkway are shown in the diagram.
>
>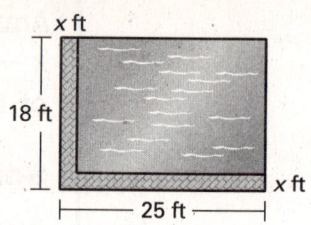
>
> - Write a polynomial that represents the area of the swimming pool.
> - What is the area of the swimming pool if the walkway is 2 feet wide?
>
> **Solution**
>
> **Step 1** Write a polynomial using the formula for the area of a rectangle. The length is _____. The width is _____.
>
> Area = _____ • _____
>
>   = _____
>
>   = _____
>
>   = _____
>
> **Step 2** Substitute ___ for x and evaluate.
>
> Area = _____ = ____
>
> The area of the swimming pool is _____.

✓ **Checkpoint** Complete the following exercise.

---

5. Swimming Pool Your neighbor has a walkway around his entire pool as shown in the diagram. The width of the walkway is the same on every side. Write a polynomial that represents the area of the pool. What is the area of the pool if the walkway is 3 feet wide?

Homework

9.3 Find Special Products of Polynomials

Goal • Use special product patterns to multiply polynomials.

Your Notes

SQUARE OF A BINOMIAL PATTERN

Algebra

$(a + b)^2 = a^2$ _____ $+ b^2$

$(a - b)^2 = a^2$ _____ $+ b^2$

Example

$(x + 4)^2 = x^2$ _____ $+ 16$

$(3x - 2)^2 = 9x^2$ _____ $+ 4$

Example 1 *Use the square of a binomial pattern*

Find the product.

Solution

a. $(4x + 3)^2 = (4x)^2$ _____ $+ 3^2$

   $= 16x^2$ _____ $+ 9$

b. $(3x - 5y)^2 = (3x)^2$ _____ $+ (5y)^2$

   $= 9x^2$ _____ $+ 25y^2$

> When you use special product patterns, remember that *a* and *b* can be numbers, variables, or variable expressions.

✓ **Checkpoint** Find the product.

1. $(x + 9)^2$

2. $(2x - 7)^2$

3. $(5r + s)^2$

Your Notes

SUM AND DIFFERENCE PATTERN

Algebra

$(a + b)(a - b) = \underline{}^2 - \underline{}^2$

Example

$(x + 4)(x - 4) = \underline{}^2 - \underline{}$

Example 2   *Use the sum and difference pattern*

Find the product.

Solution

a. $(n + 3)(n - 3) = \underline{}^2 - \underline{}^2$ Sum and difference pattern

$ = \underline{}^2 - \underline{}$ Simplify.

b. $(4x + y)(4x - y) = \underline{}^2 - \underline{}^2$ Sum and difference pattern

$ = \underline{}^2 - \underline{}^2$ Simplify.

Example 3   *Use special products and mental math*

Use special products to find the product $17 \cdot 23$.

Solution

Notice that 17 is 3 less than $\underline{}$ while 23 is 3 more than $\underline{}$.

$17 \cdot 23 = (\underline{} - 3)(\underline{} + 3)$ Write as product.

$ = \underline{}$ Sum and difference pattern

$ = \underline{}$ Evaluate powers.

$ = \underline{}$ Simplify.

Your Notes

✓ **Checkpoint** Complete the following exercises.

4. Find the product $(z + 6)(z - 6)$.

5. Find the product $(4x + 3)(4x - 3)$.

6. Find the product $(x + 5y)(x - 5y)$.

7. *Describe* how you can use special products to find 39^2.

Your Notes

Example 4 Solve a multi-step problem

Eye Color An offspring's eye color is determined by a combination of two genes, one inherited from each parent. Each parent has two color genes, and the offspring has an equal chance of inheriting either one.

The gene *B* is for brown eyes, and the gene *b* is for blue eyes. Any gene combination with a *B* results in brown eyes. Suppose each parent has the same gene combination *Bb*. The Punnett square shows the possible gene combinations of the offspring and the resulting eye color.

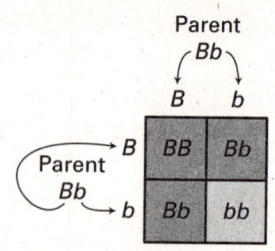

- What percent of the possible gene combinations of the offspring result in blue eyes?
- Show how you could use a polynomial to model the possible gene combinations of the offspring.

Solution

Step 1 Notice that the Punnett square shows that ___ out of 4, or _____ of the possible gene combinations result in blue eyes.

Step 2 Model the gene from each parent with _____. The possible gene of the offspring can be modeled by _____. Notice that this product also represents the area of the Punnett square.

_____

= _____

= _____

The coefficients show that _____ of the possible gene combinations will result in blue eyes.

Homework

✓ **Checkpoint** Complete the following exercise.

8. **Eye Color** Look back at Example 4. What percent of the possible gene combinations of the offspring result in brown eyes?

9.4 Solve Polynomial Equations in Factored Form

Goal • Solve polynomial equations.

Your Notes

VOCABULARY

Roots _____

_____

Vertical motion model

ZERO-PRODUCT PROPERTY

Let a and b be real numbers. If $ab = 0$, then ___ $= 0$ or ___ $= 0$.

Example 1 *Use the zero-product property*

Solve $(x - 5)(x + 4) = 0$.

Solution

$(x - 5)(x + 4) = 0$ Write original equation.

_____ $= 0$ or   _____ $= 0$ _____ property

$x =$ ___   or $x =$ ___   Solve for x.

The solutions of the equation are _____.

CHECK Substitute each solution into the original equation to check.

$(\_\_ - 5)(\_\_ + 4) \stackrel{?}{=} 0$ $(\_\_ - 5)(\_\_ + 4) \stackrel{?}{=} 0$

$\_\_\_\_ \stackrel{?}{=} 0$ $\_\_\_\_ \stackrel{?}{=} 0$

$\_\_ = 0$ $\_\_ = 0$

Your Notes

Example 2 — Find the greatest common monomial factor

Factor out the greatest common monomial factor.

a. $16x + 40y$
b. $6x^2 + 30x^3$

Solution

a. The GCF of 16 and 40 is ____. The variables x and y have _____. So, the greatest common monomial factor of the terms is ____.

$16x + 40y = $ _____

b. The GCF of 6 and 30 is ____. The GCF of x^2 and x^3 is ____. So, the greatest common monomial factor of the terms is ____.

$6x^2 + 30x^3 = $ _____

Example 3 — Solve an equation by factoring

Solve the equation.

a.
$3x^2 + 15x = 0$	Original equation
_____ $= 0$	Factor left side.
____ $= 0$ or ____ $= 0$	Zero-product property
$x = $ ____ or $x = $ ____	Solve for x.

The solutions of the equation are _____.

b.
$9b^2 = 24b$	Original equation
_____ $= 0$	Subtract ____ from each side.
_____ $= 0$	Factor left side.
____ $= 0$ or ____ $= 0$	Zero-product property
$b = $ ____ or $b = $ ____	Solve for b.

The solutions of the equation are _____.

> To use the zero-product property, you must write the equation so that one side is 0. For this reason, ____ must be subtracted from each side of the equation.

Your Notes

✓ **Checkpoint** Solve the equation.

1. $(x + 6)(x - 3) = 0$

2. $(x - 8)(x - 5) = 0$

✓ **Checkpoint** Factor out the greatest common monomial factor.

3. $10x^2 - 24y^2$

4. $3t^6 + 8t^4$

VERTICAL MOTION MODEL

The height h (in feet) of a projectile can be modeled by

$$h = -16t^2 + vt + s$$

where t is the _____ (in seconds) the object has been in the air, v is the _____ (in feet per second), and s is the _____ (in feet).

> The vertical motion model takes into account the effect of gravity but ignores other, less significant, factors such as air resistance.

Your Notes

Example 4   *Solve a multi-step problem*

Fountain A fountain sprays water into the air with an initial vertical velocity of 20 feet per second. After how many seconds does it land on the ground?

Solution

Step 1 Write a model for the water's height above ground.

$h = -16t^2 + vt + s$ Vertical motion model

$h = -16t^2 + \underline{}t + \underline{}$ $v = \underline{}$ and $s = \underline{}$

$h = -16t^2 + \underline{}$ Simplify.

Step 2 Substitute ___ for h. When the water lands, its height above the ground is ___ feet. Solve for t.

$\underline{} = -16t^2 + \underline{}$ Substitute ___ for h.

$\underline{} = \underline{}$ Factor right side.

$\underline{}$ or $\underline{}$ Zero-product property

$\underline{}$ or $\underline{}$ Solve for t.

The water lands on the ground _____ seconds after it is sprayed.

> The solution $t = 0$ means that before the water is sprayed, its height above the ground is 0 feet.

Checkpoint Complete the following exercises.

5. Solve $d^2 - 7d = 0$.	6. Solve $8b^2 = 2b$.

7. **What If?** In Example 4, suppose the initial vertical velocity is 18 feet per second. After how many seconds does the water land on the ground?

Homework

9.5 Factor $x^2 + bx + c$

Goal • Factor trinomials of the form $x^2 + bx + c$.

Your Notes

FACTORING $x^2 + bx + c$

Algebra

$x^2 + bx + c = (x + p)(x + q)$ provided ____ = b and ____ = c.

Example

$x^2 + 6x + 5 = ($____$)($____$)$ because ____ = 6 and ____ = 5.

Example 1 Factor when b and c are positive

Factor $x^2 + 10x + 16$.

Solution

Find two ____ factors of ____ whose sum is ____. Make an organized list.

Factors of ____	Sum of factors
16, ____	16 + ____ = ____
8, ____	8 + ____ = ____
4, ____	4 + ____ = ____

The factors 8 and ____ have a sum of ____, so they are the correct values of p and q.

$x^2 + 10x + 16 = (x + 8)($____$)$

CHECK

$(x + 8)($____$) = $ _____   Multiply.

$ = $ _____   Simplify.

Your Notes

Example 2 — **Factor when b is negative and c is positive**

Factor $a^2 - 5a + 6$.

Solution

Because b is negative and c is positive, p and q must _____.

Factors of ___	Sum of factors
_____	____ + (____) = ____
_____	____ + (____) = ____

$a^2 - 5a + 6 = ($ _____ $)($ _____ $)$

Example 3 — **Factor when b is positive and c is negative**

Factor $y^2 + 3y - 10$.

Solution

Because c is negative, p and q must _____ _____.

Factors of _____	Sum of factors
−10, ____	−10 + ____ = ____
10, ____	10 + ____ = ____
−5, ____	−5 + ____ = ____
5, ____	5 + ____ = ____

$y^2 + 3y - 10 = ($ _____ $)($ _____ $)$

✓ **Checkpoint** Factor the trinomial.

1. $x + 7x + 12$	2. $x + 9x + 8$

Your Notes

✓ **Checkpoint** Factor the trinomial.

3. $x + 12x + 27$	4. $x^2 - 9x + 20$
5. $y^2 + 4y - 21$	6. $z^2 + 2z - 24$

Example 4 — Solve a polynomial equation

Solve the equation $x^2 + 7x = 18$.

$x^2 + 7x = 18$	Write original equation.
$x^2 + 7x - \underline{} = 0$	Subtract ____ from each side.
$\underline{} = 0$	Factor left side.
$\underline{}$ or $\underline{}$	Zero-product property
$\underline{}$ or $\underline{}$	Solve for x.

The solutions of the equation are 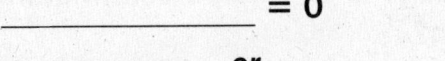.

Your Notes

Example 5 Solve a multi-step problem

Dimensions The bandage shown has an area of 16 square centimeters. Find the width of the bandage.

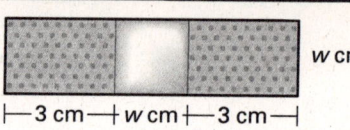

Solution

Step 1 Write an equation using the fact that the area of the bandage is 16 square centimeters.

$A = \ell \cdot w$ — Formula for area

____ = ____ · w — Substitute values.

$0 =$ ____ — Simplify.

Step 2 Solve the equation for w.

$0 =$ ____ — Write equation.

$0 =$ ____ — Factor right side.

____ or ____ — Zero-product property

____ or ____ — Solve for w.

The bandage cannot have a negative width, so the width is ____ .

✓ **Checkpoint** Complete the following exercises.

7. Solve the equation $s^2 - 12s = 13$.

8. **What If?** In Example 5, suppose the area of the bandage is 27 square centimeters. What is the width?

Homework

9.6 Factor $ax^2 + bx + c$

Goal • Factor trinomials of the form $ax^2 + bx + c$.

Your Notes

Example 1 — Factor when b is negative and c is positive

Factor $2x^2 - 11x + 5$.

Solution

Because b is negative and c is positive, both factors of c must be _____. You must consider the _____ of the factors of 5, because the x-terms of the possible factorizations are different.

Factors of 2	Factors of 5	Possible factorization	Middle term when multiplied
1, 2	−1, ___	$(x - 1)(2x$ ___ $)$	___ $- 2x =$ ___
1, 2	−5, ___	$(x - 5)(2x$ ___ $)$	___ $- 10x =$ ___

$2x^2 - 11x + 5 = (x -$ ___$)(2x$ ___$)$

Example 2 — Factor when b is positive and c is negative

Factor $5n^2 + 2n - 3$.

Solution

Because b is positive and c is negative, the factors of c have _____.

Factors of 5	Factors of −3	Possible factorization	Middle term when multiplied
1, 5	1, ___	$(n + 1)(5n$ ___ $)$	
1, 5	−1, ___	$(n - 1)(5n$ ___ $)$	
1, 5	3, ___	$(n + 3)(5n$ ___ $)$	
1, 5	−3, ___	$(n - 3)(5n$ ___ $)$	

$5n^2 + 2n - 3 = (n$ ___$)(5n$ ___$)$

Your Notes

✓ **Checkpoint** Factor the trinomial.

1. $3x^2 - 5x + 2$	2. $2m^2 + m - 21$

Example 3 *Factor when a is negative*

Factor $-4x^2 + 4x + 3$.

Solution

Step 1 Factor _____ from each term of the trinomial.

$-4x^2 + 4x + 3 =$ ____(_____)

Step 2 Factor the trinomial _____. Because b and c are both _____, the factors of c must have _____.

Factors of 4	Factors of −3	Possible factorization	Middle term when multiplied
1, 4	1, ___	$(x + 1)(4x$ ___ $)$	
1, 4	3, ___	$(x + 3)(4x$ ___ $)$	
1, 4	−1, ___	$(x - 1)(4x$ ___ $)$	
1, 4	−3, ___	$(x - 3)(4x$ ___ $)$	
2, 2	1, ___	$(2x + 1)(2x$ ___ $)$	
2, 2	−1, ___	$(2x - 1)(2x$ ___ $)$	

Remember to include the _____ that you factored out in Step 1.

$-4x^2 + 4x + 3 =$ _____

✓ **Checkpoint** Complete the following exercise.

3. Factor $-2y^2 - 11y - 5$.

Your Notes

Example 4 — Write and solve a polynomial equation

Tennis An athlete hits a tennis ball at an initial height of 8 feet and with an initial vertical velocity of 62 feet per second.

a. Write an equation that gives the height (in feet) of the ball as a function of the time (in seconds) since it left the racket.

b. After how many seconds does the ball hit the ground?

Solution

a. Use the _____ to write an equation for the height h (in feet) of the ball.

$h = -16t^2 + vt + s$ _____

$h = -16t^2 + \underline{}\, t + \underline{}$ $v = \underline{}$ and $s = \underline{}$

b. To find the number of seconds that pass before the ball lands, find the value of t for which the height of the ball is ___. Substitute ___ for h and solve the equation for t.

$\underline{} = -16t^2 + \underline{}\, t + \underline{}$ Substitute ___ for h.

$\underline{} = \underline{}(\underline{})$ Factor out ___.

$\underline{} = \underline{}(\underline{})(\underline{})$ Factor the trinomial.

_____ or _____   Zero-product property

_____ or _____   Solve for t.

A negative solution does not make sense in this situation. The tennis ball hits the ground after _____.

✓ **Checkpoint** Complete the following exercise.

Homework

4. **What If?** In Example 4, suppose another athlete hits the tennis ball with an initial vertical velocity of 20 feet per second from a height of 6 feet. After how many seconds does the ball hit the ground?

9.7 Factor Special Products

Goal • Factor special products.

VOCABULARY

Perfect square trinomial

DIFFERENCE OF TWO SQUARES PATTERN

Algebra

$a^2 - b^2 = (a + b)(_____)$

Example

$9x^2 - 4 = (3x)^2 - 2^2 = (_____)(_____)$

Example 1 Factor the differences of two squares

Factor the polynomial.

a. $z^2 - 81 = z^2 - \underline{}^2$
$= (z + \underline{})(z - \underline{})$

b. $16x^2 - 9 = (\underline{})^2 - \underline{}^2$
$= (\underline{} + \underline{})(\underline{} - \underline{})$

c. $a^2 - 25b^2 = a^2 - (\underline{})^2$
$= (a + \underline{})(a - \underline{})$

d. $4 - 16n^2 = \underline{}(\underline{} - \underline{})$
$= \underline{}[(\underline{})^2 - (\underline{})^2]$
$= \underline{}(\underline{} + \underline{})(\underline{} - \underline{})$

✓ **Checkpoint** Factor the polynomial.

1. $x^2 - 100$	2. $49y^2 - 25$
3. $c^2 - 9d^2$	4. $45 - 80m^2$

210 Lesson 9.7 • Algebra 1 Notetaking Guide

Your Notes

PERFECT SQUARE TRINOMIAL PATTERN

Algebra
$a^2 + 2ab + b^2 = (\underline{})^2$
$a^2 - 2ab + b^2 = (\underline{})^2$

Example
$x^2 + 8x + 16 = x^2 + 2(x \cdot 4) + 4^2 = (\underline{})^2$
$x^2 - 6x + 9 = x^2 - 2(x \cdot 3) + 3^2 = (\underline{})^2$

Example 2 *Factor perfect square trinomials*

Factor the polynomial.

a. $x^2 - 16x + 64 = x^2 - 2(\underline{}) - \underline{}^2$
$= (\underline{})^2$

b. $4y^2 - 12y + 9 = (\underline{})^2 - 2(\underline{}) + \underline{}^2$
$= (\underline{})^2$

c. $9s^2 + 6st + t^2 = (\underline{})^2 + 2(\underline{}) + \underline{}^2$
$= (\underline{})^2$

d. $-3z^2 + 24z - 48 = \underline{}(z^2 - 8z + 16)$
$= \underline{}[z^2 - 2(\underline{}) + \underline{}^2]$
$= \underline{}(\underline{})^2$

✓ **Checkpoint** Factor the polynomial.

5. $x^2 + 14x + 49$	6. $9y^2 - 6y + 1$
7. $16x^2 - 40xy + 25y^2$	8. $-5r^2 - 20r - 20$

Lesson 9.7 • Algebra 1 Notetaking Guide

Your Notes

Example 3 — Solve a polynomial equation

Solve the equation $x^2 + x + \frac{1}{4} = 0$.

$x^2 + x + \frac{1}{4} = 0$		Write original equation.
_____ = 0		Multiply each side by ___.
_____ = 0		Write left side as $a^2 + 2ab + b^2$.
_____ = 0		Perfect square trinomial pattern
_____ = 0		Zero-product property
$x =$ _____		Solve for x.

> This equation has two identical solutions, because it has two identical factors.

Example 4 — Solve a vertical motion problem

Falling Object A brick falls off of a building from a height of 144 feet. After how many seconds does the brick land on the ground?

Solution

Use the vertical motion model. The brick fell, so its initial vertical velocity is ___. Find the value of time t (in seconds) for which the height h (in feet) is ___.

$h =$ _____		Vertical motion model
___ = _____		Substitute values.
___ = _____(_____)		Factor out _____.
___ = _____(_____)(_____)		Difference of two squares
_____ or _____		Zero-product property
_____ or _____		Solve for t.

The brick lands on the ground _____ after it falls.

Your Notes

✓ **Checkpoint** Solve the equation.

9. $m^2 - 8m + 16 = 0$

10. $w^2 + 16w + 64 = 0$

11. $t^2 - 121 = 0$

✓ **Checkpoint** Complete the following exercise.

12. **What If?** In Example 4, suppose the brick falls from a height of $\frac{225}{4}$ feet. After how many seconds does the brick lands on the ground?

Homework

9.8 Factor Polynomials Completely

Goal • Factor polynomials completely.

Your Notes

VOCABULARY

Factor by grouping _____

Factor completely _____

Example 1 *Factor out a common binomial*

Factor the expression.

a. $3x(x + 2) - 2(x + 2)$ b. $y^2(y - 4) + 3(4 - y)$

Solution

a. $3x(x + 2) - 2(x + 2) = (x + 2)(\underline{\hspace{1cm}})$

b. The binomials $y - 4$ and $4 - y$ are _____. Factor _____ from $4 - y$ to obtain a common binomial factor.

$y^2(y - 4) + 3(4 - y) = y^2(y - 4)\underline{\hspace{1cm}}$
$ = (y - 4)\underline{\hspace{1cm}}$

Example 2 *Factor by grouping*

Factor the expression.

a. $y^3 + 7y^2 + 2y + 14$ b. $y^2 + 2y + yx + 2x$

Solution

a. $y^3 + 7y^2 + 2y + 14 = (\underline{\hspace{1cm}}) + (\underline{\hspace{1cm}})$
$ = \underline{\hspace{0.3cm}}(\underline{\hspace{1cm}}) + \underline{\hspace{0.3cm}}(\underline{\hspace{1cm}})$
$ = (\underline{\hspace{1cm}})(\underline{\hspace{1cm}})$

b. $y^2 + 2y + yx + 2x = (\underline{\hspace{1cm}}) + (\underline{\hspace{1cm}})$
$ = \underline{\hspace{0.3cm}}(\underline{\hspace{1cm}}) + \underline{\hspace{0.3cm}}(\underline{\hspace{1cm}})$
$ = (\underline{\hspace{1cm}})(\underline{\hspace{1cm}})$

> Remember that you can check a factorization by multiplying the factors.

Your Notes

> **Example 3** *Factor by grouping*
>
> Factor $x^3 - 12 + 3x - 4x^2$.
>
> **Solution**
>
> The terms x^3 and -12 have no common factor. Use the _____ to rearrange the terms so that you can group terms with a common factor.
>
> $x^3 - 12 + 3x - 4x^2$ = _____
> = _____
> = _____
> = _____

✓ **Checkpoint** *Factor the expression.*

1. $5z(z - 6) + 4(z - 6)$	2. $2y^2(y - 1) + 7(1 - y)$
3. $x^3 - 4x^2 + 5x - 20$	4. $n^3 + 48 + 6n + 8n^2$

GUIDELINES FOR FACTORING POLYNOMIALS COMPLETELY

To factor a polynomial completely, you should try each of these steps.

1. Factor out the _____ common monomial factor.
2. Look for a difference of two squares or a _____ _____.
3. Factor a trinomial of the form $ax^2 + bx + c$ into a product of _____ factors.
4. Factor a polynomial with four terms by _____.

Your Notes

> **Example 4** **Factor completely**
>
> **Factor the polynomial completely.**
> a. $x^2 + 3x - 1$
> b. $3r^3 - 21r^2 + 30r$
> c. $9d^4 - 4d^2$
>
> **Solution**
>
> a. The terms of the polynomial have no common monomial factor. Also, there are no factors of ____ that have a sum of ____. This polynomial _____ be factored.
>
> b. $3r^3 - 21r^2 + 30r = $ _____
>
> $= $ _____
>
> c. $9d^4 - 4d^2 = $ _____
>
> $= $ _____

> **Example 5** **Solve a polynomial equation**
>
> **Solve** $5x^3 - 25x^2 = -30x$.
>
> **Solution**
>
> | | |
> |---|---|
> | $5x^3 - 25x^2 = -30x$ | Write original equation. |
> | $5x^3 - 25x^2$ ____ $30x = 0$ | ____ $30x$ to each side. |
> | _____ $= 0$ | Factor out ____. |
> | _____ $= 0$ | Factor trinomial. |
> | _____ or _____ or _____ | Zero-product property |
> | $x = $ ____ $x = $ ____ $x = $ ____ | Solve for x. |

Remember that you can check your answers by substituting each solution for x in the original equation.

Your Notes

Example 6 — Solve a multi-step problem

Volume A crate in the shape of a rectangular prism has a volume of 180 cubic feet. The crate has a width of w feet, a length of $(9 - w)$ feet, and a height of $(w + 4)$ feet. The length is more than half the width. Find the crate's length, width, and height.

Solution

Step 1 Write and solve an equation for w.

Volume = _____ · _____ · _____

____ = _____

0 = _____

0 = _____

0 = _____

0 = _____

0 = _____

_____ = 0 or _____ = 0 or _____ = 0

$w =$ ___ $w =$ ___ $w =$ ____

Step 2 Choose the solution that is the correct value for w. Disregard _____, because the width cannot be _____.

You know that the length is more than half the width. Test the solutions _____ in the length expression.

Length = _____ = ___ or
Length = _____ = ___.

The solution ___ gives a length of ___ feet, which is more than half the width.

Step 3 Find the height.

Height = _____ = _____ = ___.

The width is _____, the length is _____, and the height is _____.

Your Notes

✓ **Checkpoint** Factor the polynomial.

5. $-2x^3 + 6x^2 + 108x$

6. $12y^4 - 75y^2$

✓ **Checkpoint** Complete the following exercises.

7. Solve $2x^3 + 2x^2 = 40x$.

8. **What If?** A box in the shape of a rectangular prism has a volume of 180 cubic feet. The box has a length of x feet, a width of $(x + 9)$ feet, and a height of $(x - 4)$ feet. Find the dimensions of the box.

Homework

Words to Review

Give an example of the vocabulary word.

Monomial	Degree of a monomial
Polynomial	Degree of a polynomial
Leading coefficient	Binomial
Trinomial	Roots
Vertical motion model	Perfect square trinomial
Factor by grouping	Factor completely

Review your notes and Chapter 9 by using the Chapter Review on pages 616–620 of your textbook.

10.1 Graph $y = ax^2 + c$

Goal • Graph simple quadratic functions.

Your Notes

VOCABULARY

Quadratic function

Parabola

Parent quadratic function

Vertex

Axis of Symmetry

PARENT QUADRATIC FUNCTION

The most basic quadratic function in the family of quadratic functions, called the _____ _____, is $y = x^2$. The graph is shown below.

The line that passes through the vertex and divides the parabola into two symmetric parts is called the _____ _____. The axis of symmetry for the graph of $y = x^2$ is the y-axis, _____.

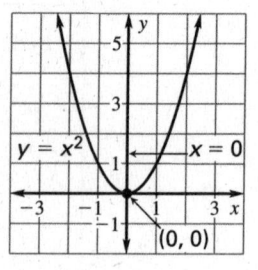

The lowest or highest point on the parabola is the _____. The vertex of the graph of $y = x^2$ is (___, ___).

220 Lesson 10.1 • Algebra 1 Notetaking Guide

Your Notes

Example 1 Graph $y = ax^2$ where $|a| < 1$

Graph $y = \frac{1}{2}x^2$. Compare the graph with the graph of $y = x^2$.

Solution

Step 1 Make a table of values for $y = \frac{1}{2}x^2$.

x	−4	−2	0	2	4
y	__	__	__	__	__

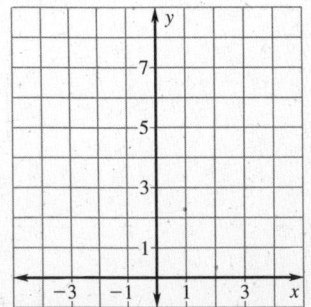

Step 2 _____ the points from the table.

Step 3 Draw a _____ through the points.

Step 4 Compare the graphs of $y = \frac{1}{2}x^2$ and $y = x^2$. Both graphs have the same vertex, (___, ___), and axis of symmetry, _____. However, the graph of $y = \frac{1}{2}x^2$ is _____ than the graph of $y = x^2$. This is because the graph of $y = \frac{1}{2}x^2$ is a vertical _____ (by a factor of ___) of the graph of $y = x^2$.

✓ **Checkpoint** Graph the function. Compare the graph with the graph of $y = x^2$.

1. $y = -5x^2$

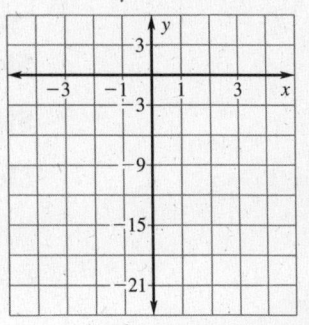

Your Notes

Example 2   Graph $y = x^2 + c$

Graph $y = x^2 - 2$. Compare the graph with the graph of $y = x^2$.

Step 1 Make a table of values for $y = x^2 - 2$.

x	-2	-1	0	1	2
y	__	__	__	__	__

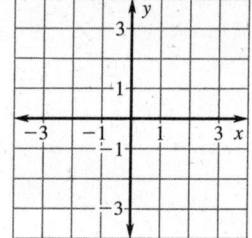

Step 2 _____ the points from the table.

Step 3 Draw a _____ through the points.

Step 4 Compare the graphs of $y = x^2 - 2$ and $y = x^2$. Both graphs open ____ and have the same axis of symmetry, _____. However, the vertex of the graph of $y = x^2 - 2$, (___, ___), is different than the vertex of the graph of $y = x^2$, (___, ___), because the graph of $y = x^2 - 2$ is a _____ (of ___ units _____) of the graph of $y = x^2$.

Example 3   Graph $y = ax^2 + c$

Graph $y = -3x^2 + 3$. Compare the graph with the graph of $y = x^2$.

Step 1 Make a table of values for $y = -3x^2 + 3$.

x	-2	-1	0	1	2
y	__	__	__	__	__

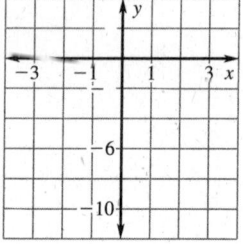

Step 2 _____ the points from the table.

Step 3 Draw a _____ through the points.

Step 4 Compare the graphs. Both graphs have the same axis of symmetry. However, the graph of $y = -3x^2 + 3$ is _____ and has a _____ vertex than the graph of $y = x^2$ because the graph of $y = -3x^2 + 3$ is a _____ and a _____ of the graph of $y = x^2$.

222   Lesson 10.1 • Algebra 1 Notetaking Guide

Your Notes

✓ **Checkpoint** Graph the function. Compare the graph with the graph of $y = x^2$.

2. $y = \frac{1}{4}x^2 - 6$

Compared with the graph of $y = x^2$, the graph of $y = ax^2$ is:

- a vertical _____ if $a > 1$,
- a vertical _____ if $0 < a < 1$.

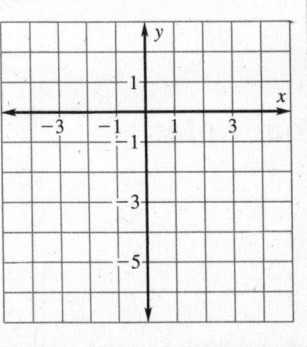

$y = ax^2, a > 0$

$a > 1$
$a = 1$
$0 < a < 1$

Compared with the graph of $y = x^2$, the graph of $y = ax^2$ is:

- a vertical _____ and a _____ in the x-axis if $a < -1$,
- a vertical _____ and a _____ in the x-axis if $-1 < a < 0$.

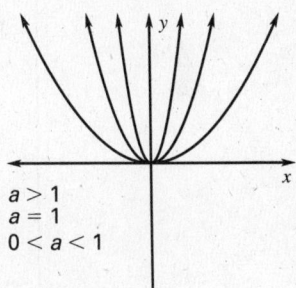

$y = ax^2, a < 0$

$a < -1$
$a = -1$
$-1 < a < 0$

Compared with the graph of $y = x^2$, the graph of $y = x^2 + c$ is:

- an _____ vertical translation if $c > 0$,
- a _____ vertical translation if $c < 0$.

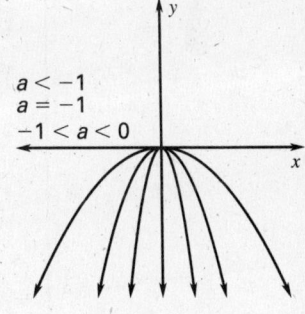

$y = x^2 + c$

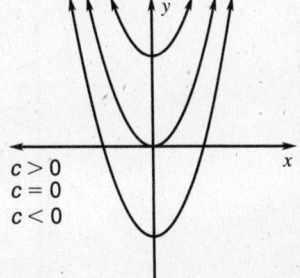

$c > 0$
$c = 0$
$c < 0$

Homework

Lesson 10.1 • Algebra 1 Notetaking Guide 223

10.2 Graph $y = ax^2 + bx + c$

Goal • Graph general quadratic functions.

Your Notes

VOCABULARY

Minimum value

Maximum value

PROPERTIES OF THE GRAPH OF A QUADRATIC FUNCTION

The graph of $y = ax^2 + bx + c$ is a parabola that:

• opens _____ if $a > 0$ and opens _____ if $a < 0$.

• is narrower than the graph of $y = x^2$ if $|a|$ ___ 1 and wider if $|a|$ ___ 1.

• has an axis of symmetry of
  $x =$ _____ .

• has a vertex with an
  x-coordinate of _____ .

• has a y-intercept of ___.
  So, the point (___, ___) is on the parabola.

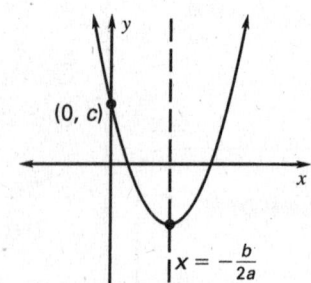

Your Notes

Example 1 — Graph $y = ax^2 + bx + c$

Graph $y = -x^2 + 4x - 1$.

Step 1 Determine whether the parabola opens up or down. Because a ___ 0, the parabola opens _____.

Step 2 Find and draw the axis of symmetry:

$$x = -\frac{b}{2a} = \underline{\qquad} = \underline{\;\;}.$$

Step 3 Find and plot the vertex. The x-coordinate of the vertex is _____, or ___.

To find the y-coordinate, substitute ___ for x in the function and simplify.

$$y = -(\underline{\;\;})^2 + 4(\underline{\;\;}) - 1 = 3$$

So, the vertex is (___, ___).

Step 4 Plot two points. Choose two x-values less than the x-coordinate of the vertex. Then find the corresponding y-values.

x	1	0
y	___	___

Step 5 _____ the points plotted in Step 4 in the axis of symmetry.

Step 6 Draw a _____ through the plotted points.

✓ Checkpoint Complete the following exercise.

1. Graph the function $y = 4x^2 + 8x + 3$. Label the vertex and axis of symmetry.

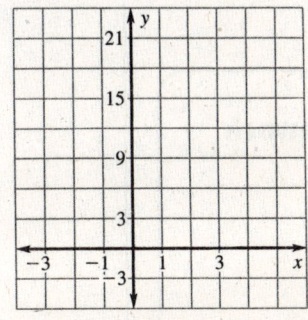

Your Notes

MINIMUM AND MAXIMUM VALUES

For $y = ax^2 + bx + c$, the y-coordinate of the vertex is the _____ value of the function if a ___ 0 and the _____ value of the function if a ___ 0.

Example 2 Find the minimum or maximum value

Tell whether the function $f(x) = 5x^2 - 20x + 17$ has a *minimum value* or a *maximum value*. Then find the minimum or maximum value.

Solution

Because $a =$ ___ and _____, the parabola opens ___ and the function has a _____ value. To find the _____ value, find the _____.

$x = -\dfrac{b}{2a} = \underline{} = \underline{}$ The x-coordinate is $-\dfrac{b}{2a}$.

$f(\underline{}) = 5(\underline{})^2 - 20(\underline{}) + 17$ Substitute ___ for x.

$= \underline{}$ Simplify.

The _____ value of the function is _____.

✓ **Checkpoint** Complete the following exercise.

2. Tell whether the function $f(x) = -\dfrac{1}{2}x^2 + 6x + 8$ has a *minimum value* or a *maximum value*. Then find the minimum or maximum value.

Homework

10.3 Solve Quadratic Equations by Graphing

Goal • Solve quadratic equations by graphing.

Your Notes

VOCABULARY

Quadratic equation

Example 1 Solve a quadratic equation having two solutions

Solve $-x^2 + 2x = -8$ by graphing.

Step 1 Write the equation in _____.

$-x^2 + 2x = -8$ Write original equation.

$-x^2 + 2x + 8 = $ ___   Add ___ to each side.

Step 2 Graph the function $y = -x^2 + 2x + 8$.
The x-intercepts are ____ and ___.

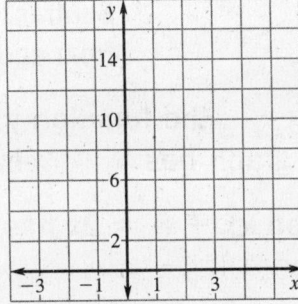

The solutions of the equation $-x^2 + 2x = -8$ are ____ and ___.

CHECK You can check ____ and ___ in the original equation.

$-x^2 + 2x = -8$ $-x^2 + 2x = -8$

$-(\underline{})^2 + 2(\underline{}) \stackrel{?}{=} -8$ $-(\underline{})^2 + 2(\underline{}) \stackrel{?}{=} -8$

$\underline{} = \underline{}$ $\underline{} = \underline{}$

Your Notes

Example 2 *Solve a quadratic equation having one solution*

Solve $x^2 - 4x = -4$ by graphing.

Step 1 Write the equation in standard form.

$x^2 - 4x = -4$ Write original equation.

$x^2 - 4x + 4 = $ ___   Add ___ to each side.

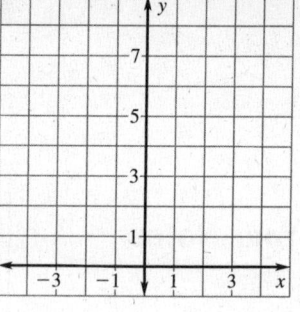

Step 2 _____ the function $y = x^2 - 4x + 4$. The x-intercept is ___.

The solution of the equation $x^2 - 4x = -4$ is ___.

Example 3 *Solve a quadratic equation having no solution*

Solve $x^2 + 8 = 2x$ by graphing.

Step 1 Write the equation in standard form.

$x^2 + 8 = 2x$ Write original equation.

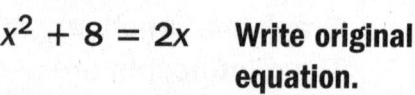   Subtract ___ from each side.

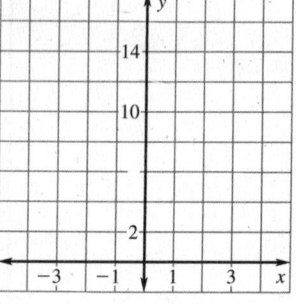

Step 2 _____ the function $y = $ _____. The graph has ___ x-intercepts.

The equation $x^2 + 8 = 2x$ has _____.

✓ **Checkpoint** Complete the following exercise.

1. Solve $x^2 - 6 = -5x$ by graphing.

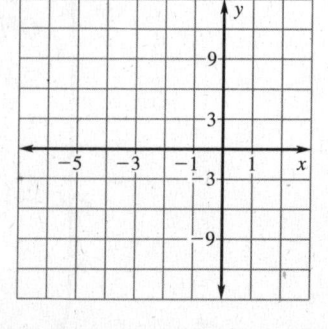

228   Lesson 10.3 • Algebra 1 Notetaking Guide

Your Notes

NUMBER OF SOLUTIONS OF A QUADRATIC EQUATION

A quadratic equation has two solutions if the graph of its related function has _____.

A quadratic equation has one solution if the graph of its related function has _____.

A quadratic equation has no solution if the graph of its related function has _____.

Example 4 *Find the zeros of a quadratic function*

Find the zeros of $f(x) = -x^2 - 8x - 7$.

Graph the function $f(x) = -x^2 - 8x - 7$. The x-intercepts are ____ and ____.

The zeros of the function are ____ and ____.

CHECK Substitute ____ and ____ in the original function.

$f(\_\_\_) = -(\_\_\_)^2 - 8(\_\_\_) - 7 = \_\_\_$

$f(\_\_\_) = -(\_\_\_)^2 - 8(\_\_\_) - 7 = \_\_\_$

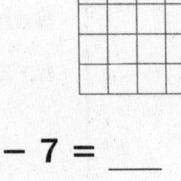

RELATING SOLUTIONS OF EQUATIONS, x-INTERCEPTS OF GRAPHS, AND ZEROS OF FUNCTIONS

Solutions of an Equation

The solutions of the equation $x^2 - 11x + 18$ are ____ and ____.

x-Intercepts of a Graph

The x-intercepts of the graph of $y = x^2 - 11x + 18$ occur where $y = \_\_\_$, so the x-intercepts are ____ and ____, as shown.

Zeros of a Function

The zeros of the function $f(x) = x^2 - 11x + 18$ are the values of x for which $f(x) = \_\_\_$, so the zeros are ____ and ____.

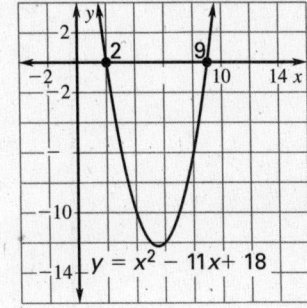

Homework

10.4 Use Square Roots to Solve Quadratic Equations

Goal • Solve a quadratic equation by finding square roots.

Your Notes

SOLVING $x^2 = d$ BY TAKING SQUARE ROOTS
- If $d > 0$, then $x^2 = d$ has _____ solutions: _____.
- If $d = 0$, then $x^2 = d$ has _____ solution: _____.
- If $d < 0$, then $x^2 = d$ has _____ solution.

Example 1 *Solve quadratic equations*

Solve the equation.

a. $z^2 - 5 = 4$ b. $r^2 + 7 = 4$ c. $25k^2 = 9$

Solution

a. $z^2 - 5 = 4$ Write original equation.
    $z^2 = $ _____   Add ___ to each side.
    $z = $ _____   Take square roots of each side.
    $z = $ _____   Simplify. The solutions are _____ and ___.

b. $r^2 + 7 = 4$ Write original equation.
    $r^2 = $ _____   Subtract ___ from each side.

Negative real numbers do not have real _____. So, there is _____.

c. $25k^2 = 9$ Write original equation.
    $k^2 = $ _____   Divide each side by ____.
    $k = $ _____   Take square roots of each side.
    $k = $ _____   Simplify. The solutions are _____ and ___.

Your Notes

✓ **Checkpoint** Solve the equation.

1. $3x^2 = 108$	2. $t^2 + 17 = 17$	3. $81p^2 = 4$

Example 2 Approximate solutions of a quadratic equation

Solve $4x^2 + 3 = 23$. Round the solutions to the nearest hundredth.

Solution

$4x^2 + 3 = 23$ Write original equation.

$4x^2 = $ _____   Subtract ___ from each side.

$x^2 = $ _____   Divide each side by ___.

$x = $ _____   Take square roots of each side.

$x \approx $ _____   Use a calculator. Round to the nearest hundredth.

The solutions are about _____ and _____.

✓ **Checkpoint** Solve the equation. Round the solutions to the nearest hundredth.

4. $2x^2 - 7 = 9$	5. $6g^2 + 1 = 19$

Your Notes

Example 3 Solve a quadratic equation

Solve $5(x + 1)^2 = 30$. Round the solutions to the nearest hundredth.

Solution

$5(x + 1)^2 = 30$	Write original equation.
$(x + 1)^2 = $ ___	Divide each side by ___.
$x + 1 = $ ___	Take square roots of each side.
$x = $ ___	Subtract ___ from each side.

The solutions are ___ $\approx$ ___ and ___ $\approx$ ___.

CHECK To check the solutions, first write the equation so that _____ as follows: $5(x + 1)^2 - 30 = 0$. Then graph the related function $y = 5(x + 1)^2 - 30$. The x-intercepts appear to be about ___ and about ___. So, each solution checks.

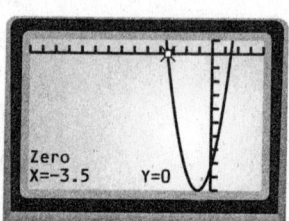

✓ **Checkpoint** Solve the equation. Round the solutions to the nearest hundredth, if necessary.

6. $3(m - 4)^2 = 12$	7. $4(a - 3)^2 = 32$

Homework

10.5 Solve Quadratic Equations by Completing the Square

Goal • Solve quadratic equations by completing the square.

Your Notes

VOCABULARY

Completing the square

COMPLETING THE SQUARE

Words To complete the square for the expression $x^2 + bx$, add the _____ of the term bx.

Algebra $x^2 + bx + \left(\dfrac{b}{2}\right)^2 = \left(x + \dfrac{b}{2}\right)^2$

Example 1 Complete the square

Find the value of c that makes the expression $x^2 - 5x + c$ a perfect square trinomial. Then write the expression as the square of the binomial.

Solution

Step 1 Find the value of c. For the expression to be a perfect square trinomial, c needs to be the square of half the coefficient of the term bx.

$c = \left(\dfrac{\Box}{2}\right)^2 = \underline{}$ Find the square of half the coefficient of bx.

Step 2 Write the expression as a perfect square trinomial. Then write the expression as the square of a binomial.

$x^2 - 5x + c = x^2 - 5x + \underline{}$ Substitute _____ for c.

$= \underline{}^2$ Square of a binomial

Your Notes

✓ **Checkpoint** Find the value of c that makes the expression a perfect square trinomial. Then write the expression as the square of a binomial.

1. $x^2 + 7x + c$	2. $x^2 - 6x + c$

Example 2   *Solve a quadratic equation*

Solve $t^2 + 6t = -5$ by completing the square.

Solution

$t^2 + 6t = -5$ Write original equation.

$t^2 + 6t +$ ___ $= -5 +$ ___   Add $\left(\dfrac{}{}\right)^2$, or ___, to each side.

_____ $= -5 +$ ___   Write left side as the square of a binomial.

_____ $=$ ___   Simplify the right side.

_____ $=$ ___   Take square roots of each side.

$t =$ _____   Subtract ___ from each side.

The solutions of the equation are _____ and _____.

Your Notes

Example 3 *Solve a quadratic equation in standard form*

Solve $4m^2 - 16m + 8 = 0$ by completing the square.

Solution

$4m^2 - 16m + 8 = 0$	Write original equation.
$4m^2 - 16m = $ ___	Subtract ___ from each side.
$m^2 - 4m = $ ___	Divide each side by ___.
$m^2 - 4m + $ ___ $= -2 + $ ___	Add $\left(\underline{}\right)^2$, or ___, to each side.
___ $= $ ___	Write left side as the square of a binomial.
___ $= $ ___	Take square roots of each side.
$m = $ ___	Add ___ to each side.

The solutions are ___ $\approx$ ___ and ___ $\approx$ ___ .

✓ **Checkpoint** Solve the equation by completing the square. Round your solutions to the nearest hundredth, if necessary.

3. $r^2 - 8r = 9$

4. $5s^2 + 60s + 125 = 0$

Homework

10.6 Solve Quadratic Equations by the Quadratic Formula

Goal • Solve quadratic equations using the quadratic formula.

Your Notes

VOCABULARY

Quadratic formula

THE QUADRATIC FORMULA

The solutions of the quadratic equation $ax^2 + bx + c = 0$ are $x = \dfrac{-b \pm \sqrt{b^2 - 4ac}}{2a}$ when $a \neq 0$ and $b^2 - 4ac \geq 0$.

Example 1 *Solve a quadratic equation*

Solve $2x^2 - 5 = 3x$.

$2x^2 - 5 = 3x$ Write original equation.

$\underline{\hspace{3cm}}$ Write in standard form.

$x = \dfrac{-b \pm \sqrt{b^2 - 4ac}}{2a}$ Quadratic formula

$= \dfrac{-\underline{} \pm \sqrt{\underline{}^2 - 4(\underline{})(\underline{})}}{2(\underline{})}$ Substitute values in the quadratic formula: $a = \underline{}$, $b = \underline{}$, and $c = \underline{}$.

$= \dfrac{\underline{} \pm \sqrt{\underline{}}}{\underline{}}$ Simplify.

$= \dfrac{\underline{} \pm \underline{}}{\underline{}}$ Simplify the square root.

The solutions are $\dfrac{\underline{} + \underline{}}{\underline{}} = \underline{}$ and $\dfrac{\underline{} - \underline{}}{\underline{}} = \underline{}$.

> Check your solution by graphing the related function and finding the *x*-intercepts.

Your Notes

Example 2 *Use the quadratic formula*

Crabbing A crabbing net is thrown from a bridge, which is 35 feet above the water. If the net's initial velocity is 10 feet per second, how long will it take the net to hit the water?

Solution

The net's initial velocity is $v =$ ____ feet per second and the net's initial height is $s =$ ____ feet. The net will hit the water when the height is ____ feet.

$h = -16t^2 + vt + s$ Vertical motion model

____ $= -16t^2 +$ ____ $t +$ ____   Substitute for h, v, and s.

$t = \dfrac{-\_\_\_ \pm \sqrt{\_\_\_^2 - 4(\_\_\_)(\_\_\_)}}{2(\_\_\_)}$ Substitute values in the quadratic formula: $a =$ ____, $b =$ ____, and $c =$ ____.

$= \dfrac{\_\_\_ \pm \sqrt{\_\_\_}}{\_\_\_}$ Simplify.

The solutions are $\dfrac{\_\_\_ + \sqrt{\_\_\_}}{\_\_\_} \approx$ ____ and

$\dfrac{\_\_\_ - \sqrt{\_\_\_}}{\_\_\_} \approx$ ____. So, the net will hit the water in about ____ seconds.

> Because time cannot be a negative number, disregard the negative solution.

✓ **Checkpoint** Complete the following exercises.

1. Use the quadratic formula to solve $2x^2 + x = 3$.

2. In Example 2, suppose the net was thrown with an initial velocity of 5 feet per second from a height of 20 feet. How long would it take the net to hit the water?

Your Notes

METHODS FOR SOLVING QUADRATIC EQUATIONS

Methods	When to Use
Factoring	Use when a quadratic equation can be _____ easily.
Graphing	Use when _____ solutions are adequate.
Finding square roots	Use when solving an equation that can be written in the form _____.
Completing the square	Can be used for any quadratic equation $ax^2 + bx + c = 0$ but is simplest to apply when _____ and b is an _____ number.
Quadratic formula	Can be used for _____ quadratic equation.

Example 3   Choose a solution method

Tell what method(s) you would use to solve the quadratic equation. *Explain* your choice(s).

a. $6x^2 - 11x + 7 = 0$ b. $4x^2 - 36 = 0$

Solution

a. The quadratic equation _____ be factored easily and completing the square would result in _____ _____. So, the equation can be solved using the _____.

b. The quadratic equation can be solved using _____ _____ because the equation can be written in the form $x^2 = d$.

✓ **Checkpoint** Complete the following exercise.

3. Tell what method(s) you would use to solve $x^2 + 8x = 9$. *Explain* your choices(s).

Homework

10.7 Interpret the Discriminant

Goal • Use the value of the discriminant.

Your Notes

VOCABULARY

Discriminant

USING THE DISCRIMINANT OF $ax^2 + bx + c = 0$

Value of the discriminant	Number of solutions	Graph of $y = ax^2 + bx + c$
$b^2 - 4ac > 0$	_____	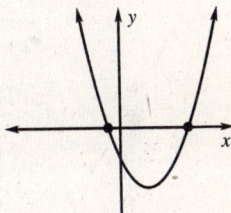
$b^2 - 4ac = 0$	_____	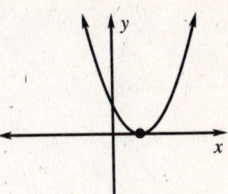
$b^2 - 4ac < 0$	_____	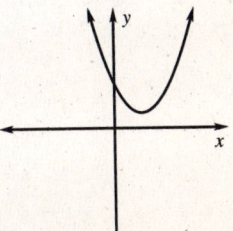

Lesson 10.7 • Algebra 1 Notetaking Guide 239

Your Notes

Example 1 — Use the discriminant

Equation $ax^2 + bx + c = 0$	Discriminant $b^2 - 4ac$
a. $x^2 - 3x - 2 = 0$	___^{2} − 4(___)(___) = ___
b. $3x^2 + 2 = 0$	___^{2} − 4(___)(___) = ___
c. $2x^2 + 8x + 8 = 0$	___^{2} − 4(___)(___) = ___

Number of solutions

a. _____   b. _____   c. _____

Example 2 — Find the number of solutions

Tell whether the equation $-2x^2 + 4x = 2$ has *two solutions, one solution,* or *no solution.*

Step 1 Write the equation in _____.

$-2x^2 + 4x = 2$ Write equation.

$-2x^2 + 4x - 2 = 0$ Subtract ___ from each side.

Step 2 Find the value of the _____.

$b^2 - 4ac =$ ___^{2} − 4(___)(___)   Substitute ___ for *a*, ___ for *b*, and ___ for *c*.

= ___   Simplify.

The discriminant is ___, so the equation has _____.

✓ **Checkpoint** Tell whether the equation has *two solutions, one solution,* or *no solution.*

1. $x^2 + 2x = 1$	2. $3x^2 + 7x = -5$
3. $5x^2 - 6 = 0$	4. $-x^2 - 9 = 6x$

Your Notes

Example 3   Find the number of x-intercepts

Find the number of x-intercepts of the graph of $y = -x^2 + 3x + 4$.

Solution

Find the _____ of the equation $0 = -x^2 + 3x + 4$.

$b^2 - 4ac = $ ___$^2 - 4($___$)($___$)$ Substitute ___ for a, ___ for b, and ___ for c.

= ___   Simplify.

The discriminant is _____, so the equation has _____. This means that the graph of $y = -x^2 + 3x + 4$ has ___ x-intercepts.

CHECK You can use a graphing calculator to check the answer. Notice that the graph of $y = -x^2 + 3x + 4$ has ___ intercepts.

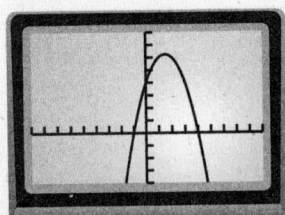

✓ **Checkpoint** Find the number of x-intercepts of the graph of the function.

5. $y = -x^2 + 3x - 3$	6. $y = x^2 - 4x + 4$

Homework

10.8 Compare Linear, Exponential, and Quadratic Models

Goal • Compare linear, exponential, and quadratic models.

Your Notes

LINEAR, EXPONENTIAL, AND QUADRATIC FUNCTIONS

Linear Function	Exponential Function	Quadratic Function
$y = $ _____	$y = $ _____	$y = $ _____

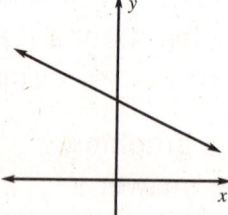 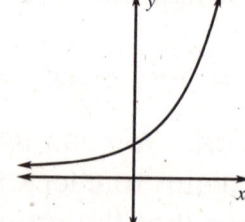 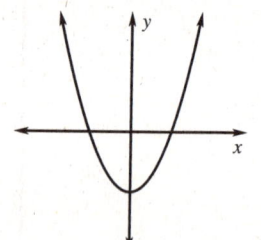

Example 1 *Choose functions using sets of ordered pairs*

Use a graph to tell whether the ordered pairs represent a *linear function*, an *exponential function*, or a *quadratic function*.

a. $(-2, 7), (-1, 1), (0, -1), (1, 1), (2, 7)$

b. $(-2, 4), (-1, 2), (0, 1), \left(1, \frac{1}{2}\right), \left(2, \frac{1}{4}\right)$

c. $(-2, 5), (-1, 3), (0, 1), (1, -1), (2, -3)$

Solution

a.
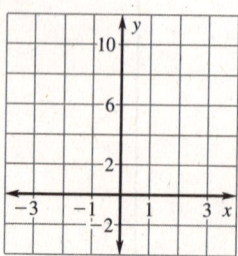

_____ function

b.
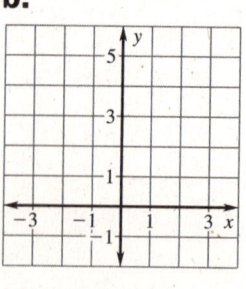

_____ function

c.
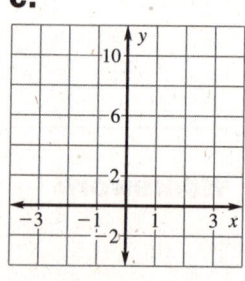

_____ function

Your Notes

> ### Example 2 — Identify functions using differences or ratios
>
> Use differences or ratios to tell whether the table of values represents a *linear function*, an *exponential function*, or a *quadratic function*.
>
> a.
>
> | x | -2 | -1 | 0 | 1 | 2 |
> |---|-----|----|----|---|---|
> | y | -12 | -8 | -4 | 0 | 4 |
>
> Differences: ___ ___ ___ ___
>
> The table of values represents _____ function.
>
> b.
>
> | x | -2 | -1 | 0 | 1 | 2 |
> |---|------|-----|---|---|---|
> | y | 0.25 | 0.5 | 1 | 2 | 4 |
>
> Ratios: $\dfrac{\square}{\square}$ = ___ ___ ___ ___
>
> The table of values represents _____ function.

✓ Checkpoint Complete the following exercises.

1. Tell whether the ordered pairs represent a *linear function*, an *exponential function*, or a *quadratic function*: (−2, −1), (−1, 1), (0, 3), (1, 5), (2, 7).

2. Tell whether the table of values represents a *linear function*, an *exponential function*, or a *quadratic function*:

x	-2	-1	0	1	2
y	3	0.75	0	0.75	3

Your Notes

Example 3 Write an equation for a function

Tell whether the table of values represents a *linear function*, an *exponential function*, or a *quadratic function*. Then write an equation for the function.

x	−2	−1	0	1	2
y	32	8	2	0.5	0.125

Step 1 Determine which type of function the values in the table represent.

x	−2	−1	0	1	2
y	32	8	2	0.5	0.25

Ratios: $\dfrac{\square}{\square}$ = _____ _____ _____ _____

The table of values represents _____ function.

Step 2 Write an equation for the _____ function. The ratio of successive *y*-values is _____, so *b* = _____. Find the value of *a* using the coordinates of a point that lies on the graph, such as (0, 2).

$y =$ _____   Write equation for _____ function.

___ = ___   Substitute _____ for *b*, _____ for *x*, and _____ for *y*.

___ = *a*   Solve for *a*.

The equation is _____.

✓ **Checkpoint** Complete the following exercise.

3. Write an equation for the function in Checkpoint 2.

Homework

Words to Review

Give an example of the vocabulary word.

Quadratic function	Parent quadratic function
Parabola	**Vertex**
Axis of symmetry	**Minimum value**
Maximum value	**Quadratic equation**

Completing the square	Quadratic formula

Discriminant

Review your notes and Chapter 10 by using the Chapter Review on pages 696–700 of your textbook.

11.1 Graph Square Root Functions

Goal • Graph square root functions.

Your Notes

VOCABULARY

Radical expression

Radical function

Square root function

Parent square root function

PARENT FUNCTION FOR SQUARE ROOT FUNCTIONS

The most basic square root function in the family of all square root functions, called the _____ _____, is y = ____.
The graph of the parent square root function is shown.

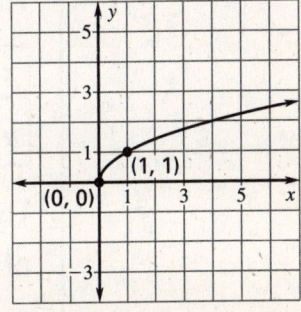

Lesson 11.1 • Algebra 1 Notetaking Guide 247

Your Notes

Example 1 — Graph a function of the form $y = a\sqrt{x}$

Graph the function $y = -4\sqrt{x}$ and identify its domain and range. Compare the graph with the graph of $y = \sqrt{x}$.

Solution

Step 1 Make a table. Because the square root of a negative number is _____, x must be nonnegative. So, the domain is _____.

x	0	1	2	3
y	__	__	__	__

Step 2 Plot the points.

Step 3 Draw a _____ through the points. From either the table or the graph, you can see the range of the function is _____.

Step 4 Compare the graph with the graph of $y = \sqrt{x}$. The graph of $y = -4\sqrt{x}$ is vertical _____ (by a factor of ____) and a _____ of the graph $y = \sqrt{x}$.

Example 2 — Graph a function of the form $y = \sqrt{x} + k$

Graph the function $y = \sqrt{x} - 2$ and identify its domain and range. Compare the graph with the graph of $y = \sqrt{x}$.

Solution

To graph the function, make a table, then plot and connect the points. The domain is _____.

x	0	1	2	3
y	__	__	__	__

The range is _____. The graph of $y = \sqrt{x} - 2$ is a _____ (of ____ units _____) of the graph of $y = \sqrt{x}$.

Your Notes

✓ **Checkpoint** Graph the function and identify its domain and range. Compare the graph with the graph of $y = \sqrt{x}$.

1. $y = 0.25\sqrt{x}$

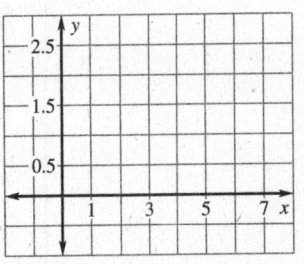

2. $y = \sqrt{x} + 4$

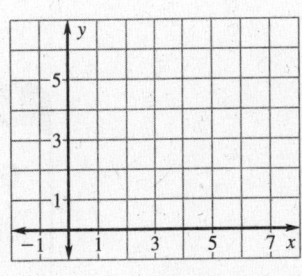

Example 3 Graph a function of the form $y = \sqrt{x - h}$

Graph the function $y = \sqrt{x + 5}$ and identify its domain and range. Compare the graph with the graph of $y = \sqrt{x}$.

Solution

To graph the function, make a table, then plot and connect the points. To find the domain, find the values of x for which the radicand, $x + 5$, is _____. The domain is _____.

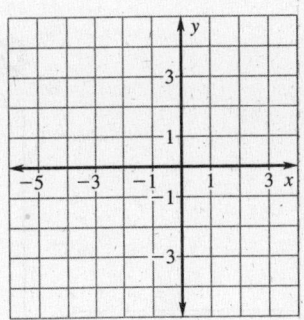

x	−5	−4	−3	−2
y	__	__	__	__

The range is _____. The graph of $y = \sqrt{x + 5}$ is a _____ (of ___ units to the _____) of the graph of $y = \sqrt{x}$.

Your Notes

GRAPHS OF SQUARE ROOT FUNCTIONS

To graph a function of the form $y = a\sqrt{x - h} + k$, you can follow these steps.

Step 1 **Sketch** the graph of $y = a\sqrt{x}$. The graph of $y = a\sqrt{x}$ starts at the _____ and passes through the point _____.

Step 2 **Shift** the graph $|h|$ units _____ (to the right if h is _____ and to the left if h is _____) and $|k|$ units _____ (____ if k is positive and _____ if k is negative).

Example 4   Graph a function of the form $y = a\sqrt{x - h} + k$

Graph the function $y = 3\sqrt{x - 1} + 2$.

Step 1 Sketch the graph of $y = 3\sqrt{x}$.

Step 2 Shift the graph $|h|$ units horizontally and $|k|$ units vertically. Notice that $h =$ ___ and $k =$ ___. Shift the graph _____ and _____.

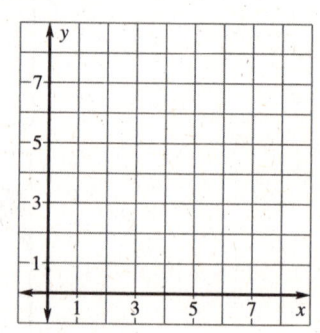

✓ **Checkpoint** Complete the following exercises.

3. Graph the function $y = \sqrt{x} - 3$ and identify its domain and range. Compare the graph with the graph of $y = \sqrt{x}$.

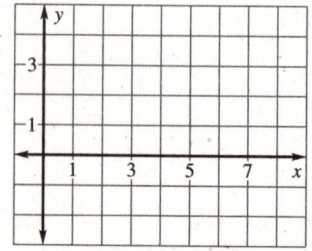

Homework

4. Identify the domain and range of the function in Example 4.

11.2 Simplify Radical Expressions

Goal • Simplify radical expressions.

Your Notes

VOCABULARY

Simplest form of a radical expression

Rationalizing the denominator

PRODUCT PROPERTY OF RADICALS

Words The square root of a product equals the _____ of the _____ of the factors.

Algebra $\sqrt{ab} =$ ____ • ____ where $a \geq 0$ and $b \geq 0$

Example $\sqrt{9x} =$ ____ • ____ $=$ ____

Example 1   *Use the product property of radicals*

Simplify $\sqrt{12x^2}$.

Solution

$\sqrt{12x^2} = \sqrt{\_\_\_ \cdot \_\_\_ \cdot \_\_\_}$ Factor using perfect square factors.

$\phantom{\sqrt{12x^2}} = \_\_\_ \cdot \_\_\_ \cdot \_\_\_$ _____ of radicals

$\phantom{\sqrt{12x^2}} = \_\_\_$ Simplify.

Your Notes

Example 2 Multiply radicals

a. $\sqrt{8} \cdot \sqrt{2} = \sqrt{\underline{} \cdot \underline{}}$

$= \sqrt{\underline{}}$

$= \underline{}$

b. $\sqrt{5x^3y} \cdot 2\sqrt{x} = \underline{}\sqrt{\underline{} \cdot \underline{}}$

$= \underline{}\sqrt{\underline{}}$

$= \underline{} \cdot \underline{} \cdot \underline{} \cdot \underline{}$

$= \underline{}$

QUOTIENT PROPERTY OF RADICALS

Words The square root of a quotient equals the _____ of the _____ of the numerator and denominator.

Algebra $\sqrt{\dfrac{a}{b}} = \dfrac{\boxed{}}{\boxed{}}$ where $a \geq 0$ and $b > 0$

Example $\sqrt{\dfrac{4}{9}} = \dfrac{\boxed{}}{\boxed{}} = \underline{}$

Example 3 Use the quotient property of radicals

a. $\sqrt{\dfrac{11}{49}} = \dfrac{\boxed{}}{\boxed{}}$ Quotient property of radicals

$= \dfrac{\boxed{}}{\boxed{}}$ Simplify.

b. $\sqrt{\dfrac{t^2}{36}} = \dfrac{\boxed{}}{\boxed{}}$ Quotient property of radicals

$= \underline{}$ Simplify.

Your Notes

✓ **Checkpoint** Simplify the expression.

1. $\sqrt{16z^4}$	2. $4\sqrt{mn} \cdot \sqrt{5m}$	3. $\sqrt{\dfrac{15}{25}}$

Example 4 Rationalize the denominator

a. $\dfrac{\sqrt{2}}{\sqrt{5}} = \dfrac{\sqrt{2}}{\sqrt{5}} \cdot \dfrac{\boxed{}}{\boxed{}}$ Multiply by $\dfrac{\sqrt{5}}{\sqrt{5}}$.

$= \dfrac{\boxed{}}{\boxed{}}$ Product property of radicals

$= \dfrac{\boxed{}}{\boxed{}}$ Simplify.

b. $\dfrac{1}{\sqrt{7r}} = \dfrac{1}{\sqrt{7r}} \cdot \dfrac{\sqrt{7r}}{\sqrt{7r}}$ Multiply by ____.

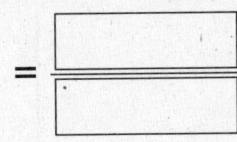   Product property of radicals

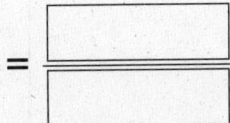   Product property of radicals

$= \dfrac{}{}$ Simplify.

Your Notes

Example 5 *Add and subtract radicals*

a. $7\sqrt{5} - \sqrt{11} + 4\sqrt{5}$

$= \underline{}$ Commutative property

$= \underline{}$ Distributive property

$= \underline{}$ Simplify.

b. $2\sqrt{2} - \sqrt{18}$

$= \underline{}$ Factor using perfect square factors.

$= \underline{}$ Product property of radicals

$= \underline{}$ Simplify.

$= \underline{}$ Distributive property

$= \underline{}$ Simplify.

✓ **Checkpoint** Simplify the expression.

4. $\dfrac{2}{\sqrt{5y}}$	5. $3\sqrt{11} + 2\sqrt{44}$

Your Notes

Example 6 — Multiply radical expressions

Multiply $(4 + \sqrt{3})(3 - \sqrt{3})$.

Solution

$(4 + \sqrt{3})(3 - \sqrt{3})$

= ___ + _____ + ___ + _____   Multiply.

= _____   Product property of radicals

= _____   Simplify.

= _____   Simplify.

✓ **Checkpoint** Simplify the expression.

6. $\sqrt{7}(2\sqrt{7} + \sqrt{3})$

7. $(3\sqrt{5} + 7)^2$

8. $(2 + \sqrt{6})(8 - \sqrt{6})$

Homework

11.3 Solve Radical Equations

Goal • Solve radical equations.

Your Notes

VOCABULARY

Radical equation

Extraneous solution

SQUARING BOTH SIDES OF AN EQUATION

Words If two expressions are equal, then their squares are _____.

Algebra If $a = b$, then _____.

Example If $\sqrt{x} = 4$, then _____.

Example 1 Solve a radical equation

Solve $3\sqrt{x + 1} - 15 = -6$.

Solution

$3\sqrt{x + 1} - 15 = -6$		Write original equation.
$3\sqrt{x + 1} = \underline{}$		Add _____ to each side.
$\sqrt{x + 1} = \underline{}$		Divide each side by ___.
$\underline{} = \underline{}$		Square each side.
$\underline{} = \underline{}$		Simplify.
$x = \underline{}$		Subtract ___ from each side.

The solution is ___.

Check the solution by substituting it in the original equation.

Your Notes

✓ **Checkpoint** Complete the following exercise.

1. Solve $\sqrt{4x - 19} - 2 = 5$.

Example 2 Solve an equation with a radical on both sides

Solve $\sqrt{3x - 3} = \sqrt{2x + 8}$.

Solution

$\sqrt{3x - 3} = \sqrt{2x + 8}$ Write original equation.

____ = ____   Square each side.

____ = ____   Simplify.

____ = ____   Subtract ____ from each side.

$x =$ ____   Add ____ to each side.

The solution is ____.

> To solve a radical equation that contains two radical expressions, be sure that each side of the equation has only one radical expression before squaring each side.

✓ **Checkpoint** Solve the equation.

2. $\sqrt{5x - 4} = \sqrt{3x + 20}$

3. $\sqrt{13 - x} = \sqrt{3x - 15}$

Your Notes

Example 3 *Solve an equation with an extraneous solution*

Solve $x = \sqrt{2x + 15}$.

Solution

$x = \sqrt{2x + 15}$ Write original equation

____ = _____   Square each side.

____ = _____   Simplify.

_____ = 0   Write in standard form.

(_____)(_____) = 0   Factor.

(_____) = 0   or   (_____) = 0

$x =$ ___   or $x =$ ____

CHECK Check ___ and ____ in the original equation.

$x =$ ___ : $x =$ ____ :

___ $\stackrel{?}{=} \sqrt{2(\_\_\_) + 15}$ ____ $\stackrel{?}{=} \sqrt{2(\_\_\_\_) + 15}$

$5 = $ ___ ✓ $-3 = $ ___ ✗

Because ____ does not check in the original equation, it is an _____. The only solution to the equation is ___.

✓ **Checkpoint** *Solve the equation.*

4. $\sqrt{20 - x} = x$

5. $\sqrt{7 + 6x} = x$

Homework

11.4 Apply the Pythagorean Theorem and its Converse

Goal • Use the Pythagorean theorem and its converse.

Your Notes

VOCABULARY

Hypotenuse

Legs of a right triangle

Pythagorean theorem

THE PYTHAGOREAN THEOREM

Words If a triangle is a right triangle, then the _____ equals the _____.

Algebra _____

Example 1 — Use the Pythagorean theorem

The lengths of the legs of a right triangle are $a = 8$ and $b = 15$. Find c.

Solution

$c^2 = a^2 + b^2$	Pythagorean theorem
$c^2 = \_\_\_^2 + \_\_\_^2$	Substitute ___ for a and ___ for b.
$c^2 = \_\_\_$	Simplify.
$c = \_\_\_$	Take positive square root of each side.

The side length of c is ___.

Your Notes

✓ **Checkpoint** Complete the following exercises.

1. The lengths of the legs of a right triangle are $a = 7$ and $b = 9$. Find c.

2. The length of a leg of a right triangle is $a = 20$ and the length of the hypotenuse is $c = 52$. Find b.

Example 2 *Use the Pythagorean theorem*

A right triangle has one leg that is 4 inches longer than the other leg. The hypotenuse is $\sqrt{106}$ inches. Find the unknown lengths.

Solution

Sketch a right triangle and label the sides with their lengths. Let x be the length of the shorter leg.

$a^2 + b^2 = c^2$ **Pythagorean theorem**

___^{2} + (___)^2 = (___)^2 **Substitute.**

___ + ___ = ___   **Simplify.**

___ = 0   **Write in standard form.**

___ = 0   **Factor.**

(___) = 0   or (___) = 0   **Zero-product property**

$x =$ ___   or $x =$ ___   **Solve for x.**

Because length is nonnegative, the solution $x =$ ___ does not make sense. The legs have lengths of ___ inches and ___ + 4 = ___ inches.

Your Notes

✓ **Checkpoint** *Complete the following exercise.*

> 3. A right triangle has one leg that is 2 centimeters shorter than the other leg. The length of the hypotenuse is 10 centimeters. Find the unknown lengths.

CONVERSE OF THE PYTHAGOREAN THEOREM

If a triangle has side lengths a, b, and c such that _____, then the triangle is a _____ triangle.

Example 3 *Determine right triangles*

Tell whether the triangle with the given side lengths is a right triangle.

a. 10, 11, 15

$$10^2 + 11^2 \stackrel{?}{=} 15^2$$

____ + ____ $\stackrel{?}{=}$ ____

_____

The triangle _____ a right triangle.

b. 3, 4, 5

$$3^2 + 4^2 \stackrel{?}{=} 5^2$$

___ + ___ $\stackrel{?}{=}$ ___

_____

The triangle _____ a right triangle.

✓ **Checkpoint** *Tell whether the triangle with the given side lengths is a right triangle.*

4. 9, 40, 41	5. 10, 15, 18

6. A triangular mirror has side lengths of 1.2 meters, 1.6 meters, and 2 meters. Is the mirror a right triangle? Explain.

Homework

11.5 Apply the Distance and Midpoint Formulas

Goal • Use the distance and midpoint formulas.

Your Notes

VOCABULARY

Distance formula

Midpoint

Midpoint formula

THE DISTANCE FORMULA

The distance between any two points (x_1, y_1) and (x_2, y_2) is _____.

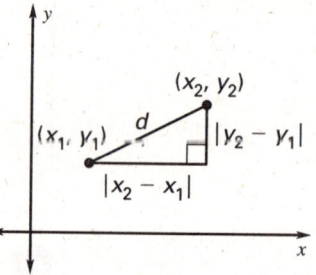

Example 1 *Find the distance between two points*

Find the distance between $(4, -3)$ and $(-7, 2)$.

Let $(x_1, y_1) = (4, -3)$ and $(x_2, y_2) = (-7, 2)$.

$d = \sqrt{(x_2 - x_1)^2 + (y_2 - y_1)^2}$ Distance formula

$= \sqrt{(\underline{\quad} - \underline{\quad})^2 + (\underline{\quad} - \underline{\quad})^2}$ Substitute.

$= \sqrt{(\underline{\quad})^2 + (\underline{\quad})^2} = \underline{\quad}$ Simplify.

The distance between the points is _____ units.

Your Notes

Example 2: Find a missing coordinate

The distance between $(5, a)$ and $(9, 6)$ is $4\sqrt{2}$ units. Find the value of a.

Solution

Use the distance formula with $d = 4\sqrt{2}$. Let $(x_1, y_1) = (5, a)$ and $(x_2, y_2) = (9, 6)$.

$d = \sqrt{(x_2 - x_1)^2 + (y_2 - y_1)^2}$ Distance formula

____ $= \sqrt{(\_\_ - \_\_)^2 + (\_\_ - \_\_)^2}$ Substitute.

____ $= \sqrt{\rule{2cm}{0.4pt}}$ Multiply.

____ $= \sqrt{\rule{2cm}{0.4pt}}$ Simplify.

____ $=$ ____   Square each side.

$0 =$ ____   Write in standard form.

$0 =$ ____   Factor.

____ $= 0$ or   ____ $= 0$ Zero-product property

$a =$ ____   or $a =$ ____   Solve for a.

The value of a is ____ or ____.

✓ Checkpoint Complete the following exercises.

1. Find the distance between $(2, -3)$ and $(5, 1)$.	2. The distance between $(-1, 2)$ and $(3, b)$ is $\sqrt{41}$ units. Find the value of b.

Your Notes

THE MIDPOINT FORMULA

The midpoint M of the line segment with endpoints $A(x_1, y_1)$ and $B(x_2, y_2)$ is

$$M\left(\underline{}, \underline{}\right).$$

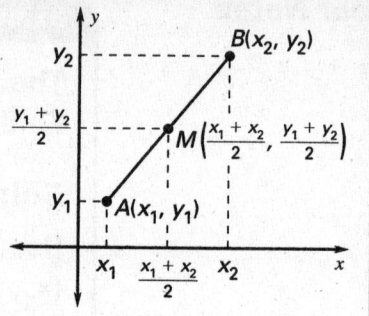

Example 3 Find the midpoint between two points

Find the midpoint of the line segment with endpoints $(-3, 7)$ and $(-1, 11)$.

Solution

Let $(x_1, y_1) = (-3, 7)$ and $(x_2, y_2) = (-1, 11)$.

$$\left(\frac{x_1 + x_2}{2}, \frac{y_1 + y_2}{2}\right) = \left(\frac{\boxed{} + \boxed{}}{\boxed{}}, \frac{\boxed{} + \boxed{}}{\boxed{}}\right)$$

$$= (\underline{}, \underline{})$$

The midpoint is $(\underline{}, \underline{})$.

✓ Checkpoint Find the midpoint of the line segment with the given endpoints.

3. $(1, -2)$, $(5, -4)$	4. $(5, 12)$, $(13, 8)$

Homework

Words to Review

Give an example of the vocabulary word.

Radical expression	Radical function
Square root function	Parent square root function
Simplest form of a radical expression	Rationalizing the denominator
Radical equation	Extraneous solution
Hypotenuse	Legs of a right triangle

Pythagorean theorem	Distance formula
Midpoint	Midpoint formula

Review your notes and Chapter 11 by using the Chapter Review on pages 754–756 of your textbook.

12.1 Model Inverse Variation

Goal • Write and graph inverse variation equations.

Your Notes

VOCABULARY

Inverse variation

Constant of variation

Hyperbola

Branches of a hyperbola

Asymptotes of a hyperbola

Example 1 Identify direct and inverse variation

Tell whether the equation represents *direct variation, inverse variation,* or *neither*.

a. $xy = -2$ Write original equation.

     $y = \underline{}$ Divide each side by ___.

Because $xy = -2$ ___ be written in the form $y = \dfrac{a}{x}$, $xy = -2$ represents _____. The constant of variation is ___.

b. $\dfrac{y}{4} = x$ Write original equation.

     $y = \underline{}$ Multiply each side by ___.

Because $\dfrac{y}{4} = x$ ___ be written in the form $y = ax$, $\dfrac{y}{4} = x$ represents _____.

Your Notes

✓ **Checkpoint** Tell whether the equation represents *direct variation*, *inverse variation*, or *neither*.

1. $\dfrac{y}{-5} = x$	2. $y = 3x - 1$	3. $xy = 8$

Example 2 *Graph an inverse variation equation*

Graph $y = \dfrac{-2}{x}$.

Step 1 Make a table by choosing several integer values of x and finding the values of y. Then plot the points. To see how the function behaves for values of x very close to 0 and very far from 0, make a second table for such values and plot the points.

x	y
−4	_____
−2	_____
−1	_____
0	_____
1	_____
2	_____
4	_____

x	y
−10	_____
−5	_____
−0.5	_____
−0.2	_____
0.2	_____
0.5	_____
5	_____
10	_____

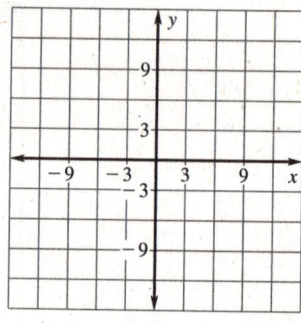

Step 2 Connect the points in Quadrant II by drawing a smooth curve through them. Repeat for points in Quadrant IV.

Your Notes

GRAPHS OF DIRECT VARIATION AND INVERSE VARIATION EQUATIONS

Direct Variation

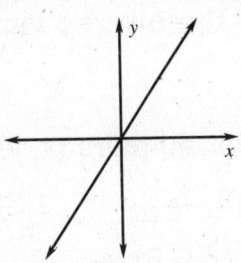
$y = ax, a > 0$

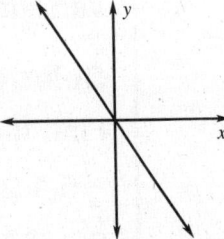
$y = ax, a < 0$

Inverse Variation

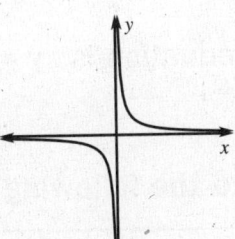
$y = \frac{a}{x}, a > 0$

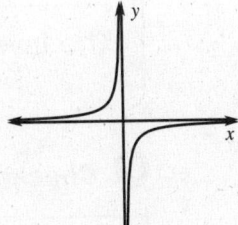
$y = \frac{a}{x}, a < 0$

Example 3 Use an inverse variation equation

The variables x and y vary inversely, and $y = -4$ when $x = 6$. Write an inverse variation equation that relates x and y. Find the value of y when $x = 3$.

Solution

Because y varies _____ with x, the equation has the form $y = \frac{a}{x}$. Use the fact that $x = 6$ and $y = -4$ to find the value of a.

$y = \frac{a}{x}$ Write inverse variation equation.

____ = $\frac{a}{\Box}$ Substitute ___ for x and ____ for y.

____ = a   Multiply each side by ___.

An equation that relates x and y is $y =$ _____ .

When $x = 3$, $y = \dfrac{\Box}{\Box} =$ _____ .

Your Notes

Example 4 *Write an inverse variation equation*

Tell whether the ordered pairs (−5, 1.2), (−2, 3), (1.5, −4), (8, −0.75), (10, −0.6) represent inverse variation. If so, write the inverse variation equation.

Solution

Find the products xy for all pairs (x, y):

$-5(1.2) =$ _____, $-2(3) =$ _____, $1.5(-4) =$ _____,

$8(-0.75) =$ _____, $10(-0.6) =$ _____

The products are equal to the same number, _____. So, _____.

The inverse variation equation is $xy =$ _____, or $y =$ _____.

✓ **Checkpoint** Complete the following exercises.

4. Graph $y = \dfrac{3}{x}$.

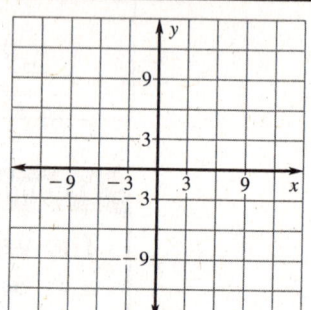

5. The variables x and y vary inversely, and $y = 5$ when $x = -3$. Write an inverse variation equation that relates x and y. Then find the value of y when $x = 9$.

Homework

6. Tell whether the ordered pairs (−20, −3), (−12, −5), (10, 6), (15, 4), (40, 1.5) represent inverse variation. If so, write the inverse variation equation.

12.2 Graph Rational Functions

Goal • Graph rational functions.

Your Notes

VOCABULARY

Rational function

PARENT RATIONAL FUNCTION

The function $y = \frac{1}{x}$ is the _____ for any rational function whose numerator has degree 0 or 1 and whose denominator has degree 1. The function and its graph has the following characteristics:

- The domain and range are all _____ real numbers.

- The horizontal asymptote is the ___-axis. The vertical asymptote is the ___-axis.

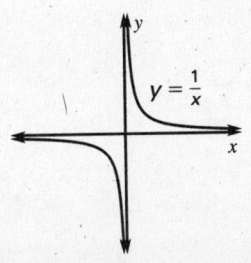

Example 1 Compare graph of $y = \frac{a}{x}$ with graph of $y = \frac{1}{x}$

The graph of $y = \frac{-1}{2x}$ is a vertical _____ with a reflection in the _____ of the graph of $y = \frac{1}{x}$.

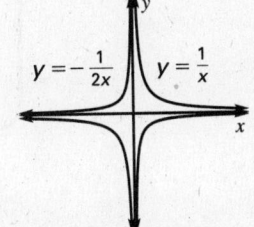

Your Notes

✓ **Checkpoint** Complete the following exercise.

1. Identify the domain and range of $y = \dfrac{1}{4x}$. Compare the graph with the graph of $y = \dfrac{1}{x}$.

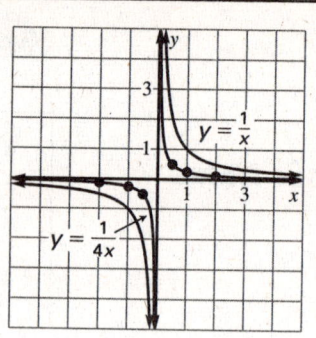

Example 2   Graph $y = \dfrac{1}{x} + k$

Graph $y = \dfrac{1}{x} - 2$ and identify its domain and range. Compare the graph with the graph of $y = \dfrac{1}{x}$.

Solution

Graph the function using a table of values. The domain is all real numbers except ____. The range is all real numbers except ____.

The graph of $y = \dfrac{1}{x} - 2$ is a _____ translation (of ___ units _____) of the graph of $y = \dfrac{1}{x}$.

x	y
-2	____
-1	____
-0.5	____
0	____
0.5	____
1	____
2	____

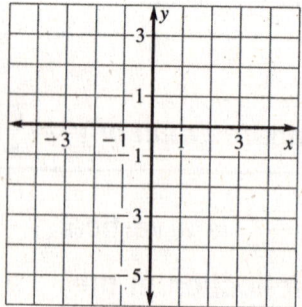

272 Lesson 12.2 • Algebra 1 Notetaking Guide

Your Notes

✓ **Checkpoint** Complete the following exercise.

2. Graph $y = \dfrac{1}{x} + 2$ and identify its domain and range. Compare the graph with the graph of $y = \dfrac{1}{x}$.

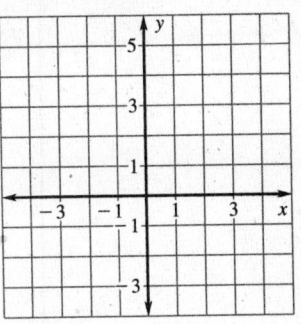

Example 3 Graph $y = \dfrac{1}{x - h}$

Graph $y = \dfrac{1}{x + 3}$ and identify its domain and range. Compare the graph with the graph of $y = \dfrac{1}{x}$.

Solution

Graph the function using a table of values. The domain is all real numbers except _____. The range is all real numbers except _____.

The graph of $y = \dfrac{1}{x + 3}$ is a _____ translation (of ___ units _____) of the graph of $y = \dfrac{1}{x}$.

x	y
−5	_____
−4	_____
−3.5	_____
−3	_____
−2.5	_____
−2	_____
−1	_____

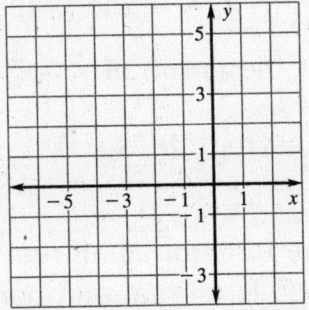

Lesson 12.2 • Algebra 1 Notetaking Guide 273

Your Notes

✓ **Checkpoint** Complete the following exercise.

3. Graph $y = \dfrac{1}{x-1}$ and identify its domain and range. Compare the graph with the graph of $y = \dfrac{1}{x}$.

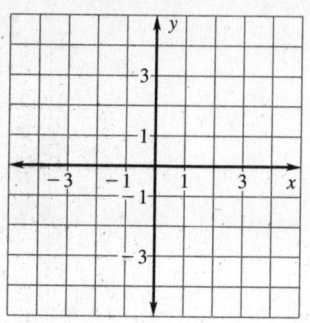

GRAPH OF $y = \dfrac{1}{x-h} + k$

The function $y = \dfrac{a}{x-h} + k$ is a _____ that has the following characteristics:

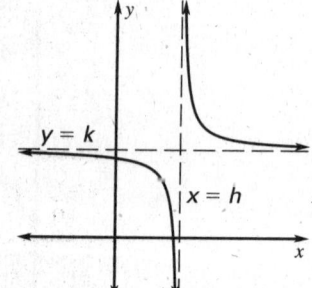

- If $|a| > 1$, the graph is a vertical _____ of the graph of $y = \dfrac{1}{x}$. If $0 < |a| < 1$, the graph is a vertical _____ of the graph of $y = \dfrac{1}{x}$. If $|a| < 0$, the graph is a reflection in the _____ of the graph of $y = \dfrac{1}{x}$.

- The horizontal asymptote is $y =$ ___. The vertical asymptote is $x =$ ___.

The domain of the function is all real numbers except $x =$ ___. The range is all real numbers except $y =$ ___.

Your Notes

Example 4 Graph $y = \dfrac{a}{x-h} + k$

Graph $y = \dfrac{2}{x-3} + 4$.

Solution

Step 1 Identify the asymptotes of the graph. The vertical asymptote is $x = $ ___. The horizontal asymptote is $y = $ ___.

Step 2 Plot several points on each side of the _____ asymptote.

Step 3 Graph two branches that pass through the plotted points and approach the _____.

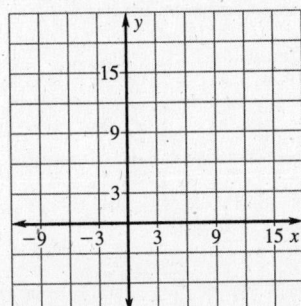

✓ **Checkpoint** Complete the following exercise.

4. Graph $y = \dfrac{3}{x+2} - 1$.

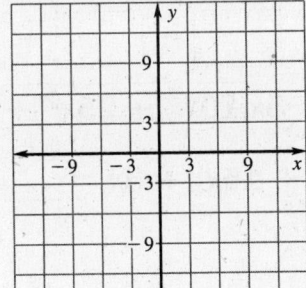

Homework

12.3 Divide Polynomials

Goal • Divide polynomials.

Your Notes

Example 1 Divide a polynomial by a monomial

Divide $10x^3 - 25x^2 + 15x$ by $5x$.

Solution

Method 1: Write the division as a fraction.

$(10x^3 - 25x^2 + 15x) \div 5x$

= _____   Write as a fraction.

= ____ − ____ + ____   Divide each term by ____.

= _____   Simplify.

Method 2: Use long division.

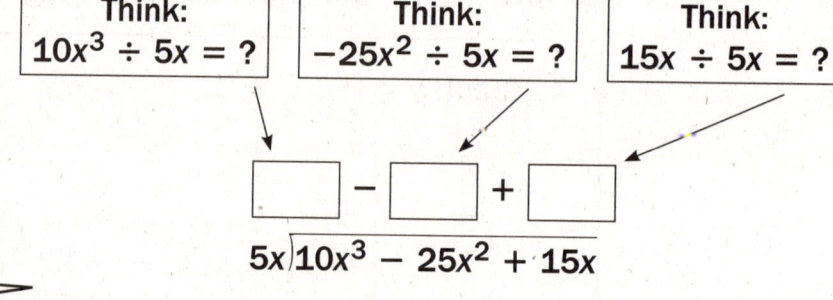

$(10x^3 - 25x^2 + 15x) \div 5x =$ _____

> To check your answer, multiply the quotient by the divisor.

✓ **Checkpoint** Complete the following exercise.

1. Divide $(12x^3 + 9x^2 - 3x)$ by x.

Your Notes

Example 2 — Divide a polynomial by a binomial

Divide $4x^2 - 4x - 3$ by $2x + 1$.

Solution

Step 1 Divide the first term of $4x^2 - 4x - 3$ by the first term of $2x + 1$.

$2x + 1 \overline{) 4x^2 - 4x - 3}$

Think: $4x^2 \div 2x = ?$
Multiply _____ and _____.
Subtract.

Step 2 Bring down _____. Then divide the first term of _____ by the first term of $2x + 1$.

$2x + 1 \overline{) 4x^2 - 4x - 3}$

Think: $-6x \div 2x = ?$
Multiply _____ and _____.
Subtract.

$(4x^2 - 4x - 3) \div (2x + 1) =$ _____

Example 3 — Divide a polynomial by a binomial

Divide $2x^2 + 9x - 6$ by $2x + 3$.

Solution

$2x + 3 \overline{) 2x^2 + 9x - 6}$

Multiply _____ and _____.
Subtract _____. Bring down _____.
Multiply _____ and _____.
Subtract _____.

$(2x^2 + 9x - 6) \div (2x + 3) =$ _____

Your Notes

✓ **Checkpoint** Divide.

> 2. $(3x^2 - x - 14) \div (3x - 7)$
>
> _____
>
> 3. $(6x^2 - 13x + 11) \div (3x - 5)$

Example 4 *Rewrite polynomials*

Divide $2x + 2 + 3x^2$ by $1 + x$.

$x + 1 \overline{\smash{)}3x^2 + 2x + 2}$

Rewrite polynomials.

Multiply _____ and _____.

Subtract _____. Bring down ___.

Multiply _____ and _____.

Subtract.

$(2x + 2 + 3x^2) \div (1 + x) =$ _____

Example 5 *Insert missing terms*

Divide $-24 + 6x^2$ by $-6 + 3x$.

$3x - 6 \overline{\smash{)}6x^2 + 0x - 24}$

Rewrite polynomials. Insert missing term.

Multiply _____ and _____.

Subtract _____. Bring down _____.

Multiply _____ and _____.

Subtract.

$(-24 + 6x^2) \div (-6 + 3x) =$ _____

Your Notes

✓ **Checkpoint** Divide.

4. $(6 - 2x + x^2) \div (2 + x)$

---

5. $(-11 + 3x^2) \div (-3 + x)$

Example 6 Rewrite and graph a rational function

Graph $y = \dfrac{4x - 3}{x - 1}$.

Solution

Step 1 Rewrite the rational function in the form

$$y = \dfrac{a}{x - h} + k.$$

$$x - 1 \overline{\smash{\big)}\, 4x - 3}^{\;\square}$$

So, $y = $ _____.

Step 2 Graph the function.

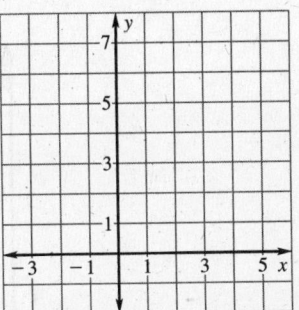

✓ **Checkpoint** Complete the following exercise.

6. Graph $y = \dfrac{5x + 13}{x + 3}$.

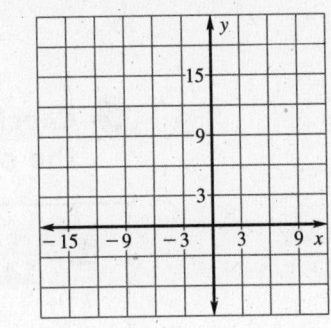

Homework

12.4 Simplify Rational Expressions

Goal • Simplify rational expressions.

Your Notes

VOCABULARY

Rational expression

Excluded value

Simplest form of a rational expression

Example 1 Find excluded values

Find the excluded values, if any, of the expression.

a. $\dfrac{x}{4x-8}$ b. $\dfrac{3x}{x^2-16}$

Solution

a. The expression $\dfrac{x}{4x-8}$ is undefined when
 _____ = 0, or $x =$ ____. The excluded value is ____.

b. The expression $\dfrac{3x}{x^2-16}$ is undefined when
 _____ = 0, or (____)(____) = 0.
 The solutions of the equation are ____ and ____.
 The excluded values are ____ and ____.

✓ **Checkpoint** Find the excluded values, if any, of the expression.

1. $\dfrac{x+6}{14x}$

2. $\dfrac{9x+1}{x^2-x-20}$

Your Notes

SIMPLIFYING RATIONAL EXPRESSIONS

Let a, b, and c be polynomials where $b \neq 0$ and $c \neq 0$.

Algebra

$$\frac{ac}{bc} = \frac{\boxed{}}{\boxed{}} = \underline{}$$

Example

$$\frac{3x - 9}{4x - 12} = \frac{\boxed{}}{\boxed{}} = \underline{}$$

Example 2 *Simplify expressions by dividing out monomials*

Simplify the rational expression, if possible. State the excluded values.

a. $\dfrac{18x}{6x^2} = \dfrac{\boxed{}}{\boxed{}}$ Divide out common factors.

   $= \underline{}$ Simplify.

The excluded value is ___.

b. $\dfrac{12x^2 - 6x}{24x} = \dfrac{\boxed{}}{\boxed{}}$ Factor numerator and denominator.

   $= \dfrac{\boxed{}}{\boxed{}}$ Divide out common factors.

   $= \underline{}$ Simplify.

The excluded value is ___.

✓ **Checkpoint** Simplify the rational expression, if possible. State the excluded values.

3. $\dfrac{7}{5x + 3}$	4. $\dfrac{5x}{5x^2 - 25}$	5. $\dfrac{6x^3}{2x + 4}$

Lesson 12.4 • Algebra 1 Notetaking Guide

Your Notes

Example 3 *Simplify an expression by dividing out binomials*

Simplify $\dfrac{x^2 + x - 12}{x^2 - 5x + 6}$. State the excluded values.

$\dfrac{x^2 + x - 12}{x^2 - 5x + 6} = \dfrac{}{}$ Factor and divide out common factor.

$= \underline{}$ Simplify.

The excluded values are ___ and ___.

Example 4 *Recognize opposites*

Simplify $\dfrac{10 + 3x - x^2}{x^2 - 25}$. State the excluded values.

$\dfrac{10 + 3x - x^2}{x^2 - 25} = \dfrac{}{}$ Factor numerator and denominator.

$= \dfrac{}{}$ Rewrite _____ as _____.

$= \dfrac{}{}$ Divide out common factor.

$= \dfrac{}{} = \underline{}$ Simplify.

The excluded values are ___ and ___.

✓ **Checkpoint** Simplify the rational expression. State the excluded values.

Homework

6. $\dfrac{x^2 + 7x + 6}{x^2 + 3x - 18}$

7. $\dfrac{4 - x^2}{x^2 + 5x - 14}$

12.5 Multiply and Divide Rational Expressions

Goal • Multiply and divide rational expressions.

Your Notes

MULTIPLYING AND DIVIDING RATIONAL EXPRESSIONS

Let a, b, c, and d be polynomials.

Algebra

$$\frac{a}{b} \cdot \frac{c}{d} = \boxed{} \text{ where } b \neq 0 \text{ and } d \neq 0$$

$$\frac{a}{b} \div \frac{c}{d} = \frac{a}{b} \cdot \boxed{} = \boxed{} \text{ where } b \neq 0, c \neq 0, \text{ and } d \neq 0$$

Examples

$$\frac{2x}{x+1} \cdot \frac{x}{5} = \boxed{} \qquad \frac{3}{x^2} \div \frac{x}{5} = \frac{3}{x^2} \cdot \boxed{} = \boxed{}$$

Example 1 Multiply rational expressions involving monomials

Find the product $\dfrac{3x^4}{4x^3} \cdot \dfrac{2x^2}{5x^3}$.

Solution

$\dfrac{3x^4}{4x^3} \cdot \dfrac{2x^2}{5x^3} = \boxed{}$ Multiply numerators and denominators.

$= \boxed{}$ Product of powers property

$= \boxed{}$ Factor and divide out common factors.

$= $    Simplify.

Your Notes

Example 2 — Multiply rational expressions involving polynomials

Find the product $\dfrac{x}{5x^2 - 6x - 8} \cdot \dfrac{2x^2 - 4x}{7x^2}$.

Solution

$\dfrac{x}{5x^2 - 6x - 8} \cdot \dfrac{2x^2 - 4x}{7x^2}$

= ▭   Multiply numerators and denominators.

= ▭   Factor and divide out common factors.

= ▭   Simplify.

Example 3 — Multiply a rational expression by a polynomial

Find the product $\dfrac{4x}{x^2 - x - 12} \cdot (x - 4)$.

Solution

$\dfrac{4x}{x^2 - x - 12} \cdot (x - 4)$

= $\dfrac{4x}{x^2 - x - 12} \cdot \dfrac{\Box}{\Box}$ Rewrite polynomial as a fraction.

= ▭   Multiply numerators and denominators.

= ▭   Factor and divide out common factor.

= ▭   Simplify.

Your Notes

✓ **Checkpoint** Find the product.

1. $\dfrac{2x^4}{5x^2} \cdot \dfrac{6x}{3x^3}$

2. $\dfrac{x^2 - 5x + 4}{3x^2 - 12x} \cdot \dfrac{2x^2 + 2}{x^2 + 6x - 7}$

3. $\dfrac{2x}{x^2 + 5x - 24} \cdot (x + 8)$

Example 4 *Divide rational expressions involving polynomials*

Find the quotient $\dfrac{x^2 + 5x - 24}{x^2 + 9x + 8} \div \dfrac{x^2 - 9}{6x - 18}$.

Solution

$\dfrac{x^2 + 5x - 24}{x^2 + 9x + 8} \div \dfrac{x^2 - 9}{6x - 18}$

$= \dfrac{x^2 + 5x - 24}{x^2 + 9x + 8} \cdot \dfrac{\boxed{}}{\boxed{}}$ Multiply by multiplicative inverse.

$= \dfrac{\boxed{}}{\boxed{}}$ Multiply numerators and denominators.

$= \dfrac{\boxed{}}{\boxed{}}$ Factor and divide out common factors.

$= \underline{}$ Simplify.

Your Notes

Example 5 *Divide a rational expression by a polynomial*

Find the quotient $\dfrac{x^2 - 25}{x - 3} \div (x - 5)$.

Solution

$\dfrac{x^2 - 25}{x - 3} \div (x - 5)$

$= \dfrac{x^2 - 25}{x - 3} \div \dfrac{\boxed{}}{\boxed{}}$ Rewrite polynomial as fraction.

$= \dfrac{x^2 - 25}{x - 3} \cdot \dfrac{\boxed{}}{\boxed{}}$ Multiply by multiplicative inverse.

$= \dfrac{\boxed{}}{\boxed{}}$ Multiply numerators and denominators.

$= \dfrac{\boxed{}}{\boxed{}}$ Factor and divide out common factors.

$= \boxed{}$ Simplify.

✓ **Checkpoint** Find the quotient.

4. $\dfrac{x^2 + 2x - 15}{x^2 + 4x - 5} \div \dfrac{x^2 - 4}{7x - 14}$

5. $\dfrac{x^2 + 8x + 7}{x^2 - 1} \div (x + 7)$

Homework

12.6 Add and Subtract Rational Expressions

Goal • Add and subtract rational expressions.

Your Notes

VOCABULARY

Least common denominator of rational expressions (LCD)

ADDING AND SUBTRACTING RATIONAL EXPRESSIONS WITH THE SAME DENOMINATOR

Let a, b, and c be polynomials where $c \neq 0$.

Algebra

$$\frac{a}{c} + \frac{b}{c} = \boxed{} \qquad \frac{a}{c} - \frac{b}{c} = \boxed{}$$

Example 1 Add and subtract with the same denominator

a. $\dfrac{3}{8x} + \dfrac{4}{8x} = \dfrac{\boxed{}}{8x}$ Add numerators.

   $= \underline{}$ Simplify.

b. $\dfrac{2x + 9}{x + 1} - \dfrac{7}{x + 1} = \dfrac{\boxed{}}{x + 1}$ Subtract numerators.

   $= \dfrac{\boxed{}}{x + 1}$ Simplify.

   $= \dfrac{\boxed{}}{\boxed{}}$ Factor and divide out common factor.

   $= \underline{}$ Simplify.

Your Notes

✓ **Checkpoint** Find the sum or difference.

1. $\dfrac{x+8}{4x} + \dfrac{3}{4x}$	2. $\dfrac{6x-5}{x} - \dfrac{2x-5}{x}$

Example 2 *Find the LCD of rational expressions*

Find the LCD of the rational expressions.

a. $\dfrac{1}{3x^3}, \dfrac{5}{4x^4}$

b. $\dfrac{7}{x^2-4}, \dfrac{x+3}{x^2+x-2}$

Solution

a. Find the _____ of $3x^3$ and $4x^4$.

$3x^3 = $ _____

$4x^4 = $ _____

LCM = _____ = _____

The LCD of $\dfrac{1}{3x^3}$ and $\dfrac{5}{4x^4}$ is _____.

b. Find the _____ of $x^2 - 4$ and $x^2 + x - 2$.

$x^2 - 4 = $ _____

$x^2 + x - 2 = $ _____

LCM = _____

The LCD of $\dfrac{7}{x^2-4}$ and $\dfrac{x+3}{x^2+x-2}$ is

_____.

✓ **Checkpoint** Find the LCD of the rational expressions.

3. $\dfrac{5}{36x}, \dfrac{x+2}{4x^3}$	4. $\dfrac{7x}{x-8}, \dfrac{x-1}{x+3}$

Your Notes

Example 3 *Add expressions with different denominators*

Find the sum $\dfrac{1}{3x^3} + \dfrac{5}{4x^4}$.

Solution

$\dfrac{1}{3x^3} + \dfrac{5}{4x^4}$

$= \dfrac{1 \cdot \boxed{}}{3x^3 \cdot \boxed{}} + \dfrac{5 \cdot \boxed{}}{4x^4 \cdot \boxed{}}$ Rewrite fractions using LCD, _____.

$= \dfrac{\boxed{}}{\boxed{}} + \dfrac{\boxed{}}{\boxed{}}$ Simplify numerators and denominators.

$= \dfrac{\boxed{}}{\boxed{}}$ Add fractions.

Example 4 *Subtract expressions with different denominators*

Find the difference $\dfrac{x+1}{x^2+5x+6} - \dfrac{x-4}{x^2-9}$.

Solution

$\dfrac{x+1}{x^2+5x+6} - \dfrac{x-4}{x^2-9}$

$= \dfrac{x+1}{(\boxed{})(\boxed{})} - \dfrac{x-4}{(\boxed{})(\boxed{})}$

$= \dfrac{(x+1)(\boxed{})}{\boxed{}(\boxed{})} - \dfrac{(x-4)(\boxed{})}{\boxed{}(\boxed{})}$

$= \dfrac{\boxed{}}{\boxed{}}$

$= \dfrac{\boxed{}}{\boxed{}}$

$= \dfrac{\boxed{}}{\boxed{}}$

Your Notes

✓ **Checkpoint** Find the sum or difference.

5. $\dfrac{9}{x-1} - \dfrac{15}{3x+1}$

6. $\dfrac{12}{5x} + \dfrac{3x}{x-4}$

7. $\dfrac{x-1}{x^2-2x-24} + \dfrac{4}{x^2-5x-6}$

8. $\dfrac{x+2}{x^2+2x-15} - \dfrac{x-6}{x^2+4x-21}$

Homework

12.7 Solve Rational Equations

Goal • Solve rational equations.

Your Notes

VOCABULARY

Rational equation

Example 1 *Use the cross products property*

Solve $\dfrac{5}{x-1} = \dfrac{x}{4}$. Check your solution.

Solution

$\dfrac{5}{x-1} = \dfrac{x}{4}$ Write original equation.

$20 = \underline{\hspace{2cm}}$ Cross products property

$0 = \underline{\hspace{3cm}}$ Subtract ___ from each side.

$0 = (\underline{\hspace{1cm}})(\underline{\hspace{1cm}})$ Factor polynomial.

$\underline{\hspace{1cm}} = 0$ or $\underline{\hspace{1cm}} = 0$ Zero-product property

$x = \underline{\hspace{0.5cm}}$ or $x = \underline{\hspace{0.5cm}}$ Solve for x.

The solutions are ___ and ___.

CHECK   If $x = \underline{\hspace{0.5cm}}$:   If $x = \underline{\hspace{0.5cm}}$:

$\dfrac{5}{\boxed{} - 1} \stackrel{?}{=} \dfrac{\boxed{}}{4}$ $\dfrac{5}{\boxed{} - 1} \stackrel{?}{=} \dfrac{\boxed{}}{4}$

$\underline{\hspace{1cm}} = \underline{\hspace{1cm}}$ $\underline{\hspace{1cm}} = \underline{\hspace{1cm}}$

Your Notes

✓ **Checkpoint** Solve the equation. Check your solution.

1. $\dfrac{-2}{x+9} = \dfrac{x}{7}$

2. $\dfrac{6}{x-4} = \dfrac{3}{x}$

Example 2 Multiply by the LCD.

Solve $\dfrac{x}{x+6} - \dfrac{1}{2} = \dfrac{4}{x+6}$.

Solution

$$\dfrac{x}{x+6} - \dfrac{1}{2} = \dfrac{4}{x+6}$$

$$\dfrac{x}{x+6} \cdot \boxed{} - \dfrac{1}{2} \cdot \boxed{} = \dfrac{4}{x+6} \cdot \boxed{}$$

$$\dfrac{\boxed{}}{\cancel{x+6}} - \dfrac{\boxed{}}{\cancel{2}} = \dfrac{\boxed{}}{\cancel{x+6}}$$

$$\underline{} = \underline{}$$

$$\underline{} = \underline{}$$

$$x = \underline{}$$

The solution is ___.

✓ **Checkpoint** Complete the following exercise.

3. Solve $\dfrac{3}{x-3} - \dfrac{1}{x+3} = \dfrac{14}{x^2-9}$. Check your solution.

Your Notes

Example 3 — Factor to find the LCD

Solve $\dfrac{3}{x+2} - 1 = \dfrac{-5}{x^2 - 3x - 10}$.

Solution

Write each denominator in factored form. The LCD is _____.

$$\dfrac{3}{x+2} - 1 = \dfrac{-5}{(x+2)(x-5)}$$

$$\dfrac{3 \cdot \boxed{}}{x+2} - 1 \cdot \boxed{}$$

$$= \dfrac{-5 \cdot \boxed{}}{(x+2)(x-5)}$$

$$\dfrac{\boxed{}}{\boxed{}} - \boxed{}$$

$$= \dfrac{\boxed{}}{\boxed{}}$$

_____ − (_____) = _____

_____ = _____

_____ = 0

_____ (_____) = 0

_____ = 0   or   _____ = 0

_____ = _____

x = _____   or   x = _____

The solutions are ____ and ____.

✓ Checkpoint Complete the following exercise.

4. Solve $\dfrac{1}{x+6} + 2 = \dfrac{x^2 - 38}{x^2 + 2x - 24}$

Homework

Words to Review

Give an example of the vocabulary word.

Inverse variation	Constant of variation
Hyperbola	**Asymptotes of a hyperbola**
Branches of a hyperbola	**Rational function**
Rational expression	**Excluded value**

| Simplest form of a rational expression | Least common denominator of rational expressions |
|---|---|//
| Rational equation ||

Review your notes and Chapter 12 by using the Chapter Review on pages 831–834 of your textbook.

13.1 Find Probabilities and Odds

Goal • Find sample spaces and probabilities.

Your Notes

VOCABULARY

Outcome

Event

Sample space

Probability

Odds

Example 1 *Find a sample space*

You flip 2 coins. How many possible outcomes are in the sample space? List the possible outcomes.

Solution

Use a tree diagram to find the outcomes in the sample space.

Coin flip _____   _____

Coin flip ___ ___   ___ ___

The sample space has ___ possible outcomes. They are listed below.

____ , ____   ____ , ____

____ , ____   ____ , ____

Your Notes

✓ **Checkpoint** Complete the following exercise.

> 1. You flip 3 coins. How many possible outcomes are in the sample space? List the possible outcomes.

Example 2 *Find a theoretical probability*

Marbles You reach into a bag containing 4 yellow marbles, 5 green marbles, and 6 blue marbles. What is the probability of choosing a blue marble?

Solution

There are a total of _____ = ____ marbles. So, there are ____ possible outcomes. Of all the marbles, ___ marbles are blue. There are ___ favorable outcomes.

P(blue marble) = $\dfrac{\rule{3cm}{0.4pt}}{\rule{3cm}{0.4pt}}$

$= \dfrac{\rule{3cm}{0.4pt}}{\rule{3cm}{0.4pt}}$

$= \dfrac{\square}{\square}$

$= \dfrac{}{}$

✓ **Checkpoint** Complete the following exercise.

> 2. In Example 2, what is the probability of selecting a green marble?

Your Notes

Example 3 Find the odds

Telephone Calls A study indicates that out of every 60 telephone calls, 6 result in busy signals and 12 result in no answer. What are the odds in favor of someone answering?

Solution

There are 3 possible outcomes: _____, _____, and _____. _____ is the favorable outcome. The number of favorable outcomes is _____ = ____ . _____ or _____ are unfavorable outcomes. The number of unfavorable outcomes is _____ = ____ .

Odds in favor of someone answering

$= \dfrac{\rule{3cm}{0.4pt}}{\rule{3cm}{0.4pt}}$

$= \dfrac{\rule{1cm}{0.4pt}}{\rule{1cm}{0.4pt}}$

$=$ ____ or ____ .

✓ **Checkpoint** Complete the following exercises.

3. In Example 3, what are the odds against someone answering?

4. In Example 3, what are the odds in favor of a busy signal?

Homework

13.2 Find Probabilities Using Permutations

Goal • Use the formula for the number of permutations.

Your Notes

> **VOCABULARY**
>
> Permutation
>
> _____
>
> n factorial
>
> _____

Example 1 Count permutations

Consider the number of permutations of the letters in the word DOG.

a. In how many ways can you arrange all of the letters?

b. In how many ways can you arrange 2 of the letters?

Solution

a. Use the counting principle to find the number of permutations of the letters in the word DOG.

$$\text{Number of permutations} = \text{Choices for 1st letter} \cdot \text{Choices for 2nd letter} \cdot \text{Choices for 3rd letter}$$

$$= \underline{} \cdot \underline{} \cdot \underline{}$$

$$= \underline{}$$

There are ___ ways you can arrange all of the letters.

b. When arranging 2 letters of the word DOG, you have ___ choices for the first letter and ___ choices for the second letter.

$$\text{Number of permutations} = \text{Choices for 1st letter} \cdot \text{Choices for 2nd letter}$$

$$= \underline{} \cdot \underline{}$$

$$= \underline{}$$

There are ___ ways you can arrange 2 of the letters.

Your Notes

PERMUTATIONS

Formulas

The number of permutations of n objects is given by:

$_nP_n = $ _____

The number of permutations of n objects taken r at a time, where $r \leq n$, is given by:

$_nP_r = \dfrac{\boxed{}}{\boxed{}}$

Example 2   *Use permutations formula*

Codes A garage door has a keypad with 10 different digits. A sequence of 4 digits must be selected to open the door. How many keypad codes are possible?

Solution

To find the number of permutations of 4 digits chosen from 10, find $_{10}P_4$.

$_{10}P_4 = \dfrac{10!}{(10-4)!}$ Permutations formula

$= \dfrac{10!}{6!}$ Subtract.

$= \dfrac{10 \cdot 9 \cdot 8 \cdot 7 \cdot \cancel{6!}}{\cancel{6!}}$ Expand factorials. Simplify.

$= $ _____   Multiply.

There are _____ possible keypad codes.

✓ **Checkpoint** Complete the following exercises.

1. In how many ways can you arrange the letters in the word BEAR?

2. In Example 2, suppose the code is a sequence of 5 digits. How many keypad codes are possible?

Your Notes

Example 3 — Find a probability using permutations

Cards A bag contains 5 cards numbered 1–5. You draw one card at a time until you draw all 5 cards. What is the probability of drawing the card numbered 1 first and the card numbered 2 second?

Solution

Step 1 Write the number of possible outcomes as the number of permutations of the 5 cards. This is
$_{\_\_}P_{\_\_} = \_\_\_$.

Step 2 Write the number of favorable outcomes as the number of permutations of the other cards, given that the card numbered 1 is drawn first and the card numbered 2 is drawn second. This is
$_{\_\_}P_{\_\_} = \_\_\_$.

Step 3 Calculate the probability.

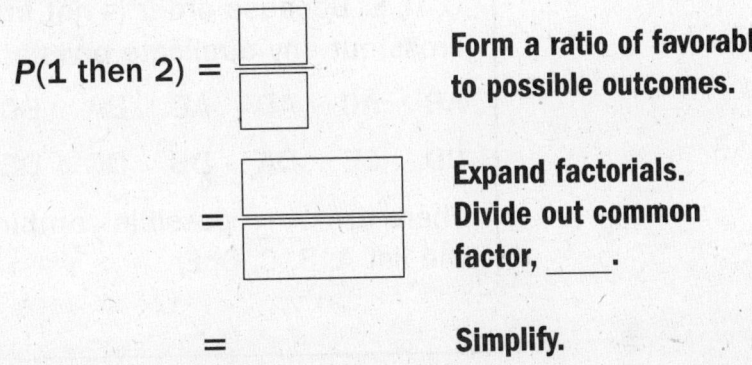

$P(1 \text{ then } 2) = \dfrac{\Box}{\Box}$ Form a ratio of favorable to possible outcomes.

$= \dfrac{\Box}{\Box}$ Expand factorials. Divide out common factor, ___.

$= \dfrac{}{\_\_\_}$ Simplify.

✓ **Checkpoint** Complete the following exercise.

3. In Example 3, suppose there are 10 cards in the bag numbered 1–10. Find the probability that the card numbered 1 is drawn first and the card numbered 2 is drawn second.

Homework

13.3 Find Probabilities Using Combinations

Goal • Use combinations to count possibilities.

Your Notes

VOCABULARY

Combination

Example 1 *Count combinations*

Count the combinations of two letters from the list A, B, C, D, E.

Solution

List all of the permutations of two letters in the list A, B, C, D, E. Because order is not important in a combination, cross out any duplicate pairs.

AB AC AD AE ~~BA~~ BC BD BE ~~CA~~ ~~CB~~
CD CE ~~DA~~ ~~DB~~ ~~DC~~ DE ~~EA~~ ~~EB~~ ~~EC~~ ~~ED~~

There are ___ possible combinations of 2 letters from the list A, B, C, D, E.

COMBINATIONS

Formula

The number of combinations of n objects taken r at a time, where $r \leq n$, is given by:

$$_nC_r = \frac{}{}$$

Example

The number of combinations of 5 objects taken 2 at a time is:

$$_5C_2 = \frac{}{} = \frac{}{} = \underline{}$$

Your Notes

Example 2 — Use the combinations formula

Toppings You order a pizza at a restaurant. You can choose 3 toppings from a list of 12. How many combinations of toppings are possible?

Solution

The order in which you choose the toppings is not important. So, to find the number of combinations of 12 toppings taken 3 at a time, find $_{12}C_3$.

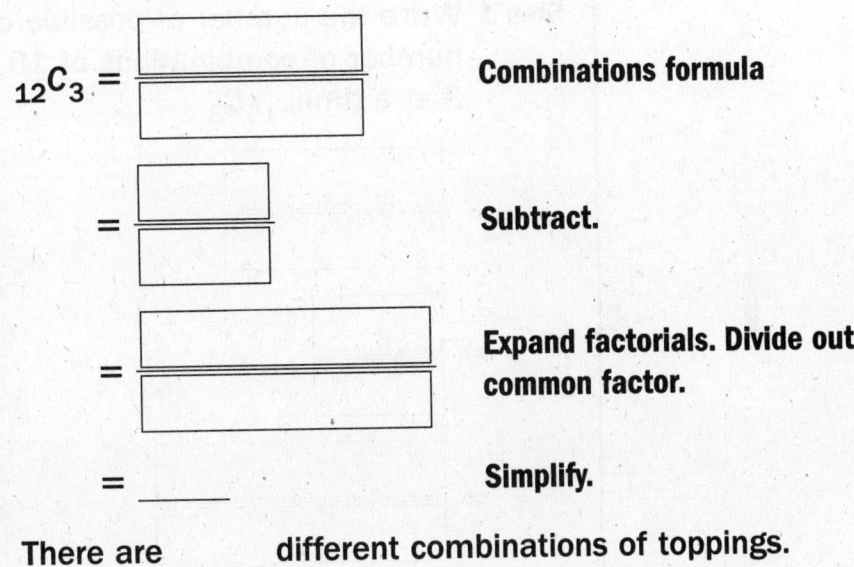

$_{12}C_3 = \dfrac{\boxed{}}{\boxed{}}$ Combinations formula

$= \dfrac{\boxed{}}{\boxed{}}$ Subtract.

$= \dfrac{\boxed{}}{\boxed{}}$ Expand factorials. Divide out common factor.

$= \underline{}$ Simplify.

There are _____ different combinations of toppings.

✓ Checkpoint Complete the following exercises.

1. Count the combinations of two letters from the list A, B, C, D, E, F.

2. In Example 2, suppose you can choose only 2 toppings out of the 12 topping choices. How many combinations are possible?

Your Notes

Example 3: Find a probability using combinations

Scholarships A committee must award three students with scholarships. Fifteen students are candidates for the scholarship including you and your two best friends. If the awardees are selected randomly, what is the probability that you and your two best friends are awarded the scholarships?

Solution

Step 1 Write the number of possible outcomes as the number of combinations of 15 candidates taken 3 at a time, $_{15}C_3$.

$$_{15}C_3 = \frac{\boxed{}}{\boxed{}}$$

$$= \frac{\boxed{}}{\boxed{}}$$

$$= \frac{\boxed{}}{\boxed{}}$$

$$= \underline{}$$

Step 2 Find the number of favorable outcomes. Only _____ of the possible combinations includes scholarships for you and your two best friends.

Step 3 Calculate the probability.

P(scholarships awarded to you and your friends) = _____

Homework

✓ **Checkpoint** Complete the following exercise.

3. In Example 3, suppose there are 20 candidates for the scholarships. Find the probability that you and your two best friends are awarded the 3 scholarships.

13.4 Find Probabilities of Compound Events

Goal • Find the probability of a compound event.

Your Notes

VOCABULARY

Compound event

Mutually exclusive events

Overlapping events

Independent events

Dependent events

Example 1 *Find the probability of A or B*

You roll a number cube. Find the probability that you roll a 4 or a prime number.

Solution

Because 4 is not a prime number, rolling a 4 and rolling a prime number are _____ events.

$P(4 \text{ or prime}) = $ _____ + _____

$= \underline{} + \underline{}$

$= \underline{}$

$= \underline{}$

Your Notes

> **Example 2** **Find the probability of A or B**
>
> You roll a number cube. Find the probability that you roll an even number or a number greater than 3.
>
> **Solution**
>
> Because ___ and ___ are both even and greater than 3, rolling an even number and rolling a number greater than three are _____ events. There are ___ even numbers, ___ numbers greater than 3, and ___ numbers that are both.
>
> P(even or > 3)
>
> = _____ + _____ − _____
>
> = ___ + ___ − ___
>
> = ___
>
> = ___

✓ **Checkpoint** Complete the following exercises.

---

1. You roll a number cube. Find the probability that you roll a 1 or a 6.

---

2. You roll a number cube. Find the probability that you roll an even number or a 2.

---

306 Lesson 13.4 • Algebra 1 Notetaking Guide

Your Notes

Example 3   *Find the probability of A and B*

You roll two number cubes. What is the probability that you roll a 1 first and a 2 second?

Solution

The events are _____. The number on one number cube does not affect the other.

$P(1 \text{ and } 2) =$ _____ $\cdot$ _____ $=$ _____ $\cdot$ _____ $=$ _____

Example 4   *Find the probability of A and B*

Miniature Golf You and a friend must each select a golf ball from a bucket to play miniature golf. There are 3 yellow balls, 4 red balls, 5 green balls, and 4 purple balls. You select a golf ball and then your friend selects a golf ball. What is the probability that both golf balls are green?

Solution

Because you do not replace the first ball, the events are _____. Before you choose a ball, there are ____ balls and ____ are green. After you choose a green ball, there are ____ balls and ____ are green.

$P(\text{green and then green})$

$=$ _____ $\cdot$ _____

$=$ _____ $\cdot$ _____ $=$ _____ $=$ _____

✓ **Checkpoint** Complete the following exercise.

Homework

3. A bag contains 6 red marbles, 5 green marbles, and 3 blue marbles. You randomly draw 2 marbles, one at a time. Find the probability that both are red if:

   a. you replace the first marble.

   b. you do not replace the first marble.

Lesson 13.4 • Algebra 1 Notetaking Guide   307

13.5 Analyze Surveys and Samples

Goal • Identify populations and sampling methods.

Your Notes

VOCABULARY

Survey

Population

Sample

Biased sample

Biased question

SAMPLING METHODS

In a _____ sample, every member of the population has an equal chance of being selected.

In a _____ sample, the population is divided into distinct groups. Members are selected at random from each group.

In a _____ sample, a rule is used to select members of the population.

In a _____ sample, only members of the population who are easily accessible are selected.

In a _____ sample, members of the population select themselves by volunteering.

Your Notes

Example 1 Classify a sampling method

Study Time A high school is conducting a survey to determine the average number of hours that their students spend doing homework each week. At the school, only the members of the sophomore class are chosen to complete the survey. Identify the population and classify the sampling method.

Solution

The population is _____. Because a rule (sophomore class only) is used to select members of the population, the sample is a _____ sample.

Example 2 Identify a potentially biased sample

Is the sampling method used in Example 1 likely to result in a biased sample?

Solution

Students in other grades may have different study habits, so the method _____ in a biased sample.

Example 3 Identify potentially biased questions

Tell whether the question is potentially biased. Explain your answer. If the question is potentially biased, rewrite it so that it is not.

a. Do you still support the school basketball team, even though the team is having its worst season in 5 years?

b. Don't you think that dogs are better pets than cats?

Solution

a. This question is biased because _____ _____ _____. An unbiased question is, "_____"

b. This question is biased because _____ _____. An unbiased question is "_____"

Your Notes

✓ **Checkpoint** Complete the following exercises.

1. In Example 1, suppose the school asks students to volunteer to take the survey. Classify the sampling method.

2. **Amusement Park** An amusement park owner wants to evaluate the customer service given by the park's ride operators. One day, every 10th customer leaving the park was asked, "Don't you think that our friendly, well-trained ride operators provided excellent customer service today?"

   a. Is this sampling method likely to result in a biased sample? Explain.

   b. Is this question potentially biased? Explain your answer. If the question is potentially biased, rewrite it so that it is not.

Homework

13.6 Use Measures of Central Tendency and Dispersion

Goal • Compare measures of central tendency and dispersion.

Your Notes

VOCABULARY

Measure of dispersion

Range

Mean absolute deviation

MEASURES OF CENTRAL TENDENCY

The _____, or *average*, of a numerical data set is denoted by $\bar{x}$, which is read as "x-bar." For the data set $x_1, x_2, \ldots, x_n$, the mean is

$$\bar{x} = \frac{}{}.$$

The _____ of a numerical data set is the _____ _____ when the numbers are written in numerical order. If the data set has an even number of values, the median is the _____.

The _____ of a data set is the value that _____ _____. There may be one mode, no mode, or more than one mode.

Your Notes

Example 1 — Compare measures of central tendency

Test Scores Your last 8 test scores are listed below. Find the mean, median, and mode(s) of the data.

81   87   91   91   93   95   98   100

Solution

$\bar{x} = \dfrac{\rule{4cm}{0.4pt}}{\rule{4cm}{0.4pt}}$

$= \dfrac{\square}{\square} = \underline{}$

The median is the mean of the two middle values, ____ and ____, or ____.

The mode is ____.

✓ Checkpoint Complete the following exercise.

1. Find the mean, median, and mode(s) of the data set.

   13, 15, 15, 19, 23, 26, 27, 30

MEASURES OF DISPERSION

The _____ of a numerical data set is the difference of the greatest value and the least value.

The _____ of the data set $x_1, x_2, \ldots, x_n$, is given by:

_____ .

Your Notes

Example 2 *Compare measures of dispersion*

Golf The 9-hole scores of golfers on two different high school teams are given. Compare the spread of the data sets using (a) the range and (b) the mean absolute deviation.

Team 1: 51, 46, 40, 49, 55, 47
Team 2: 41, 47, 54, 50, 42, 42

Solution

a. Team 1: _____   Team 2: _____

The range of set 1 is _____ the range of set 2. So, the data in _____ cover a wider interval than the data in _____.

b. The mean of set 1 is _____, so the mean absolute deviation is:

$$\frac{\rule{4cm}{0.4pt}}{\rule{4cm}{0.4pt}} = \underline{}.$$

The mean of set 2 is _____, so the mean absolute deviation is:

$$\frac{\rule{4cm}{0.4pt}}{\rule{4cm}{0.4pt}} = \underline{}.$$

The mean absolute deviation of _____ is greater, so the average variation from the mean is greater for the data in _____ than for the data in _____.

✓ **Checkpoint** Complete the following exercise.

2. **Golf** The 9-hole scores of golfers on Team 3 are 43, 52, 46, 44, 42, and 43. Compare the spread of the data with that of set 2 in Example 2 using (a) the range and (b) the mean absolute deviation.

Homework

13.7 Interpret Stem-and-Leaf Plots and Histograms

Goal • Make stem-and-leaf plots and histograms.

Your Notes

VOCABULARY

Stem-and-leaf plot _____

Frequency _____

Frequency table _____

Histogram _____

Example 1 Make a stem-and-leaf plot

Survey A survey asked people how many miles they commute to work. The results are listed below. Make a stem-and-leaf plot of the data.

5, 10, 18, 15, 9, 27, 10, 35, 12, 4, 8, 14, 23, 2, 20, 5, 15

Solution

Step 1 Separate the data into stems and leaves.

Miles
Stem	Leaves
0	_____
1	_____
2	_____
3	_____

Step 2 Write the leaves in _____.

Miles
Stem	Leaves
0	_____
1	_____
2	_____
3	_____

Key: 3 | 5 = _____

Checkpoint Complete the following exercise.

1. Make a stem-and-leaf plot of the data.
   3.4, 4.3, 5.9, 6.2, 5.3, 3.7, 3.9, 4.7, 3, 4.8, 6.3, 3.6, 3.2, 3.4

Example 2 Interpret a stem-and-leaf plot

Fundraiser Sales The back-to-back stem-and-leaf plot shows the fundraiser sales (in hundreds of dollars) of the homerooms of two different grades. Compare the sales of each grade.

```
        Fundraiser Sales
     9th Grade    10th Grade
             5 | 5 |
           7 5 | 6 | 6 8 9
         7 4 3 | 7 | 0 2 5 5 7 9
       6 5 3 3 1 | 8 | 3
```
Key: 3 | 7 | 0 = 7.3, 7.0

Solution

Consider the distribution of the data. The interval for 7.0 and 7.9 hundreds of dollars in sales contains _____ of the 10th grade homerooms, while the interval for 8.0 and 8.9 hundreds of dollars in sales contains _____ _____. The clustering of the data shows that the _____ fundraiser sales were generally higher than the _____ fundraiser sales.

Your Notes

Example 3 — Making a histogram

Birth Weight The birth weight (in ounces) of babies born at a hospital are listed below. Make a histogram of the data.

96, 128, 115, 120, 107, 125, 136, 122, 131, 112, 110

Solution

Step 1 Choose intervals of _____ size that cover all of the data values. Organize the data using a _____.

Birth weight	Babies
90–99	
100–109	
110–119	
120–129	
130–139	

Step 2 Draw the bars of the histogram using the intervals from the frequency table.

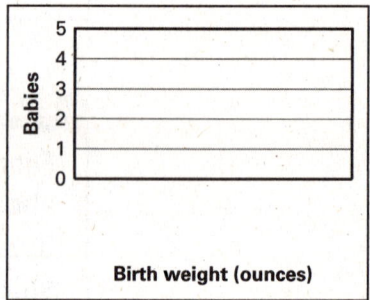

Birth weight (ounces)

✓ **Checkpoint** Complete the following exercise.

2. Make a histogram of the data.

   19.00, 18.59, 19.80, 20.52, 18.73, 20.89, 20.12, 18.17, 20.62

Homework

13.8 Interpret Box-and-Whisker Plots

Goal • Make and interpret box-and-whisker plots.

Your Notes

VOCABULARY

Box-and-whisker plot

Quartile

Interquartile range

Outlier

Example 1 Make a box-and-whisker plot

Height Make a box-and-whisker plot of the heights (in inches) of 7 family members: 34, 67, 70, 62, 46, 75, 54.

Step 1 Order the data. Then find the median and quartiles.

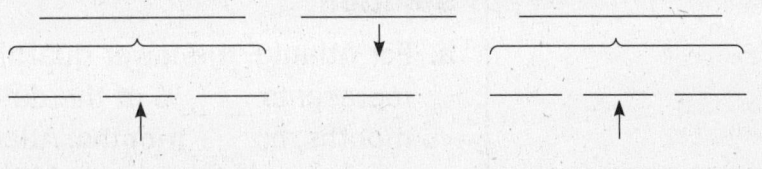

Step 2 Plot the median, the quartiles, the maximum value, and the minimum value below a number line.

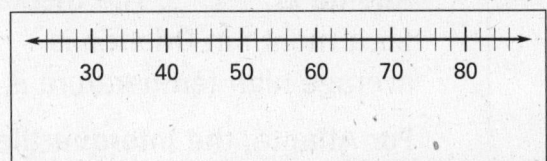

Step 3 Draw a _____ from the lower quartile to the upper quartile. Draw a vertical line through the _____. Draw a line segment from the box to the maximum and another from the box to the minumum.

Your Notes

✓ **Checkpoint** Complete the following exercise.

> 1. Make a box-and-whisker plot of the data.
>   10, 8, 2, 4, 3, 8, 6, 4, 5, 5

Example 2 *Interpret a box-and-whisker plot*

Average Temperature The box-and-whisker plots below show the average high temperature (in degrees Fahrenheit) each month in Atlanta, Georgia and Orlando, Florida.

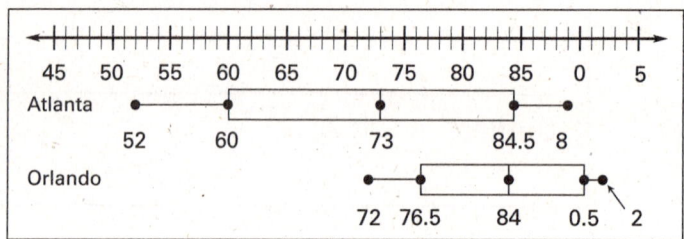

a. For how many months is Atlanta's average high temperature less than 60°F?

b. Compare the average high temperature in Atlanta with the average high temperature in Orlando.

Solution

a. For Atlanta, the lower quartile is _____. A whisker represents _____% of the data, so for _____% of _____ months, or _____ months, Atlanta has an average high temperature less than 60°F.

b. The median average high temperature for a month in Atlanta is _____. The median average high temperature for a month in Orlando is _____. In general, the average high temperature is _____ in Orlando.

For Atlanta, the interquartile range is _____, or _____°F. For Orlando, the interquartile range is _____, or _____°F. The range for Atlanta is _____ than the range for Orlando. So, Atlanta has _____ variation in average high temperature per month.

Your Notes

✓ **Checkpoint** Complete the following exercise.

> 2. In Example 2, for how many months was the average high temperature in Orlando more than 84°F?

Example 3 Identify an outlier

The average monthly high temperatures (in degrees Fahrenheit) in Atlanta are: 52, 57, 65, 73, 80, 87, 89, 88, 82, 73, 63, 55. These data were used to create the box-and-whisker plot in Example 2. Find the outlier(s) of the data set, if possible.

Solution

From Example 2, you know the interquartile range of the data is _____ °F. Find 1.5 times the interquartile range: 1.5(_____) = _____.

From Example 2, you also know that the lower quartile is _____ and the upper quartile is _____. A value less than _____ − _____ = _____ is an outlier. A value greater than _____ + _____ = _____ is an outlier.

Because there is _____ value less than _____ and there is _____ value greater than _____, this data set _____ an outlier.

✓ **Checkpoint** Complete the following exercise.

> 3. Find the outlier(s) of the data set, if possible.
>
>   22, 29, 15, 25, 9, 32, 49, 20, 33, 26, 19, 30

Homework

Words to Review

Give an example of the vocabulary word.

Outcome	Event
Sample space	Probability
Odds	Permutation
n factorial	Combination
Compound event	Mutually exclusive events

Overlapping events	Independent events
Dependent events	Survey
Population	Sample
Biased sample	Biased question

Measure of dispersion	Range
Mean absolute deviation	Stem-and-leaf plot
Frequency	Frequency table
Histogram	Quartile

Interquartile range	Outlier
Box-and-whisker plot	

Review your notes and Chapter 13 by using the Chapter Review on pages 896–900 of your textbook.

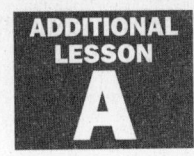

Estimation and Accuracy of Measurement

Goal • Use estimation to determine reasonable solutions and calculate the degree of accuracy with measurement and measuring tools.

Your Notes

VOCABULARY

Estimation

When to Estimate

Calculation Of Error

Example 1 Estimate a reasonable solution

Estimate: $\sqrt{53}$

Find the perfect square just less than 53 and the perfect square just greater than 53.

The perfect squares on either side of 53 are 49 . . . 53 . . . 64. Therefore $\sqrt{53}$ is between $\sqrt{49}$ and $\sqrt{64}$ which means the $\sqrt{53}$ is between 7 and 8.

The difference between 49 and 53 is 4, the difference between 49 and 64 is 15, the difference between 7 and $\sqrt{53}$ is "x" and the difference between 7 and 8 is 1.
Solve the following proportion.

$$\frac{4}{15} = \frac{x}{1}$$

$$15x = 4$$

$$x = \frac{4}{15}$$

$$x = .266$$

Therefore $\sqrt{53} = 7.3$, with accuracy to the tenths place.

Example 2 — Estimate and determine a reasonable amount of error

Estimate the measure of ∠ABC and ∠FBC in the drawing.

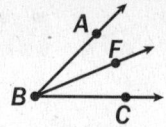

Compare ∠ABC with an angle of known measure such as a right angle or a straight angle.

If ∠DBC is a right angle, and ∠ABC appears to be approximately $\frac{1}{2}$ of ∠DBC, then ∠ABC is approximately 45°.

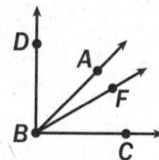

∠FBC is approximately $\frac{1}{3}$ of the right angle ∠DBC, or approximately 30°. Depending on your estimation skills, the error of the measure of the angle could be as much as 10° on either side of 30°.

Example 3 — Using tools to measure line segments and angles

What is the measure of line segment $\overline{AB}$?

If the ruler being used has increments of eighths of an inch, the measure is approximately $1\frac{5}{8}$ inches with an error of $\frac{1}{8}$ inch in either direction. If the ruler is incremented in sixteenths of an inch, the measure is $1\frac{11}{16}$ inches with an error of $\frac{1}{16}$ of an inch in either direction.

What is the measure of ∠CAB?

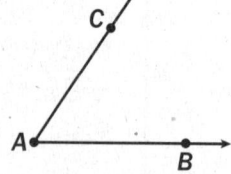

If the protractor that is being used has increments in degrees, the measure of the angle is approximately 56° with an error of 1° greater or less than 56°.

If the protractor is incremented every 5°, the angle is still approximately 56° with an error range of 5° greater or less than 56°.

✓ **Checkpoint** Complete the following exercises.

1. Estimate the $\sqrt{94}$.

2. Estimate the measure of ∠CAT.

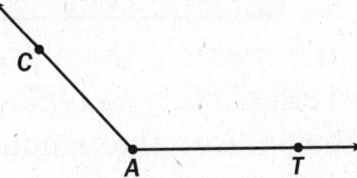

3. Measure ∠CAT.

4. Measure line segment $\overline{ME}$.

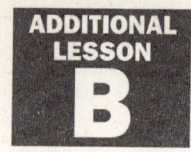

Metric/Customary Conversions

Goal • Use the Metric to Customary Conversion Tables to understand how one unit of measure relates to the other.

Your Notes

HISTORY

The metric system was developed in France in the late 18th century to replace the various systems that were being used throughout the world at that time. Today, the metric system is referred to as the International System of Units, abbreviated SI. Customary Systems grew out of the customs of the area. The system presently used in the United States is the English System and the United States is the only industrial nation using it.

ABBREVIATIONS

Customary
inch = in.
foot = ft.
mile = mi.
quart = qt.
gallon = gal.
Fahrenheit = F

Metric
centimeter = cm
meter = m
kilometer = km
liter = l or L
Celsius = C

CONVERSION TABLES

Into Metric				Into Customary		
Length						
From	multiply by	To		From	multiply by	To
in.	2.54	cm		m	39.36	in.
ft.	30.48	cm		cm	0.39	in.
mi.	1.61	km		km	0.62	mi.
Mass (Weight)						
From	multiply by	To		From	multiply by	To
qt.	.95	L		L	1.06	qt.
gal.	3.79	L		L	0.26	gal.
Temperature						
From		To		From		To
F	subtract 32 then multiply by $\frac{5}{9}$	C		C	multiply by $\frac{9}{5}$ then add 32	F

Example 1 — **Convert from Customary into Metric Units**

Convert 4.56 in. to centimeters.

$$4.56 \times 2.54 = 11.58 \text{ cm}$$

Convert 5 miles to kilometers

$$5 \times 1.61 = 8.05 \text{ km}$$

Example 2 — **Convert from Metric into Customary Units**

The Smith family is driving a rental car in Europe. They stop and put 52 liters of gas into the car. They are surprised at such a large number for the amount of gas. Determine the number of gallons they used.

$$52 \times 0.26 = 13.52 \text{ gallons}$$

Example 3 — **Convert from Celsius (C) to Fahrenheit (F)**

As they were driving through a small town, they noticed a sign at the bank indicating that the temperature was 10°. Knowing that Celsius is the unit used in Europe for temperature, what is the Fahrenheit equivalent?

$$10 \times \frac{9}{5} = 18.0, \; 18.0 + 32 = 50.0°F$$

Your Notes

 Checkpoint Complete the following exercise.

You are planning on taking a trip to Canada and driving through the country for two weeks. In order to budget enough money for the trip, you need to determine the cost of gas. You have found out that the average cost of gas in Canada is $0.78 per liter (Canadian Dollars). What is the cost of gas in gallons (in Canadian dollars)? You have also calculated that you will be driving approximately 1890 kilometers on your trip. How many miles will you be driving?

The average temperature in Canada at the time of your trip is 23°C. Are you going to dress for warm or cold weather? Determine the temperature in Fahrenheit.

You may want to bring shorts.

ADDITIONAL LESSON C

Special Right Triangles

Goal • Use special right triangles to solve problems.

Your Notes

45°–45°–90° TRIANGLE

Words In a 45°–45°–90° triangle, the length of the hypotenuse is the product of the length of a leg and $\sqrt{2}$.

Algebra hypotenuse = leg • $\sqrt{2}$
= $a\sqrt{2}$

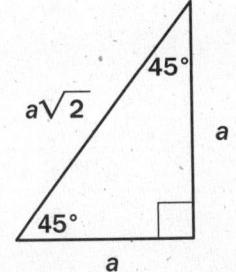

Example 1 Using a 45°–45°–90° Triangle

A 45°–45°–90° triangle used in mechanical drawing has 10-inch legs. Find the length of the hypotenuse to the nearest tenth of an inch.

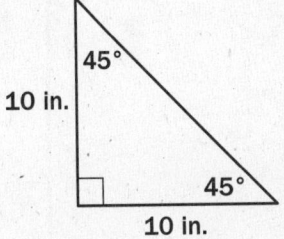

Solution

hypotenuse = leg • $\sqrt{2}$ Rule for 45°–45°–90° triangle

= _____ • $\sqrt{2}$ Substitute

≈ _____   Use a calculator

The length of the triangle's hypotenuse is about _____ inches.

Your Notes

✓ Checkpoint

1. Find the unknown length x. Write your answer in simplest form.

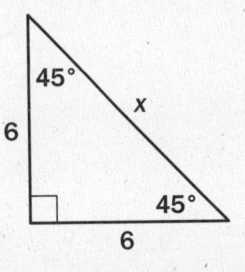

30°–60°–90° TRIANGLE

Words In a 30°–60°–90° triangle, the length of the hypotenuse is twice the length of the shorter leg. The length of the longer leg is the product of the length of the shorter leg and $\sqrt{3}$.

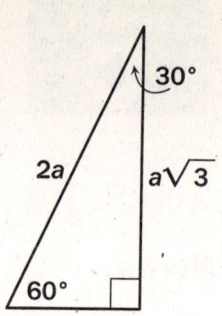

Algebra hypotenuse = 2 • shorter leg = 2a

longer leg = shorter leg • $\sqrt{3}$ = a$\sqrt{3}$

Example 2   Using a 30°–60°–90° Triangle

Find the length x of the hypotenuse and the length y of the longer leg of the triangle.

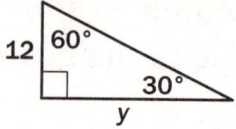

The triangle is a 30°–60°–90° triangle.

The length of the shorter leg is _____ units.

a. hypotenuse = 2 • shorter leg

    x = 2 • _____

    = _____

The length x of the hypotenuse is _____ units.

b. longer leg = shorter leg • $\sqrt{3}$

    y = _____ $\sqrt{3}$

The length y of the longer leg is _____ $\sqrt{3}$ units.

✓ **Checkpoint**

2. Find the unknown lengths x and y. Write your answers in simplest form.

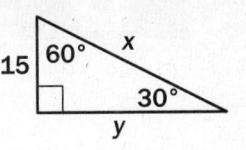

Example 3 Using a Special Right Triangle

An escalator going up to the second floor in a mall is 224 feet long and makes a 30° angle with the first floor. Find, to the nearest foot, the lengths of the triangle's legs.

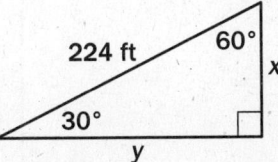

Solution

You need to find the length of the shorter leg first.

1. Find the length x of the shorter leg.

   hypotenuse = 2 • shorter leg   Rule for 30°-60°-90° triangle

   _____ = 2x   Substitute.

   _____ = x   Divide each side by _____.

2. Find the length y of the longer leg.

   longer leg = shorter leg • $\sqrt{3}$ Rule for 30°-60°-90° triangle

   y = _____ $\sqrt{3}$ Substitute.

   y ≈ _____   Use a calculator.

The length of the shorter leg is _____ feet and the length of the longer leg is about _____ feet.

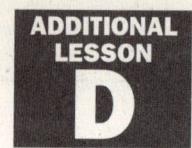

Triangle Inequalities

Goal • Use triangle measurements to decide which side is longest and which angle is largest.

Your Notes

Words If one side of a triangle is longer than another side, then the angle opposite the longer side is _____ than the angle opposite the shorter side.

Symbols If $BC > AB$, then $m\angle A$ _____ $m\angle C$.

_____

Words If one angle of a triangle is larger than another angle, then the side opposite the larger angle is _____ than the side opposite the smaller angle.

Symbols If $m\angle D > m\angle E$, then EF _____ DF.

Example 1 Order Angle Measures

Name the angles from largest to smallest.

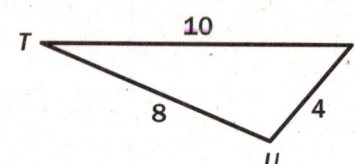

Solution

TV _____ TU, so $m\angle U$ _____ $m\angle V$.

TU _____ UV, so $m\angle V$ _____ $m\angle T$.

The order of the angles from largest to smallest is _____, _____, _____.

Example 2   Order Side Lengths

Name the sides from longest to shortest.

Solution

m∠E _____ m∠D, so DF _____ FE.

m∠D _____ m∠F, so FE _____ DE.

The order of the sides from longest to shortest is _____, _____, _____.

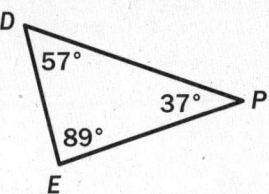

Your Notes

✓ **Checkpoint** Name the angles from largest to smallest.

1.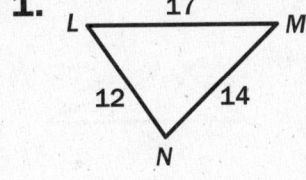

2.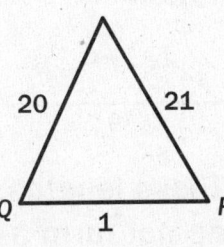

3.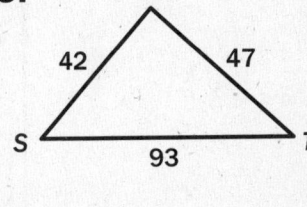

Name the sides from longest to shortest.

4.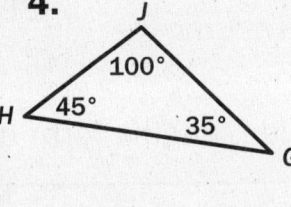

5.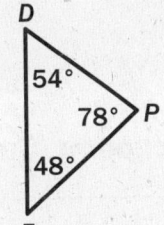

6.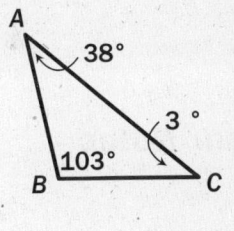

Words The sum of the lengths of any two sides of a triangle is _____ than the length of the third side.

Symbols

CA + AB _____ BC

AB + BC _____ CA

BC + CA _____ AB

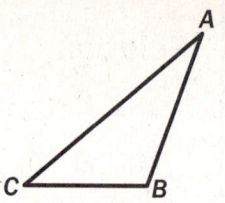

Example 3 Use the Triangle Inequality

Can the side lengths form a triangle? Explain.

a. 3, 5, 9   b. 3, 5, 8   c. 3, 5, 7

Solution

a.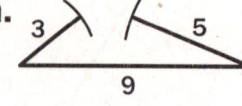

b.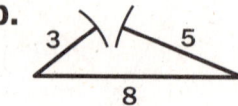

c.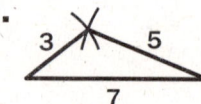

These lengths do not form a triangle, because 3 + 5 _____ 9.

These lengths do not form a triangle, because 3 + 5 _____ 8.

These lengths do form a triangle, because 3 + 5 _____ 7, 3 + 7 _____ 5, and 5 + 7 _____ 3.

Your Notes

 Checkpoint Can the side lengths form a triangle? Explain.

7. 5, 7, 13	8. 6, 9, 12	9. 10, 15, 25

A12   Algebra 1 Notetaking Guide • Additional Lesson D

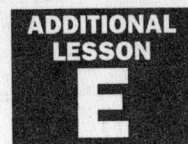

The Tangent Ratio

Goal • Use the tangent to find side lengths of right triangles.

Your Notes

VOCABULARY

Trigonometric ratio

THE TANGENT RATIO

The tangent of an acute angle of a right triangle is the ratio of the length of the side opposite the angle to the length of the side adjacent to the angle.

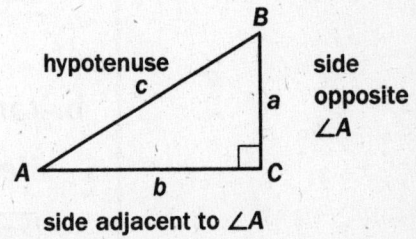

$$\tan A = \frac{\text{side opposite } \angle A}{\text{side adjacent to } \angle A} = \frac{a}{b}$$

Example 1 Finding a Tangent Ratio

For $\triangle PQR$, find the tangent $\angle P$.

$$\tan A = \frac{\text{opposite}}{\text{adjacent}} = \underline{\qquad}$$

Your Notes

✓ **Checkpoint**

1. For △PQR in Example 1, find the tangent of ∠Q.

Example 2 | **Using a Calculator**

a. tan 24°

Keystokes	Display	Answer
[2nd] [TRIG] ◄ ◄ [=] 24 [)] [=]	_____	_____

b. tan 55°

Keystokes	Display	Answer
[2nd] [TRIG] ◄ ◄ [=] 55 [)] [=]	_____	_____

Your Notes

✓ **Checkpoint** Approximate the tangent value to four decimal places.

2. tan 5°	3. tan 38°	4. tan 72°

A14 Algebra 1 Notetaking Guide • Additional Lesson E

Example 3 — Using a Tangent Ratio

Find the height *h* (in feet) of the roof to the nearest foot.

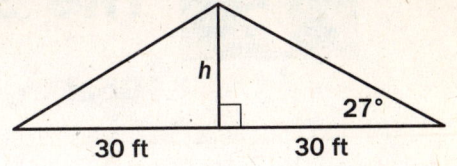

Solution

Use the tangent ratio. In the diagram, the length of the leg opposite the 27° angle is *h*. The length of the adjacent leg is 30 feet.

$\tan 27° = \dfrac{\text{opposite}}{\text{adjacent}}$ Definition of tangent ratio

$\tan 27° =$ _____   Substitute

_____ ≈ _____   Use a calculator to approximate tan 27°

_____ = *h*   Multiply each side by _____

The height of the roof is about _____ feet.

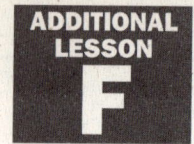

The Sine and Cosine Ratios

Goal • Use sine and cosine to find triangle side lengths.

Your Notes

THE SINE AND COSINE RATIOS

The **sine** of an acute angle of a right triangle is the ratio of the length of the side opposite the angle to the length of the hypotenuse.

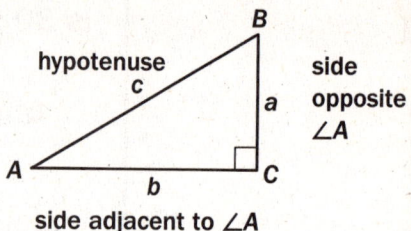

$$\sin A = \frac{\text{side opposite } \angle A}{\text{hypotenuse}} = \frac{a}{c}$$

The **cosine** of an acute angle of a right triangle is the ratio of the length of the angle's adjacent side to the length of the hypotenuse.

$$\cos A = \frac{\text{side adjacent } \angle A}{\text{hypotenuse}} = \frac{b}{c}$$

Example 1 Finding Sine and Cosine Ratios

For △PQR, find the sine and cosine of ∠P.

$$\sin P = \frac{\text{opposite}}{\text{hypotenuse}} = \underline{\hspace{2cm}}$$

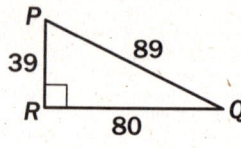

$$\cos P = \frac{\text{adjacent}}{\text{hypotenuse}} = \underline{\hspace{2cm}}$$

Your Notes

✓ **Checkpoint**

1. For △PQR in Example 1, find the sine and cosine of ∠Q.

Example 2 — Using a Calculator

a. sin 60°

Keystokes	Display	Answer
[2nd] [TRIG] [=]		
60 [ )] [=]		

b. cos 45°

Keystokes	Display	Answer
[2nd] [TRIG] [◄] [◄]		
[=] 45 [ )] [=]		

Checkpoint Approximate the sine or cosine value to four decimal places.

2. cos 9°	3. cos 78°	4. sin 13°	5. sin 88°

Example 3 Using a Cosine Ratio

Find the value of x in the triangle.

In $\triangle DEF$, $\overline{DE}$ is adjacent to $\angle D$. Because you know the length of the hypotenuse, use cos D and the definition of the cosine ratio to find the value of x. Round your answer to the nearest tenth of a unit.

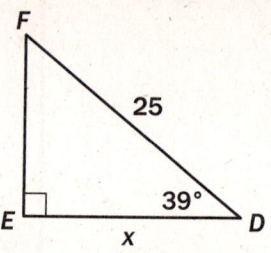

$\cos D = \dfrac{\text{adjacent}}{\text{hypotenuse}}$ Definition of cosine ratio

_____ = _____ Substitute

_____ ≈ _____ Use a calculator to approximate cos 39°

_____ = x Multiply each side by _____

Example 4 Using a Sine Ratio

A ski jump is 140 meters long and makes an angle of 25° with the ground. To the nearest meter, estimate the height *h* of the ski jump.

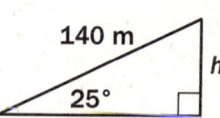

Solution

To estimate the height of the ski jump, find the length of the side _____ the 25° angle. Because you know the length of the hypotenuse, use sin 25°.

$\sin 25° = \dfrac{\text{opposite}}{\text{hypotenuse}}$ Definition of cosine ratio

$\sin 25° = $ _____ Substitute

_____ ≈ _____ Use a calculator to approximate sin 25°

_____ = h Multiply each side by _____

The height of the ski jump is about _____ meters.

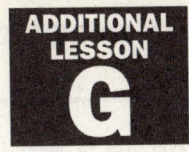

Vertex-Edge Graphs, Circuits, Networks, and Routing

 • Apply the characteristics of vertex-edge graphs to circuits and networks. Include using subscripts to name the ordinal postion of a vertex.

Your Notes

VOCABULARY

Graph

Vertex

Edge

Adjacent Vertices

Adjacent Edges

Degree of a vertex

Path

Circuit

Ordinal

Subscript

Route

Network

| Example 1 | Determine if a graph is a circuit by using the degree of each vertex |

If a graph has any odd vertices, then it cannot be a circuit (starting and ending at the same point and traveling over each edge only once). If a graph has more than two odd vertices, then it cannot have a path.

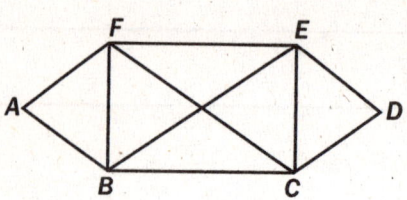

Degree of each vertex

$A = 2$ Since all of the vertices
$B = 4$ are even, the figure can
$C = 4$ be traced starting at
$D = 2$ one vertex returning to
         the same vertex without
$E = 4$ tracing over one edge
$F = 4$ more than once.

Your Notes

✓ **Checkpoint** Complete the following exercises.

Find the degree of each vertex and determine if the graph is a circuit. Trace the graph and show that it forms a circuit or a path.

1.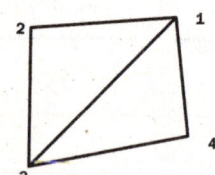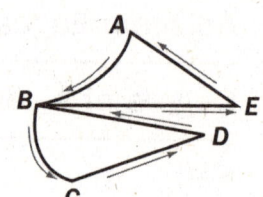

2. Place appropriate letters on this graph using subscript notation. Find the degree of each vertex and determine if the graph is a circuit. Trace the graph and show that it forms a circuit or a path.

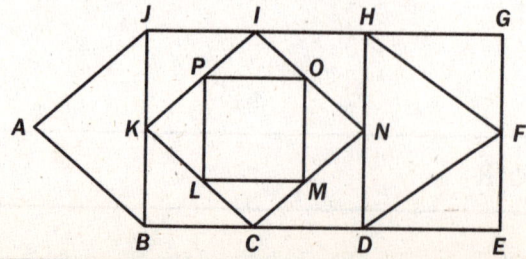

Example 2 — Determine if a network presents the best route basing the solution on the number of vertices and edges

The following network shows several cities and the paths connecting them. The vertices represent cities and the edges indicate nonstop airline routes between them.

Drawing 1

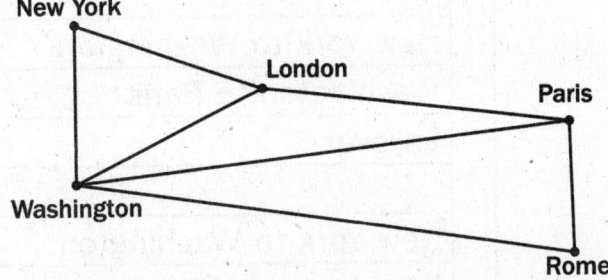

An alternate method is to mark the graph using subscripts.

Drawing 2

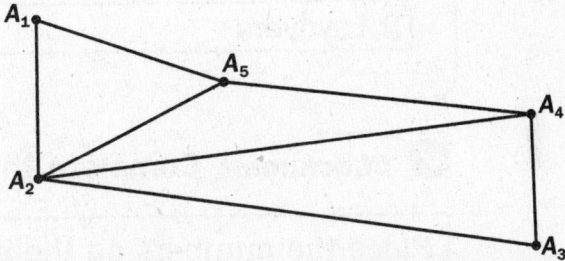

Another alternate method is to mark the graph using the first letter of each city.

Drawing 3

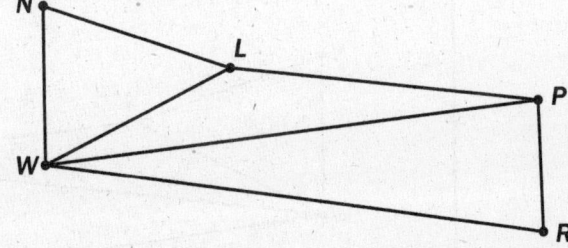

According to this particular airlines network, there are direct flights between New York and London, between Washington and London, between Washington and Paris, and between Washington and Rome. There are no direct flights between New York and Paris and New York and Rome.

There are several paths that describe a trip from New York to Paris, using drawing 2; $A_1A_5A_4$, $A_1A_2A_4$, $A_1A_2A_5A_4$, and $A_1A_2A_3A_4$ or using drawing 3; NLP, NWP, NWLP, and NWRP. The path that seems the most direct is NLP however, depending on cost, layover time and availability (see chart 1) one of the other paths may be a better choice. The consideration of these values determines a routing problem.

(continued)

Example 2 (continued)

Chart 1: The prices and times are listed below.

New York to London	$1414.00	6 hr. 50 min.
London to Paris	$147.00	1 hr. 15 min.
Layover		2 hr. 25 min.
New York to Washington	$142.00	1 hr. 15 min.
Washington to Paris	$1370.00	6 hr. 57 min.
Layover		2 hr. 47 min.
New York to Washington	$142.00	1 hr. 15 min.
Washington to Rome	$2321.00	11 hr. 20 min.
Rome to Paris	$393.00	2 hr. 10 min.
2 Layovers		4 hr. 25 min.

Your Notes

✓ **Checkpoint** Complete the following exercise.

Place the numbers on the graph and compare the different routes with respect to total cost and total time of each trip. Use the chart above for the total prices and time. Which route would you take and why?

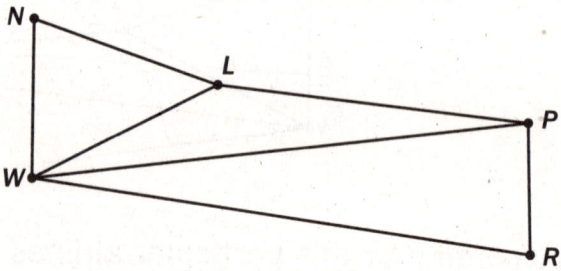

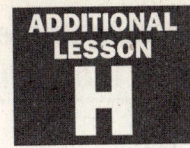

Introduction to Vectors

Goal • Sketch vectors; determine the magnitude and the direction of a resultant vector and draw vectors with a given bearing.

Your Notes

VOCABULARY

Vector

Initial Point

Terminal Point

Magnitude of a vector

Direction of a vector

Resultant

Example 1 — Sketch vectors and determine the magnitude and the direction using the Pythagorean Theorem

Sketch the following vectors. A(3, 5) and B(5, 0)

The direction of **A** can be measured using a protractor.

$\angle X = 59°$

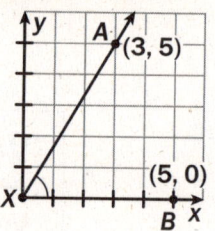

Since the vector B is on the x-axis, its direction is 0°. Determine its length (magnitude) of vector A by using the Pythagorean Theorem.

$\|A\| = \sqrt{3^2 + 5^2} = \sqrt{9 + 25} = \sqrt{34}$ $\|B\| = 5$

Example 2 — Add vectors to determine the end point of the resultant vector, determine the magnitude of the resultant vector and the degree of the direction angle

Add vector A(3, 5) and vector B(−1, −4). To determine the end point of the resultant vector, add the coordinates of the two vectors, that is $C(x, y) = A(x_1, y_1) + B(x_2, y_2)$

$C(x, y) = A(3, 5) + B(-1, -4)$

$C(X, Y) = (3 + (-1), 5 + (-4)) = (2, 1)$

To determine the magnitude of C, use the Pythagorean Theorem.

$\|C\| = \sqrt{2^2 + 1^2} = \sqrt{4 + 1} = \sqrt{5}$

Measure $\angle COX$ using a protractor.

$\angle COX = 27°$

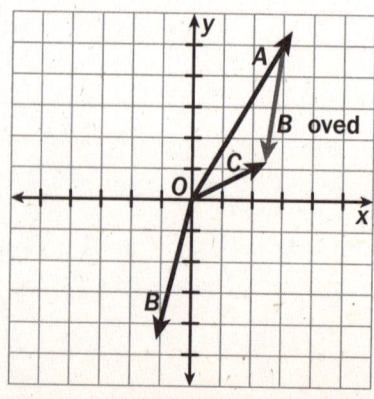

Checkpoint Complete the following exercise.

1. Find the magnitude and direction of the resultant vector, C, of adding vectors A(3, 5) and B(5, 2).

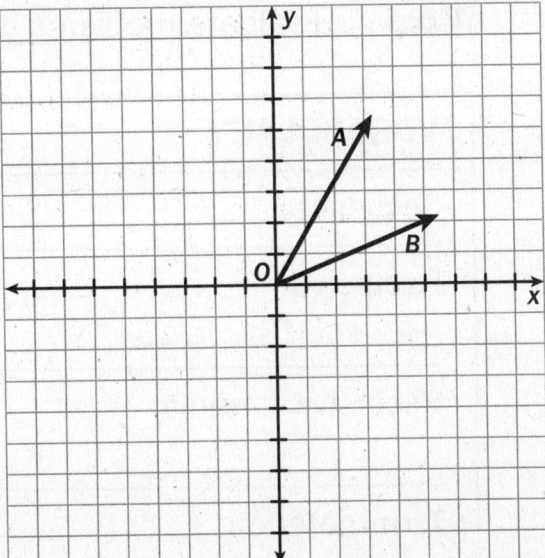

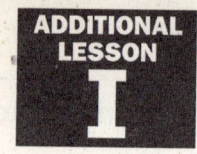

Introduction To Recursive Functions For Sequences

Goal • Evaluate problems using basic recursive formulas.

Your Notes

VOCABULARY

Sequence

Recursive

Recursive formula

Term notation

Example 1 — Write terms of sequences

a. Write the first 6 terms of the sequence 1, 4, 7, . . . where $t_n = t_{n-1} + 3$, that is, any term is determined by adding 3 to the previous term.

$t_4 = t_3 + 3$ $t_4 = 7 + 3 = 10$

$t_5 = t_4 + 3$ $t_5 = 10 + 3 = 13$

$t_6 = t_5 + 3$ $t_6 = 13 + 3 = 16$

Thus the first 6 terms are 1, 4, 7, 10, 13, 16

b. Write the first 5 terms of the sequence 1, 2, 5, . . . where $t_n = (t_{n-1})^2 + 1$, that is, 1 is added to the previous term squared.

$t_4 = (t_3)^2 + 1$ $t_4 = 5^2 + 1 = 25 + 1 = 26$

$t_5 = (t_4) + 1$ $t_5 = 26^2 + 1 = 676 + 1 = 677$

Thus the first 5 terms are 1, 2, 5, 26, 677

Your Notes

> ✓ **Checkpoint** Complete the following exercises.
>
> 1. Write the first 6 terms of the sequence 1, 5, . . . where $t_n = t_{n-1} + 4$
>
> 2. The *Fibonacci numbers* are shown below. Use the Fibonacci numbers to answer the following questions.
>
>   1, 1, 2, 3, 5, 8, 13, 21, 34, 55, 89 . . .
>
>   a. Copy and complete: After the first two numbers, each number is the _____ of the _____ previous numbers.
>
>   b. Write the next three numbers in the pattern.

Example 2   **Write a rule for the *n*th term of a sequence**

Find the *n*th term, that is, the formula or rule that is used to determine the next term in the sequence 1, 3, 7, 15, 31, 63 . . .

Examine each term. How do you get the second term from the first? How do you get the third term from the second? And so on.

$1 \times 2 + 1 = 3$

$3 \times 2 + 1 = 7$

$7 \times 2 + 1 = 15$

$15 \times 2 + 1 = 31$

$31 \times 2 + 1 = 63$

the previous term is multiplied by 2 and 1 is added to it.

The *n*th term $t_n = 2(t_{n-1}) + 1$

Additional Lesson l • Algebra 1 Notetaking Guide

Your Notes

✓ **Checkpoint** Complete the following exercise.

1. Find the *n*th term, that is, the formula for determining the next term for the sequence 1, 6, 11, 16, 21, 26 . . .

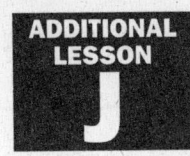

Introduction to Limits

Goal • Determine the limits of a function as it approaches a given value.

Your Notes

VOCABULARY

Limit

Unique

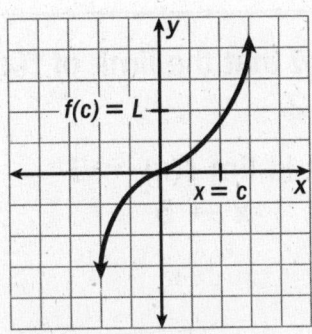

Written as: $\lim\limits_{x \to c} f(x) = L$

Example 1 — Calculate the limit of a given function choosing values of x as it approaches c from both sides

Determine the limit of $f(x) = x^3 + 2$ as x approaches 3, from both sides of 3, that is, numbers less than 3 and numbers just greater than 3.

$f(2.5)$	17.625	$f(3.5)$	44.875
$f(2.7)$	21.683	$f(3.3)$	37.937
$f(2.9)$	26.389	$f(3.1)$	31.791
$f(2.99)$	28.97	$f(3.01)$	29.271
$f(2.999)$	28.997	$f(3.001)$	29.027

Therefore the limit of $f(x)$ as x approaches 3 is 29. That is, the value $f(x)$, the y value, gets closer to 29 as the value of x gets closer to 3. Mathematically this is written as

$$\lim_{x \to 3} f(x) = 29$$

Additional Lesson J • Algebra 1 Notetaking Guide

Example 2
Calculate the limit of a function as x approaches a given value

Determine the limit of $f(x) = -x^2 + 4x + 1$ as x approaches 2.

$f(1.5)$	4.75	$f(2.5)$	4.75
$f(1.7)$	4.91	$f(2.3)$	4.91
$f(1.9)$	4.99	$f(2.1)$	4.99
$f(1.99)$	4.999	$f(2.01)$	4.999
$f(1.999)$	4.9999	$f(2.001)$	4.9999

Therefore the limit of $f(x)$ as x approaches 2 is 5.

Written as $\lim\limits_{x \to 2} f(x) = 5$

Your Notes

✓ **Checkpoint** Complete the following exercise.

Show that the limit of $f(x) = \dfrac{x^2 - 3x - 10}{x - 5}$ as x approaches 5 is 2.

That is $\lim\limits_{x \to 5} f(x) = 5$

Two-Way Tables of Probability

Goal • Determine the degree of dependence of two quantities specified by a two-way table.

Your Notes

VOCABULARY

Experiment

Outcome

Sample Space

Probability

Two-way Table

HISTORY

Two-way tables are tables that contain information about two categorical (or categorized) variables. They are designed to allow comparisons between one set of data and two others. The need to learn about two-way tables came about because it was determined that students needed a better way to develop an understanding of probability and appreciate it as a measure of chance. In the past, students in introductory probability courses rarely experienced applications from the world that made sense. Two-way tables provide an organized way to record data, which then leads to drawing conclusions based on findings. They serve as a preparation for more formal hypothesis testing and the grounds for analyzing information to help make decisions. Two-way tables are a practical and sense-making way to help students develop an understanding of probability.

Example 1 — Interpret the two-way table to determine probabilities of compound events

A high school cafeteria surveyed the students for their soft drink preferences. The following two-way table summarizes the results.

	Do not drink soft drinks	Prefer diet soft drinks	Prefer regular soft drinks	Total
Female	28	278	134	440
Male	12	194	295	501
Total	40	472	429	941

A student is selected at random from the group surveyed.

1) What is the probability that the student drinks diet soft drinks?

$$\frac{\text{total students drinking diet}}{\text{total number of students}} : \frac{472}{941} = 0.502$$

2) What is the probability that a male does not drink soft drinks?

$$\frac{\text{total males not drinking}}{\text{total number male students}} : \frac{12}{941} = 0.013$$

3) What is the probability that a student selected from the males does not drink soft drinks?

$$\frac{\text{total males not drinking}}{\text{total number of males}} : \frac{12}{501} = 0.024$$

4) What is the probability that a student selected from the females prefers diet?

$$\frac{\text{total number of female students drinking diet}}{\text{total number of females}} :$$

$$\frac{278}{440} = 0.632$$

Your Notes

✓ **Checkpoint** Complete the following exercise.

A standardized test was given to a group of freshmen and sophomores students. A summary of the results is listed below.

	Scoring below grade level	Scoring at grade level	Scoring above grade level	Total
Freshmen	32	175	82	289
Sophomores	15	208	72	295
Total	47	383	154	584

A student is selected at random from the group surveyed.

1) What is the probability that the student scores below grade level?

2) What is the probability that a sophomore scores above average?

3) What is the probability that a student selected from the freshmen class scores at grade level?

4) What is the probability that a student is above grade level when the student is selected from the sophomore class?

Additional Lesson K • Algebra 1 Notetaking Guide

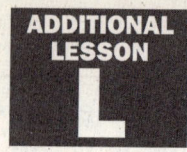

Quantitative vs. Qualitative Data

Goal • Understand the difference between qualitative and quantitative data.

Your Notes

VOCABULARY

Quantitative

Qualitative

Example 1 Classify Data

Classify the following data as qualitative or quantitative.

Number of freshmen, sophomores, juniors or seniors	Qualitative
Test scores on the SAT exam for the junior class of 2006	Quantitative
Heights of students in the freshman class	Quantitative
Number of college freshmen majoring in Science, Arts, Language, Social Studies, Other	Qualitative
Cost of textbooks for each freshman student	Quantitative

Your Notes

✓ **Checkpoint** Complete the following exercise.

1. Determine whether the following graphs represent qualitative or quantitative data

   A) scores on the AP Calculus exam for the year 2006

   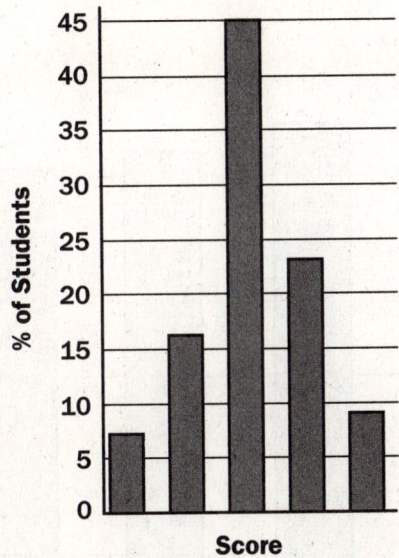

   B) The students' hair color at Washington High School.

   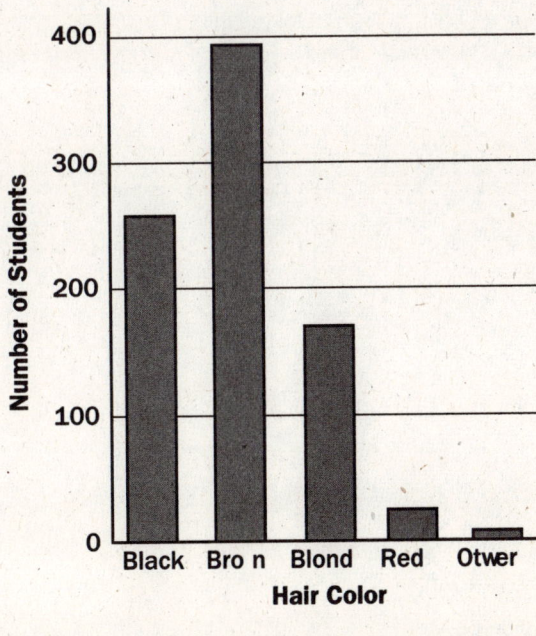

Additional Lesson L • Algebra 1 Notetaking Guide

Your Notes

✓ **Checkpoint** (continued)

C) The number of students in each class watching TV during prime time (8 PM–11 PM).

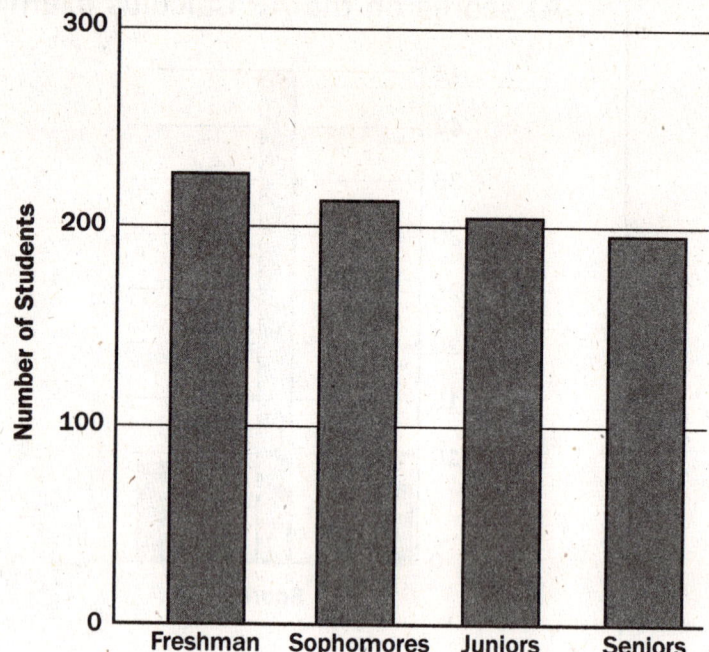

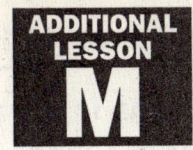

Caustion vs. Correlation

Goal • Understand the difference between correlation and causation.

Your Notes

VOCABULARY

Correlation

Causation

Example 1 Analyze a set of data to determine a correlation

Given is the following set of data for the weight in ounces and age in months of hamsters.

Age (in mo.)	1	2	3	4	5	6	7	8	9
Weight (in oz)	6.9	9.3	12.4	12.9	14.6	17.8	20.1	21.4	22.0

The data is plotted on the graph and the line of best fit is drawn. The linear regression equation can be determined using a graphing calculator.

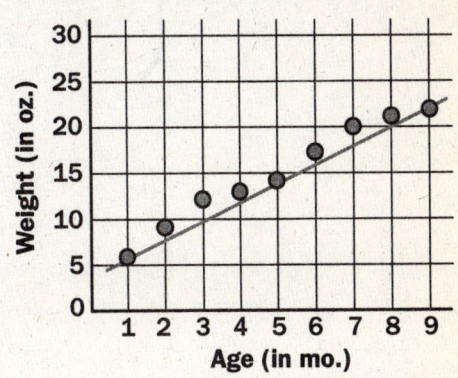

As can be seen from the graph, there appears to be a very strong correlation between age and weight.

Additional Lesson M • Algebra 1 Notetaking Guide   A37

Example 2 — Analyze a set of data to determine a causation

The following data lists the number of televisions in particular groups of countries and the life expectancy of the inhabitants of those countries.

	Least Developed Countries	Developing Countries	Industrial Countries
Number of TVs (per 100 people)	2	14	50
Life expectancy (in years)	48.9	60.9	77.7

The graph of this data is shown below with the linear regression equation graphed on it. There also appears to be a strong correlation between countries with TVs and life expectancy of the inhabitants. However, there is not a causal relationship. The life expectancy in the least developed countries will not improve even if the Industrial Countries sent TVs to the them.

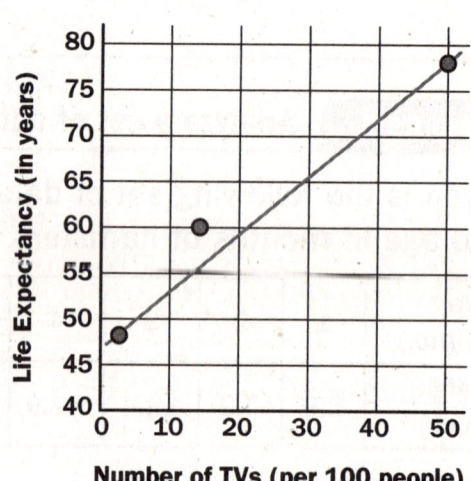

Your Notes

✓ **Checkpoint** Complete the following exercise.

The following data represents the number of hours that seven students spent playing frisbee and their respective grade point average. Is there a correlation? If there is, is there a cause and effect relationship?

Student	Hours of Frisbee	GPA
A	2	3.54
B	8	2.48
C	10	2.05
D	6	2.76
E	16	.68
F	12	1.67
G	4	3.31

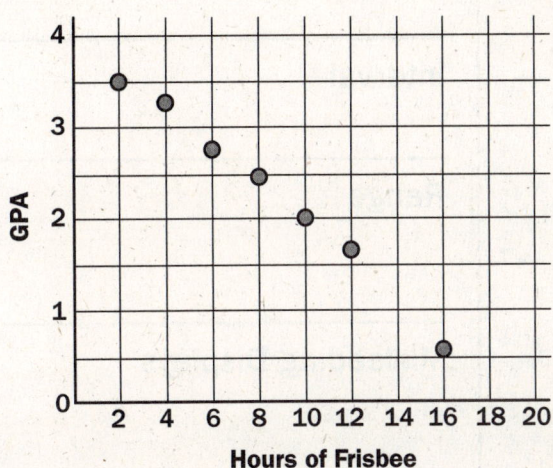

Additional Lesson M • Algebra 1 Notetaking Guide   A39

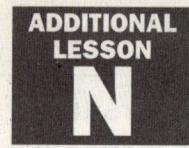

Misleading Data Displays

Goal • Determine if the data displayed is giving a misleading impression.

Your Notes

VOCABULARY

Data

Display

Scale

Interval

Range

Misleading Displays

Example 1 — Analyze a graph to determine how an incorrect conclusion may be drawn

The graph on the left displays the number of calories burned **down** a set of stairs while the graph on the right displays the number of calories burned walking **up** a set of stairs.

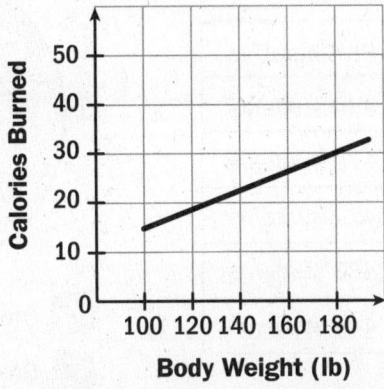
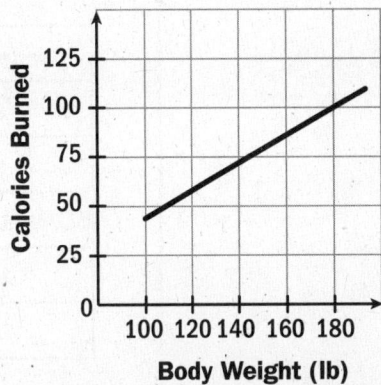

The two graphs appear to be very similar therefore implying that walking up or down the stairs burn the same amount of calories. This is an incorrect conclusion since the scales on the vertical axis are different. The choice of interval affects the slope of the lines.

Example 2 — Analyze a set of data to determine if the display is appropriate

The following data indicates the number of families with zero, one, two, or three pets.

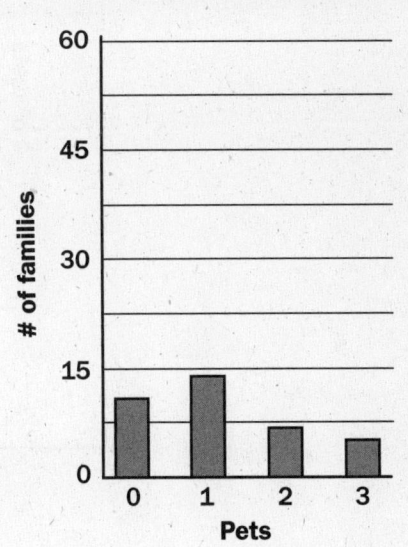

From the display, the number having zero, one, two or three pets is difficult to determine. The upper level on the scale used for the vertical axis is too large and the size of the intervals is also too large to make an accurate estimate.

Your Notes

✓ **Checkpoint** Complete the following exercises.

1. The table and the circle graph shows the same data about student participation in a school district's sports program. Explain how the graph could be misleading.

Grade Level	Participation
8	440 students
9	172 students
10	412 students
11	433 students
12	444 students

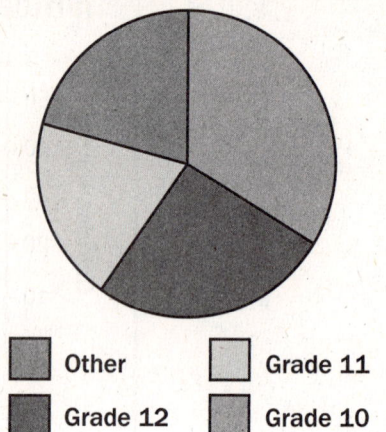

Other | Grade 11
Grade 12 | Grade 10

2. The scores of a student's last 10 math tests are given below. Explain how the display could be misleading.

Test Scores: 90, 62, 65, 75, 83, 80, 61, 82, 85, 68

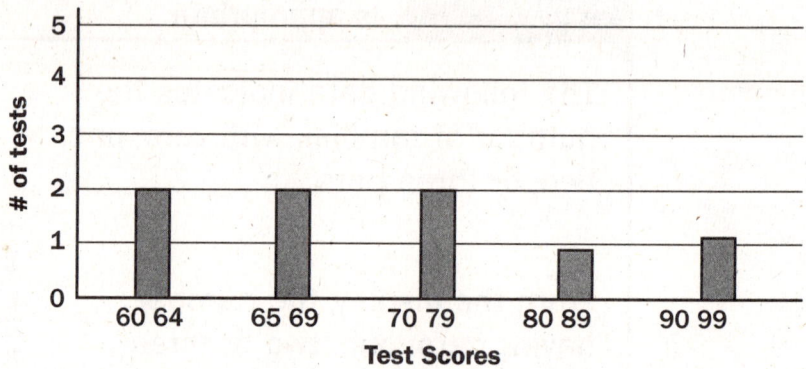